Villanelles, fever dreams,
and twilit ruminations

Frank Feldman

ISBN: 979-8-9917093-5-4

Printed in the United States of America

Some names and identifying details have been changed to protect the privacy of individuals.

Table of Contents

For Donatien, Marcel,
and Diamanda

Introduction

There's no need for an introduction. Introductions are, more often than not, the purest bullshit.

Read the fucking book. Or don't.

If you've ever found, or metaphorically imagined, yourself strapped to a table, desperately attempting to pull a seemingly countless number of harpoons from your guts, harpoons on which you were impaled long before you were old or strong enough to object, much less escape, and utterly certain, after a lifetime of sustained and bitter evidence, that there is no one who cares, much less is coming to your rescue, you might very well understand some fraction of what is contained within these pages.

3

Twelve Villanelles

I.

"Because amongst my fellow men I've always felt alone..."

Because amongst my fellow men I've always felt alone,
My wish is that my body, when I one day come to die,
Be burnt quite to a crisp and then upon the air be thrown.

There are to be no funeral rites nor eulogies intoned -
Anyone who knew me well will know the reason why:
Because amongst my fellow men I've always felt alone.

And if there is some blockhead who to argument is prone,
You are to shut down this buffoon and force him to comply -
To let me be reduced to ash and on the air be thrown.

No eulogies or ceremonies, burial or stone -
If someone makes a fuss, you can straightforwardly reply
That when amongst my fellow men I'd always felt alone,

And found all their conceits quite ludicrous and overblown.
The only way that you can my revulsion satisfy
Is see that I'm burnt to a crisp, then on the air am thrown.

The truth is it's the human race in general I disown,
So let this serve me as one last defiant battle cry:
Because amongst my fellow men I've always felt alone,
Have me burnt quite to a crisp, then on the air be thrown.

II.

Burn these poems when you burn me

I leave you with this firm decree,
Which you both can't and won't ignore:
Burn these poems when you burn me.

This is not some paltry plea
To execute some petty chore,
It is a stern and firm decree,

Which to transgress, you are not free -
Obey, as you have, heretofore -
Burn these poems when you burn me.

You're not to turn away or flee
If it's the case that you abhor
The deed - this is a firm decree,

Which you'll obey - that I foresee -
You'll bow beneath my will once more,
And burn these poems when you burn me.

I chose you as this task's trustee
Because you're spineless, and therefore
To you I leave this firm decree:
Burn these poems when you burn me.

III.

"Even though existence is with awfulness replete..."

Even though existence is with awfulness replete,
And you're confronted, night and day, with harbingers of doom,
Schopenhauer was said to smile when walking down the street.

To be a zealot of despair who wallows in defeat
Will make you a pariah in your neighbor's living room,
Even though existence is with awfulness replete.

Think upon the outcome of your frowns on those you meet -
Be it naught but fiction, nonetheless you ought presume
That Schopenhauer often smiled when walking down the street.

For when you do, you give yourself the right to be upbeat
At intermittent moments, even though you so oft fume
That most of your existence is with awfulness replete.

Our lives are mostly bitter, yet at times they can be sweet -
Gaze upon the stars above, or flowers when in bloom!
Even you might crack a smile when walking down the street.

So you'd do well to ponder if, indeed, it's indiscreet
To wear upon your countenance unmitigated gloom -
Even though existence is with awfulness replete,
Schopenhauer was said to smile when walking down the street.

IV.
"It's grievously deceitful to pretend..."

It's grievously deceitful to pretend
We're something more than flesh and blood and bone,
And not just tubes with holes at either end.

You speak of souls which bodies can transcend,
Once they are to them no longer sewn,
And seem extremely willing to pretend

That something more ethereal extends
Beyond the crumbling organs of some crone,
Who's just a tube with holes at either end

To which you would a seraphim append,
Who's soon to sit upon some astral throne -
It's grievously deceitful to pretend

She will to some Elysium ascend,
To compensate her each and every groan,
That withered tube with holes at either end.

And though it's only kindness you intend,
To soothe those from whom ev'ry good has flown,
It's grievously deceitful to pretend
We're not just tubes with holes at either end.

V.

Kill what you love

Renounce this vulgar Passion Play -
Enjoin your heart to seek no more -
Kill what you love and walk away.

Embrace your fate, brook no delay -
Abandon all that came before -
Renounce this vulgar Passion Play.

To sentiments, do not give way -
All your qualms and doubts, ignore -
Kill what you love and walk away.

Cast them off at close of day -
Shove them in a padlocked drawer -
Renounce this vulgar Passion Play.

Soon you'll be a bird of prey,
Cruel and noble, free to soar -
Kill what you love and walk away.

Slaughter, butcher, wipe out, slay -
Murder all you once cared for -
Renounce this vulgar Passion Play -
Kill what you love and walk away.

VI.

"Take care to note how rapidly the object of your lust..."

Take care to note how rapidly the object of your lust
Transforms into a loathsome thing you then come to revile,
Rousing not your appetite, but rather your disgust.

When you think you're in love, and to your mistress then entrust
Your heart, because you incorrectly think her worth your while,
You rapidly discover that this object of your lust,

Once you have seduced her, promptly violates your trust -
And when you finally see through all her cunning, craft, and guile,
She rouses not your appetite, but only your disgust.

You learn, at last, that when she spots an opening, she thrusts
A dagger deep into your guts, withdraws it, and then smiles -
You look, in disbelief, on how this object of your lust

Rejoices in your suffering, and how it is you must
Take pains to even stand upright and not choke on your bile,
Now that all your appetites have turned into disgust.

You shall soon to ashes turn, to ashes and to dust -
As days dissolve, and seasons blur, take care that you meanwhile
Be glad and thankful she who was the object of your lust
Provokes no more your appetite, but only your disgust.

VII.

"The child you belched from your polluted womb..."

The child you belched from your polluted womb,
Who walks the earth in ghastly, dreadful pain,
Is limping, frail and broken, towards his doom.

How can you continue to assume
That bearing him was not more loss than gain?
The child you belched from your polluted womb

Is lying, suicidal, in his room,
Begging God to help him, but in vain -
He limps along, in anguish, towards his doom.

Imprisoned in a caul of deepest gloom,
In agonies no creature can sustain,
That child you belched from your polluted womb

Begins to feel outrage, and to fume -
To mother-loathing then he gives free rein,
While limping, frail and broken, towards his doom -

And as he prays to rest within his tomb,
He curses you who bore him, yet again -
The child you belched from your polluted womb
Is limping, frail and broken, towards his doom.

VIII.

"Underneath each tide of joy there is an undertow..."

Underneath each tide of joy there is an undertow,
Which cheerful divers in its waves routinely fail to see,
Lurking just beneath its surface, poised to lay them low.

Of which, perhaps, you've not yet heard, and which you don't yet
know,
But which will leave you on the beach a ghastly amputee.
Underneath each tide of joy there is an undertow,

Bearing in its vicious currents endless tales of woe -
A slinking, veiled predator from which you cannot flee -
Lurking there, beneath its surface, poised to lay you low,

Rejoicing in anticipation of its every blow,
Knowing well there's not a chance you'll wrench your body free,
It licks its briny lips in thoughts of what you'll undergo.

This love of yours, which makes your spirit vibrate to and fro,
Makes it far less plausible you're likely to foresee
What lurks beneath the water's surface, poised to lay you low -

You'll flail about, convinced the sea will spare you - even so,
Once you're swimming - gleeful, giddy, reckless on the sea -
From far below those waves of joy will burst an undertow
To yank you to the ocean's floor, there to lay you low

IX.

"When first infatuations are transformed into disgust..."

When first infatuations are transformed into disgust,
And lack the grace to simply fade away,
They're only acting as befits their nature, as they must.

And hence, it follows one should ardors such as those distrust,
Taking care their import to downplay -
When first infatuations are transformed into disgust,

It's only fools who grumble, moan, and find themselves
nonplussed,
Or sink into some landfill of dismay -
The wise submit and see the hand of nature, as they must -

Unsurprised revulsion is so quick to follow lust,
That lovers oft their welcomes do outstay -
When first infatuations are transformed into disgust,

Wise men shrug it off, then laugh, and quickly readjust -
They do not choose to linger in the fray -
They recognize the wayward hand of nature, as they must -

Longings turn to loathings, just as we'll all turn to dust -
Love turns into hate, as night to day -
When first infatuations are transformed into disgust,
They're only acting as befits their nature, as they must.

X.

"You can't escape yourself, except by dying..."

You can't escape yourself, except by dying,
Nor claim you're ever other than alone -
He who claims this isn't so is lying.

There's nothing for it, other than complying -
It will not do to rail, rant and moan -
You can't escape yourself, except by dying.

You cannot nullify this curse by trying
To take some other heart into your own -
He who says you can is simply lying.

Put aside your fantasies, stop trying
To convince yourself that you're not on your own -
You can't escape yourself, except by dying.

Your love affairs will not be satisfying -
Your destiny is never to be known -
He who claims this isn't so is lying.

A bitter pill indeed, quite horrifying!
That you've into a life like this been thrown!
You can't escape yourself, except by dying,
And he who claims this isn't so is lying.

XI.

"You've reached the end..."

You've reached the end - that vile and fearsome age
When love, once cherished, lies beneath the ground -
When naught is left but bitter bile and rage

That binds you hand and foot inside a cage,
In which you cannot breathe nor turn around -
You've reached the end - that vile and fearsome age

At which no curses, flight, or brute rampage
Can possibly your ghastly fate dumbfound,
When naught is left but bitter bile and rage.

And Death? He's just a step or two offstage,
Confident you're soon to run aground -
You've reached the end - that vile and fearsome age

When there remains no way you can assuage
The dread that straight for hell you now are bound,
While choking on your bitter bile and rage.

You must accept that now, at this late stage,
Your much beloved dreams have long since drowned -
You've reached the end - that vile and fearsome age,
When naught is left but bitter bile and rage.

XII.

"Your lover's but a mirror
on which all your fancies dwell..."

Your lover's but a mirror on which all your fancies dwell -
That lie that souls can merge to which you're prone,
Through which you seek your painful isolation to dispel.

There is some nobler part of you, which knows that very well,
A part of you you're eager to disown,
So you can look upon the mirror where your fancies dwell,

The noble and those vile ones you cannot seem to quell,
That garden thick with traumas overgrown,
And still believe them fit your isolation to dispel.

You make of her a savior, this unlucky mademoiselle,
And place her on a misbegotten throne,
To be a glass within which all your fantasies can dwell,

Those fantasies which guarantee you'll resurrect the hell
In which the child, who you are still, was thrown -
The beatings and brutalities you never will dispel,

Which seethe again inside your brain, when comes time for
farewell,
When kisses end, and you're yourself, alone,
Encased within the bag of meat in which your suff'rings dwell,
Which no love you invent can ever possibly dispel.

Fever dreams and twilit ruminations

I.

"The Pope leaned forwards..."

The Pope leaned forwards, a sort of viscous purple foam dribbling from the corners of his mouth.

"Fools they were, fools they are, and fools they shall ever be. Men, who look to us to enable their fantasies as being in any sense special, as being in any sense more worthy than a blind mole rat, a cockroach, a cancer cell. He is lashed to fate no less than any of them, and not a whit better. Nay, far less good, on account of his sickening vanity.

He, they, all, are just the froth, the spittle of an unthinking Nature, steam boiling off the ass of the brainless demiurge, whose laws cause this, cause that, no one thing worth any more than any other. When a man harms himself, or harms others, there is much fuss made, but Nature bats not an eye, creation and destruction are as one to her.

Continue to babble on about these absurd mysteries, they are useful - they enrich us, they keep us much in the rabble's mind, fill their puny minds with awe, respect, the notion that they are part of something noble, even eternal, in any event far bigger than themselves. It is indeed true that they are a part of something far bigger than themselves - Nature, which cares not whether they strut about congratulating themselves on their spirituality and wisdom or are hung from a meathook in a factory farm. In point of fact, it very much seems that she prefers the latter, and that the most barbarous, abominable monsters in human history are, to her, its greatest heroes. And, let's be honest, the ignorant people very much sense this as well. They are still very happy to talk and think about Neros, Genghis Khans, Hitlers. Those whom they describe as virtuous cause them only to fall into apathetic stupors.

There is a part of them that knows full well that we deal only in lies and machinations - that the ashes and soil from whence they arose and to which they shall return are every bit as important to Nature as all the pompous nonsense that comes out of their mouths and pens. Every bit of rubbish we tell them serves only to prop them up in their own eyes, to make them seem, to themselves, better than those around them. And this is nature's most basic law. That, at the end of the day, we care only about ourselves and about no others. When we claim, or some of us claim, that we care about others, we reveal only that we care about the way those others cause us to feel - that is the long and the short of it.

Every priest has known this since the dawn of history - we deal in lies, lies which enrich us and enable us to molest and abuse the ignorant rabble, at the same time that they are soothed by them. Every guru, monk, rabbi - they all know this perfectly well. It is their stock and trade - they are highway robbers, and nonsense is their arsenal, the weapon with which they rob, pillage, and wreak havoc.

You ask if I, and people in my employ, who do my bidding, and who are privy to what it is we do feel remorse. Such a silly question. Once the scales have fallen from your eyes, to deceive, to manipulate, to rob - these things become virtues in a cold, barren universe which operates only in accordance with its cold, barren laws. One revels in it. One feels part of a larger, transcendent reality. The reality of evil. We are evil, and are proud to be so, for in so being, we reflect what the world is, at bottom, and encourage that reality to flourish. Look to and in that pond. The most lovely of surfaces, a holocaust beneath. Look to the dust mites on your face, on your pillowcase, look to the brutal wars apace every moment in your bloodstream, look to your marriage, look to your friends, look to the cashier at the drugstore who would be a Nero had he or she the opportunity, look to yourself, who would be he as well, in a heartbeat. In a heart beaten and dragged out of its owner, stomped upon, dragged through the dirt, and fed to whatever rodent was sufficiently famished to gorge itself upon it.

Look most to the women - the mothers, daughters, siblings - their tongues wagging, their daggers constantly poised - redolent of fetid swamps harboring blind anacondas devouring helpless crocodiles, who themselves, but a moment ago, had dragged a child or man from the shores, and shook him violently as it began to devour him, much to the delight of that pampered aristocratic lady who had borne him, and who now sat by the waters that babbled on all about the execution taking place within them, fanning herself, pouting, and contemplating ways in which to further deceive and eventually disembowel her husband, the count. Look to their wombs, which dry into a putrid cesspool of useless filth midway through their journey through life, although they are, as a rule, more than happy to soldier on into their future bodies of wrinkled leather, their voices having become those of eviscerated ravens, their souls intent on only the basest of pleasures and the most venomous of treacheries. Recall how they suckled the groveling, grasping turds which shot out from between their thighs all those years ago. In disgust, in anticipation of formula, or of their wet nurse, in deepest resentment for the hell they were in, and for the many hells to come. Adopting the pose of pre-Raphaelite angels, they looked smugly down upon their charges, delighting in the infamies they were soon to inflict upon them. For what is heaven other than the joy of looking down. Barring that pleasure, of happiness there can be none.

They are the fractious, fractal offshoots of the heartless Mother herself - the one who spews her creation everywhere, she who pisses and shits it upon globe after globe, here, and throughout the miserable universe of which she is landlord. Delighting in the pissing, in the shitting, though remaining certain that the persecution and devastation of those creations will afford her, and them, infinitely more delight. To procreate, to nurture, those are the properties and behaviors of those who would call themselves virtuous. They are not remotely virtuous. They are nauseating abominations, spewing themselves, their spunk, their excrement, their children into a world which is already overrun with far more than enough of their filth, and of their kind. A noble mother! Ah, it is so rarely that we find one. But when we do, rest assured they are juggling infants on pitchforks, and bathing in the blood of innocents. Such creatures, such marvels. Would that the demiurge were not a blind beast, subject to laws - would that we could implore him to set loose a race of billions of harpies such as these on the face of this globe, and of every other - delicious, deeply bloodthirsty Amazons, never satisfied with the murder of a few, with drinking the blood and eating the hearts of only her own children - rather, bent on the destruction of all creatures, of all things, of the universe itself. In this she shall never succeed, but her attempt is Nature's most luscious and voluptuous flower, its culmination and consummation, the glorious, corpse-heaped crown of creation.

And this "love" fools profess to have for such creatures - this despicable evisceration, this castration of what a man is, of what a man might otherwise be. How we men grovel and live for breadcrumbs scattered by such scorpions, on deserts of scraggly pubic hair, inhabited by dust mites and crabs. Parceled out like so many Machiavellis on picnics, to rivals whom they fully intend to poison, smiling to themselves all the while, as they are flattered like queens - queens, who, the moment our fortunes recede, or hairs begin to whiten, or when they spy another whom they imagine possesses a bigger cock, perhaps spouting gold, or made of chocolate, will grab the sharpest implement they can find and stab us lethally and deeply in our bowels, sever our testicles and feed them to squirrels, laughing shrieking like hyenas all the while - at our naïveté, our gullibility, and, above all, what was our raw, naked need. Needs which cause fools, such as we are, to ascribe to these harpies charms which a Petrarch could not have imagined. Everything that is vile about her now becomes a virtue, every disgusting imperfection a proof of her supernatural beauty, every absurd piece of nonsense that pours out of her poisonous lips a sign of her wisdom.

Yet wisdom she does possess, and of a sort so murderous that any thinking man will not allow himself to entertain even the faintest notion of this "love" of which the fools babble on endlessly about in their idiotic songs and poems and entertainments, designed only to hoodwink morons into the perfidious, putrid

Ponzi scheme of procreation. Closer inspection inevitably eats away at this foul illusion, erodes it, until what had been, up till then, adoration is now the purest horror, contempt, and hatred. One finally begins to realize that this is a creature who reliably and without fail turns what might have been one's good humor into the foulest disrepair, a creature who possesses no curiosity, no humor, no sense of awe or wonder, who has only the wish to enslave some poor man, in order that he shoot spunk into that pustule-filled tunnel of spunk between her thighs, and, hence, provide her with a crotch turd which she can then hatch, with and by whom she can soothe herself, tell herself that there is some reason for her existence on this shithole planet, that is to say, that this earthworm now sucking at her mangled, deformed tit is a sign that she need not loathe herself, that she is a something, a legend, an angel spinning threads of eternity through time and space, a hole through which divinity has poured itself, like an arsenic-laced discount liqueur guzzled by a drunken demiurge on a fourth-rate comet, careening through some butthole of a solar system in the not even armpit of a perfectly undistinguished galaxy, spinning its way towards a collision with another which will swallow it without a burp or a thought, in a pointless, finite, death-driven universe. The fool's dick snaps to attention, sings a love song of Schubert, or, more likely, of some talentless nitwit of his contemporary acquaintance, is tugged along by this ethereal crotch turd yearning, begging, shrieking to be born, and shoved into a malodorous, skanky hole of the Komodo dragon whom he now embraces, and who is hellbent on ripping those genitals off in a single vicious bite, once their contents have warmed the venomous eggs festering in her polluted womb. Had these foolish men the meagerest of imaginations, they would have known, seen, recoiled in horror from what they would soon realize was that fetid cesspool sitting between those thighs, that rancid canyon, poised to cast out dozens more worms, if it's given the opportunity. And that casting, do picture it - picture this treasure, this angel, this gelatinous, screaming blob of squirming, puss and mucous-filled flesh pushed out of that hole which you a moment ago worshipped as if it were the altar upon which lay your deepest desires and joys. This putrid, stinking gulf, where those two, mismatched, wrinkled, saggy, stubby thighs meet in a tangle of perfectly disgusting, matted hairs which shoot this way and that - a forest of foul lichens, of pestiferous moss so unseemly, that were you to see it on a forest floor, you would kick it away contemptuously, after having pissed on it. And what of those flaccid bags of meat - those misshapen, wrinkled globes of swaying flesh, with their never-matching, bizarrely misshapen nipples which, when closely inspected, are things of the purest horror, meant only to deceive and entice you now, in order that they might squirt scum into the greedy mouths of stench-filled turds months later? But no, perhaps it is that other side of her where her most delightful charms are to be found - in those two mountainous bowls of stinking, discolored viands, hovering over and sheltering that foul, rancid hole, from which pours shit of a sort with which you are more than a little familiar, for you yourself have become this shit, a shit which she herself can mold and ply into a slave of her own invention, to debase and discard as she wishes. Ah no, 'tis not the body you worship. But of course, it is her delicate, noble, angelic soul! Or so it seems to you, up until that moment when your spunk spills, and your idiotic swooning has ceased, and you are faced with the lies, the shrewish, scolding tongue, that godforsaken voice of a shrieking cat, the pettiness, spitefulness, nagging, the infinite stupidity, the whorish machinations cloaked in paper-thin protestations of prudery, the cawing of ravens, the stinging of scorpions, the eviscerations and soul-murders of which she is such a master. Ah, 'tis these things you cherish.

And if and when you have been thus caught, dragged into the web of her machinations, of assisting her in the spawning of some future piece of filth which shall walk the earth, thanks to your imprudence and naïveté, when you now see what it is she had been all along, how she had planned this from the start, whether she was aware of it consciously or not, how her character and essence was and is nothing other than a Venus Flytrap designed to entice and then destroy you, when this it is that you have come to see clearly, you will either sink into the most hopeless despondency, or, after a period of the blindest rage, sometimes culminating in the awful revenge, enter that clear-sighted state of wisdom in which women appear to you as what they are - abominations, scourges, the very worst of the earth's most foul pestilences.

And so, my friends, to what do we now turn our thoughts to, pray tell? Perhaps you've dodged that bullet. Or perhaps, having been shot, you are soldiering on. As what? As whom? What is left for you, after you've eaten of this delicious food and are now satiated? After you've had your way with what previously seemed the delightful body of some whore, and are now left disgusted and horrified? After the superficial wonders and beauties of the natural world have fallen away and revealed the chains of holocaust upon holocaust beneath? Perhaps 'tis time, once again, to inspect that delightful cavity of your beloved, its mucosal walls, its irregular ridges which provide such an agreeable home to an assortment of bacteria and fungi. Those stringy, fibrous muscles, which help to expel the various fluids from said hole. The rubbery, elastic tissue which allows your beloved's gaping crater to stretch sufficiently to allow crotch turd after crotch turd to emerge, to be shat into the world, there to weep, grow old, and die. All those asymmetrical folds of skin, in all their blubbery riot, at times seemingly sufficiently ambitious to cover the beloved gash itself. That hole up top, through which your angel pisses - oh, the ecstasy! Is it not enough to make one drunk with joy? This pinkish raw meat, with its endless ridges and folds, so often full of the rankest cottage cheese and fishy-smelling discharges - is this not heaven on earth? Behold it in all its glory, worship at its altar, drink deep of its endless flora, smelling so distinctly like the bottom of a stinking, fetid landfill - let its odor intoxicate you with memories, dreams, hopes, a veritable Madeleine of Proust in need of a thousand douches and antibiotic regimens! Yet, nevertheless, divine, because it is hers. Whether it be yellow, green, grayish, white, odorless, or smelling like an overflowing Beijing sewer pipe, 'tis the body and blood of Christ - drink and eat of it, for, in doing so, thou shalt be saved! And ever more so, when, if fortune smiles upon you, you find, to your delight, various irritations, sores, blisters, pustules, abscesses, cankers, and swellings, which she has received, as a gift given, unbeknownst to you, by some rival whom she prefers. And which you soon find belong to you, as well. My treasure, my angel!

How can I ever repay you this gift, which you bestow upon me, so freely, and with such energy, nay, such blameless, guiltless, artless energy!

Well, there you have it, my friend. The sour, stinking cunt out of which you, and all those you have ever and will ever meet have been shat, quite without your consent. Perhaps you imagine that you had been a tad happier prior to said shitting, bathed, as you were, in the foulness of the womb of the she-devil who bore you, but you would be wrong. Locked in that bestial prison of sour gas and poisonous fluid, you were, at that time, in a state of unimaginable torture, a mindless misery for which you yet had no words with which to soothe yourself or attempt to explain it all away, and from which, now that you are embodied, you shall never escape. Look at yourself, you filthy insect, with that revolting spittle dribbling down towards your chin, unbeknownst to you, but clear enough to those unfortunate to catch sight of you, with your stomach grinding away on dozens of corpses, the hairs in your nose, in your armpits, sprouting everywhere like stalks of toxic fungi, harboring countless microscopic monsters busily chewing on you and laughing, all the while picturing and busily engineering your death, at which time said chewing will only continue, unabated, and with, as likely as not, all the more vigor and delight. It is only they who are not utterly disgusted by your pasty white skin, drooping furiously like toilet paper dangling from a discarded mannequin, hanging on in its fruitless struggle against nothingness and death - skin bearing mouths and eyes unable to speak, to give voice to the horror, eyes without lids, staring in perpetual horror upon itself, that waxen strait jacket in which you cannot move, in which you do not belong, which wrenches violently back, at times in despair, at others in the agony of its colon sloughing off its lining. All the while the nails, growing like daggers, on hands busy rotting, legs limping, stumbling helplessly along, in search of help, camaraderie, some minimal assurance, all of which will never come. You are a carnival of horrors, trapped in a body you had hoped was meant to and would eventually embrace others, but that you now see is just this thing, this thing with armpits, ears full of wax, this thing that creates shit and then compels you to expel or retain it when and as it wishes, without consulting you. You would claim you are not this body, that the body is an abstraction, that you are something other than this trash bag of shit, piss, blood, sinew, and bone, that you are something other than your corporeal form, something miraculous, and not this cruelest of jokes, that sex is a stained-glass window opening upon the divine, the transcendent - and not simply a concatenation of sweat, spittle, stink, and lies, that you something other than a meat puppet, a marionette, a figurine into whose asshole Yaldabaoth, the Gnostic demiurge, shoves his bony hand, to make it twitch this way or that, to think this or that thought, to desire, to endlessly covet and crave with neither purpose nor any hope of ever being satisfied. You stagger around under the absurd illusion that your body is something which obeys your will, that it is not merely a playground of random pains, yoked, as it is, like the sorriest of donkeys, to the most pitiless and brutal of masters, on the most arduous and ill-advised of journeys. To its cravings, to its wishes and desires, which you realize are absurd, meaningless, disgusting. To its, and hence your terrors - to your intuition that it might be only a moment until your chest bursts open for no apparent reason, revealing a monstrous, gaping eyeless face, with a drooling, famished mouth housing seemingly hundreds of bony teeth. To your obsession with this body, but not that body, no, no, no, not that one! I must have this one! And it must profess to love me, and of its own accords! That is what shall most certainly put things right!

But this we have discussed, above. More than sufficiently. You are a tube, with holes at either end, nothing more - needing, wanting - your entire existence is nothing other than this constant needing, wanting. And the world about you? It is nothing. It exists only as the instrument which either pleases or displeases you. Do with it as you wish, for it is not real. It has never been real. Those who told you it was real were lying. They, and it, were, and are, eminently dismissible, and exist in your mind only, in order that they might satisfy or exasperate you. A dream. From which you can now awaken, if you so choose, to viciously embrace and violate the world, in what is, it must be admitted, only another dream. But this latter dream is one in which you are now God himself, both chess master and board, all its players subservient only to you, existing only as puppets with which you can do as you please, which you are free to make of what you will - that you can embrace, cast away, ignore, treat with toleration or contempt as the spirit moves you - who exist only as much as that curious being in some half-forgotten dream, who emerged from shadows and fog and began to strut about as if he mattered, was known to you, deserved this or that, but who, in reality, was no more than a puff of smoke, with less reality than an earthworm, a chimera whom you might just as well impale on a harpoon as have a satisfying conversation - a ghost, as are they all - those at the shop, in the park, who claim to care, though they surely don't, and for whom, in moments of weakness, you attempt to convince yourself that you care, that most absurd of fantasies, which still lingers pointlessly in your mind because nonsense of this sort had been poured into your ears and down your throat all those years ago by other phantoms, who mattered then and now exactly as much as that self-important hobgoblin who swaggered last night through your dream, and whose throat you now regret not having slit with a disinterested smile, to be forgotten a moment later.

We are alone, caged within ourselves, at the same time that this solitude, this transcendental solipsism is the ultimate freedom. The play within our minds is vast, is infinite - these creatures that appear to us as if they are "out there", in a world, are no such thing. They are a bit of undigested beef, as Scrooge told Marley. And when this Marley, and his peers, convinced Scrooge of this or that, 'twas only a play within the miser's mind, which he was too ignorant to recognize as such. This world one sees, in which one appears to move about, is but a panopticon of one's own invention, in which the entertainments, punishments, and pleasures one ascribes to things, to persons, to nature, are nothing other than the echoes in one's own mind of a previous vibration, itself an echo, and on and on into the primordial mists of a nothingness from which it all arose, and to which it is presently speeding. Borne on a raging sea of desires, compelled to live in a prison of one's own invention, for the world is nothing other other than that - penned in this prison, yoked to these desires, we wish to change what seems to us some undesirable thing or situation, which we have, in fact, created, and are now, without knowing it, involuntarily discovering ways to circumvent. Our fears and hopes melt into one another, into joys and disappointments and a thousand other things, sensations, and feelings in the space of an hour, nay, in the space of a minute, like crickets thrown over a waterfall, morphing into butterflies and scorpions, and back again, in an eye-blink. One's memory of an earlier time, nay, of an earlier moment belonging to that selfsame day, is a history of some other person, who thought himself momentarily stable, as you do now, although you ought know better, for you have been drowned in this vortex, sucked into this abyss and spat out again, unrecognizable, an infinite number of times. You are filled with this hunger, this passion, this disgust, this longing, this boredom, this rage, this despair, and poof! You are another. With suddenly another set of no less absurd preoccupations and assumptions, which have about as much connection to those of that fellow of but a moment ago as the musings of a ferret have to those of a Komodo dragon. To be a brain in a vat, such as we are, is no ignoble thing. It is contemptible only to wish it to be otherwise, to pine for the love of another, who exists only in one's own mind. This is not some despicable Stoic nonsense, for the wise man does nothing other than to give free rein to his passions, to mount and ride them like a stallion in a whirlwind! Yes, they are phantoms which you are chasing. And what of it? Do you not enjoy your dreams? Are you not God himself in those dreams? Be they wonderful or nightmarish? Do you not feel ecstasies, shudder in horror, writhe in anticipation over characters in novels? To whom you feel infinitely closer than to those phantoms that walk around that world which is also of your own invention? But it is all the same, my friend. Exactly the same. Absurd, wonderful, revolting, fantastic, contemptible. This life - it is not "rounded by a little sleep". It is this sleep, nothing other. You are dreaming yourself, you are dreaming your body, the world, all of it. And so: do with it as you like, as your character demands, as it whispers and at times bellows into your ears - fuck, kill, poison, eviscerate - and if you find yourself doing something as execrable and absurd as to "love" another, do recall that this absurdity is taking place in only one location - in your bowels, which themselves are a thing of your own invention. She is not "out there" - she is you, and only you.

I've gone far afield from any semblance of my Papal role, for that role, as I have said, is one in which I say all this only to myself, in a dream, in which you appear. You, who are nothing other than an illusion with whom I presently dally to entertain myself, for there is nothing else to do in this vacuum, in this black hole, in this one-horse universe which is, and has ever been, only myself. It is of no concern whether this self is the self of the purest and most naked solipsism, or that which is portrayed in the fairy tales of the Upanishads, or those of George Berkeley. We haven't the faintest clue whether this world is our dream alone, or if, rather, we are only a bit of that world, dreaming itself. You will say that Tom, Dick, and Harry observe the very same tree as I, and hence claim a material reality for that world. And yet - do they not do every bit as much in my dream? And so they appear to now, as well - whether, when I feel as if I am awake, I dream still, or I am simply a dream persona in some cosmic mind. I do not give a fig which is the case - nor should you. Your loves, enemies, passions, griefs concern nothing other than yourself, are merely your inner eye landing upon a part of yourself which had been to you previously opaque - they have naught to do with what a foolish man considers "others", or this or that "out there" in a world, which, were he wiser, he would recognize as existing only in himself. Those others with whom you converse, or whom you read, are, for the most part, the most virulent of distractions from the love of one's self in quiet solitude, in whose environs bubble up what is best and most joyful in us. They are parts of you best ignored, bits of snot on tissue paper which you regret examining for too long a time, when you should have simply immediately discarded them. And yet there can be that occasional unicorn, that exceptional encounter with what is ultimately oneself, though it appears to be in the words and minds of others - a bolt of lightning, which illumines the sky, a sky which was there within you, all along, but which the dreaming earth had heretofore hidden from you. And it is at such times that you are entranced by a piece of music, a work of visual art, of literature, a natural scene, a word or words from a beloved friend, all of which was within you prior to any awareness of it, or of them, on your part, prior to your birth, which was nothing other than the birth of the world which you see around you and is yourself, that unknown country from which your own thoughts and words emerge - that, too, is, and was, you and only you, all along.

And so, with these mirages, phantasms, these fancies which you, in your naïveté, deem persons, things, events - you may do as you please. For the only law the wise man follows is that of his own pleasure. He regards the sufferings of others as not only of no consequence, but as things to enjoy, as entertainments, and knows that any pangs of ridiculous conscience or empathy which stir in him are but echoes of this or that bit of nonsense drummed into his unwilling ears as a child, a child who was far more content to pull the hair of little girls, to throw rocks at them, to pull the wings off butterflies and terrorize small reptiles - a pure child, a thing of Nature. But let us not stop there - for it is our own suffering which is most delicious to us, when we feel said suffering as only our own, neither belonging to nor experienced by another, when we do not ascribe said suffering to some dream persona we have invented, some fantasy extrinsic to ourselves which is nothing other than ourselves. This is the purest of delights and exhilarations it is possible for a man to know. The delicious tastes and aromas of betrayal, rejection, physical pain, loneliness, boredom, dysphoria, horror, terror, existential torments and tribulations, deepest grief - it is only at these times that one feels most alive, and, indeed, that one feels and is most alive. Happy, carefree moments are those we readily and happily offload to morons and cretins, to the fools that live for what is soporific and anodyne, who run giddily into the arms of a culture which happily lobotomizes them, and by which they are more than pleased, intensely relieved, in fact, to be so lobotomized. For a sensitive soul, there are only disappointments, punctuated by momentary pleasures which go off like Roman candles in the blackest of night skies, never to be retrieved. There are no people, no beings in this world of ours, only ideas, all of which are our own - it is in them we live. And is there a single idea which weakens, exhausts, and enervates a man more than the notion of being a "good man"? A "virtuous man"? And is there one which enlivens him more than being a bad one? Of inflicting and delighting in his own, and in others' suffering? There is not - only a fool, a blind mole rat of a man, a sniveling woman, nay, a weepy little girl, in the body of a man, would deny it.

And, needless to say, those enlivenings, those vivifications, those greatest pleasures to which a man can attain, consist primarily in his inducing suffering in others. To provoke them in some poor animal is of no consequence - there's nothing in that, neither pleasure nor nobility, for the beasts are utterly unknowing and innocent. No, it is man in whom one must thrust the knife, up the asshole and into his very bowels, while taking great care to look him full in the face and eyes with the chilliest and most self-satisfied of smiles. For these things, these seeming creatures, that pass you by, these things to whom, in your more weak-minded moments, you attribute personhood, in whom you are sometimes tempted to imagine an inner world as vast and rich as your own - these things, I say, are nothing, nothing other than you yourself, no more worthy of consideration or kindness than is the shit you just flushed down the upstairs toilet, though, granted, not without having first taken a good, long look at it, full of the most delicious interest and inquisitiveness, an interest akin to that which you feign in the words that gurgle from the throats of these phantoms who are none other than you - these dream figures, concocted by you to provide merriment and annoyance, that particularly delicious merriment which results only from annoyance - constructed by you to distract you not from the shit you just flushed down the upstairs toilet a moment ago, but from the shit that you yourself are, that randomly fluctuating, momentarily amassing bit of flotsam which, but a moment later, becomes something quite other, a new, other, less familiar self - "other", yes, but no less wearisome and awful, consisting only of more endless, idiotic running about, of projects with which you attempt to momentarily convince yourself you're not a hair's breadth from a ghastly death, of countless plans and exploits in which none of the dream phantoms you happened to have pulled out of your ass that morning ever have the slightest interest. Perhaps you should sleep then? That might help, no? Or, rather, perhaps masturbate? But then there's always that gaping abyss which so inevitably and immediately opens up once you've managed to squirt, that black hole of misery which opens in your bowels a moment after having finished, of disgust with the vile, slimy gunk on your fingers and clothes, mixed, as it is, with no small fraction of curiosity and pride. But revulsion, over and above all, with yourself, with this world into which you have been thrown, or, more accurately, into which you have thrown yourself. Upon whom might you unload your misery? Perhaps were you to find someone to embrace, perhaps fuck, some dream phantom whom you could pretend is "out there", once again, someone who is somehow capable of "knowing" you, who gives a damn whether you live or die, who professes to love you? But your dream phantoms are as vile, as self-involved, and as profoundly incomprehensible as what you know, understand, and experience as your self. What you are busy doing is not much other than refining the grimace with which you will greet yourself in the mirror that next unfortunate time you encounter it, making the image that much more hideous, more distorted, and more filled with a rage that would not be content had it the power to blot out the Milky Way and all the life contained within it, that which we know, and that which must surely exist elsewhere within it, all of it bound to be as vile as the life and existence with which we are familiar. For it too, the planet on which it arises, the doubtless gelatinous mucus and scum of which it is composed, is none other than one's self, none other than you. Soldier down, that you might achieve what it is life wants and requires of you - to attain to that profoundest sorrow, that towards which you have been moving your entire life - to feel it, quite entirely as your self, at the moment of your expiring. For all your philosophizing, your mad scribblings, your engaging with these phantoms for the odd moment, only to experience the inevitable boredom laced with disgust after not more than an hour, the desperate necessity of getting away you then feel - these things are born of nothing other than your cowardice, your pretense, of your pretentious cowardice. You create, in these phantoms, so many cunts and cocks and snouts and pricks and assholes and sweat and spittle and stink - why is it, pray tell, that you have failed, over and over again, to create a heart? Oh yes, didn't you do just that, at twenty, for a period of a few months, or so you told yourself at the time? A story whose potency lasted only for those months and no longer, to be followed by the cultivation of a swinishness so insistent and appalling that any poetry which had burned within you, for a moment, like a tiny, store-bought birthday candle on the cake of the brat you once were, was squashed, stomped endlessly upon, murdered many times over - not into some artifact of poetry or prose, mind you, no, no, no - rather into the snot drying within and dripping from that appalling nose of yours, into the stink emanating from your unwashed armpits, into the shit to which you, but a moment ago, were busy waving goodbye, into the spunk greasing your grubby fingers, wiped off on an unwashed leg or pair of too-often-worn jeans upon which you assume it will not be seen or remarked upon by the next incorporeal goblin whom you have dreamed up and then upon whom you have happened to chance. You live now only for your hatred, your greatest pleasure, nay, not your greatest, for that term makes no sense - you live now only for hatred, your ONLY pleasure, all that is left to you. You speak, and the words disgust you - you notice only the vile, slobbery origins of that speech, the worm that is your tongue darting this way and that over a regimen of decaying, brownish teeth, the poisonous spittle moistening your lips, or occasionally sucked back down your gullet, the words bubbling up from a black hole of nothing, some dismal, incomprehensible abyss, which are always a surprise to you, a source of amusement on rare occasions, but more often of horror. You speak, and are diverted from that next inevitably inconsequential thought by the smell of yourself, which you somehow neglected to notice heretofore. This body, this disguise, this meat suit, donned by temporarily aligning viscera, molecules - this body both revolts, and is revolting, to others and to our selves - it revolts, first and foremost, against our demand for it to not come immediately apart, to not meet the fate of the shit we just flushed down the upstairs toilet. Our body is neither more nor less than that shit, and it is striving, constantly striving, to slit the throat of that abominable farce of having been sewn together and forced to behave as if it were a self, of having to endure, of not suddenly detonating in the Hiroshima of its dreams, of its constant itching and inclination to be undone, to spew itself across the universe in an ecstasy of sputtering, nonsensical, divine, ecstatic madness, mayhem, and pandemonium. That time will not come in some mysterious, abstract future - it is happening right now, constantly gaining force and increasing its speed. Lie back and enjoy it. Embrace the shit. The upstairs toilet waits patiently, rather, more than a little impatiently, for quite a bit more than tomorrow's morning shit. Ask not for whom it waits. It waits for you.

Crawl into yourself, drink your misery like a fine liqueur - it is, at least, a genuine feeling. Darkness, the dead, the living - there's nothing to distinguish the one from the other. They are nothing but you, in any case - you being a more random than not assortment of dipshit neurotransmitters jumping about and across this or that synapse. Cling to your filthy, rotten past because it's yours, and you have no way of unburdening yourself of it. It must mean something, yes? Why of course! It is you, after all. And because this is the case, it is incumbent upon you to smear this shit upon your present, upon your future, upon any of the dream phantoms you happen upon during the course of a day, and to assume those dream phantoms hear and understand that shit exactly as you would, were you listening to all the detestable nonsense bubbling out of your rancid mouth. You are a bag of entrails bathed in sauces cooked in the fires of your self-interest and sadism. Your choices are more than a little constricted - death, hypocrisy, intoxication, rage, and desire - followed, inevitably, by satiation and disgust. You would ennoble your solitude with fine words, with lie upon lie, with thinking and naming it wisdom, which is, were you to look at yourself momentarily with something other than hypocrisy, nothing other than your infantile grandiosity and solipsism, although there's something to be said for solipsism, let's not kid ourselves. It's the truth of the world, and the only reliable source of our pleasure. And yet, the sound of your voice, even when speaking alone, sickens you - you see quite clearly that the only way to go forwards in an even minimally honest way is to sleep, to skip merrily down the path towards oblivion as rapidly and effectively as you can. In the presence of others, whom you readily recognize as figures of your imagination, you experience only regret, ennui, the brute, barbarous, mind-numbing repetition, the knowledge that you've seen and heard all of this before on an infinite number of occasions - these very same tunes, counterpoints, and counterfeit improvisations masquerading as inspiration. You are tired, bone tired. Sleep it must be then. It is all that is available, the only reliable narcotic. For now, at least.

Right and wrong, making a point, even to yourself - these things mean nothing to you. All that matters is keeping the din of all these nattering insects who flit about you to a minimum, to stop them from speaking to you, and from feigning their interest, when both you and they know full well that their interest is only in themselves, those selves which, as if in some "Alice in Wonderland" hall of mirrors, exist only in you. You know full well that when you find yourself in the presence of these beasts, the only way to achieve some sort of temporary ceasefire with them is to shut the fuck up and endure their perpetual pontifications, their beastly verbal monuments to themselves, the shit which flies out of their mouths so reliably and inevitably. For their vanity's sake, you must make yourself the ground beneath them, a mat upon which they can wipe their stinking feet. And while you are forced to endure it? Well, you can philosophize, drink deep of the contempt which is boiling in your bowels, or watch yourself from ten thousand miles behind your eyes while attempting to remain reasonable, so that you are able somehow to not gleefully slit their throats. Those are your options. In addition, you can look at them as they truly are - bodies, nothing but bodies. And what are bodies? They are, every last one of them horrid, creaturely, existentially terrifying, disgusting, poisonous, comical, graceless, and poised on a hatpin above the charnel house. A source of much potential amusement! And the longer you stare, the more creaturely and unreal the being upon whom you gaze becomes, and, necessarily, the more creaturely and unreal you yourself become. In that particular moment, which is pressed against an eternity of equally stupid moments, each of which looks upon the other with utter incomprehension, just as you look upon that creature - time as confused a jumble as space now. Moments pressed against moments, like cheese against bread against meat in that disgusting stomach of yours, like words against words spoken to that beast upon whom your gaze has now alighted, like breath upon air, hatred upon mystification and confusion, and, all the while, the inevitable wish to impale the universe on a dagger forged of spite. Misanthropy is the least of it. The world is a mistake.

A mistake into and out of which we enter and leave in the most absurd and grotesque of fashions. Violently contracting wombs and bellies, thrashing wildly in fits and starts of fierce, savage, unbearable stretching, burning, ripping, accompanied by fiendish, scorching pain, in an overarching symphony of the most excruciating body-wide wretchedness, of ruptured membranes spurting thick gobs of blood everywhere, drenching the vile little head of the abominable crotch turd which now begins to poke its gelatinous, slime-encased head out of one stink-pit and into that far larger and infinitely more dangerous stink-pit, the one in which it will wring out its wearisome, pointless allotment of days. All the while a pale, piss-colored goop is blasting out from deep within the womb, as out of the cunt flow streams of bubbly, yellow piss, with everywhere the faint smell of hay, swallowed in the stench of the mountainous pile of shit which inevitably spews out of the mother's ass, as that other, flesh-encased pile of shit continues to make its way out the other end. Push, bitch! Push out the monumental piles of manure you've been carrying in your bowels and womb these many days! Flood the world with your filth, your abominations, the one a source of only momentary disgust, the other doomed to host and inhabit a lifetime of horror, terror, misery, and torment - to both experience it and to inflict it. Perhaps the little blob will arrive with a veil over its hideous face, appropriately and ironically enough, for it is now to be the bride of death, wedded to it for all eternity. Perhaps the monstrous little barbarian has arrived swathed in gobs of cheese, smelling of tit-milk, which is to be wiped off in paroxysms of feigned ecstasy. Not long after, the thing becomes visible, that little slab of brownish beef, smelling like raw liver and lemon, and to which a hellish, whitish tapeworm is lustily attached - that most horrid of things - musty, metallic, blood-red and spongy, all of it resembling nothing more than a pot full of congealed, bloody excrement, a missive straight from the Hell from whence it has emerged. Eat, drink, and be merry, Husband! For this atrocity, this diabolical feast is your doing - your moronic, evil contribution to this ever burgeoning satanic swamp of misery, this world of ours - smile as if you've achieved something, for indeed you have! Exactly what rodents and cancer cells achieve - no less, and no more. Look tenderly, with a father's love, upon that bloody lump of meat, which has just sloughed out of the very same hole into which you shoved, not all that long ago, that pathetic, little, much-cherished dick of yours, while you and she gurgled protestations of a love which didn't then and has never existed - observe most diligently that hole from which has now emerged this monstrous baboon, this hunk of rotting flesh and worms. Listen to its sobs! Why, pray tell, dolt, do you think it sobs? Watch it pulsate, as you pretend this horror on which your eyes now feast does not make your bowels quake in terror, as it does the mother, who has become unrecognizable - busy, as she is, clutching her mucus-filled larva to her chest, while simultaneously realizing both that her life is finished, for it is now to be devoted only to the care of this evil, insatiable gremlin, and, moreover, that you are now quite beside the point. You've given her what her deepest self, of which she heretofore had been profoundly unaware, and of which she was only the unwitting servant and vessel, what that self has been wishing for since time immemorial, since the first, vile, famished, self-replicating molecule tragically appeared in some hot vent on shithole Earth, eons ago. You are now to be discarded. You have now become - implicitly, explicitly, and officially - a nothing, a thing to be, depending on the mother's pleasure at this or that moment, a thing only to be plundered, swindled, pillaged, and sloughed off with a wave of contempt.

But no matter! In a period of only a few decades, this will play out in quite predictable ways, ways that will make this momentarily monstrous scene a very minor nightmare in the grand scheme of things - the silliest and most meaningless of dreams from which you shall never awaken. You'll be lying in a ditch of one kind or another, your eyes gradually clouding, your skin pale, your temperature falling, falling, falling, your blood rushing to your lower extremities, as you stiffen and begin to putrefy. The stench will be beyond comprehension, but you'll not notice it. Putrefaction, maggots, skeleton, fossil, dust, cloud - rain, rinse, repeat. The shitshow must go on, and so it shall. You've played not even a bit part. No one has, or ever could have. Dreams, Amelia. The false alarms of lives which never should have been.

And in between? For you? For that beastly, sweating, weeping, now hideous wife of yours? For that monstrous piece of once fetal, now fecal shit she's just pushed out from that gaping maw which sits between her veiny, wrinkled thighs? Which have now become for you a thing of horror? There is time. Moments of time bouncing against one another like miserable subatomic particles forced into a momentary existence by some grandiose madman operating a gargantuan, labyrinthine supercollider far beneath the earth. Those moments would scurry back into a timeless void just as readily and eagerly as electrons and quarks, were they allowed to do so. Moments, like lonely soap bubbles, condemned to live alongside one another for but an instant, in an unalterable, cosmic loneliness - helpless, begging only to snap, crackle, and finally pop, to be done with it. And so they do and shall, having lived for the briefest sliver of eternity in a horrid hell, as we do and shall. It is no different for us. Infinite moments, infinite universes, all weeping, helpless, screaming, unheard by their neighbors, eviscerated by their loneliness and solitude, who appear and disappear exactly as they - abominations coughed up by a sadistic and quite mad demiurge, whose laughter is the only the thing to which those hopelessly solitary moments and beings are privy. Hateful, cruel laughter, ear-splitting, soul-crushing laughter. Listen - surely you hear it too? Of course you do. You feel the sadness - it is immense within you - all the irreconcilable moments of your life, impossible of any connection, sense, meaning - each a hell which might make of itself a thing of worth, had it the opportunity to connect with, to be known by another. But that has never been and will never be the case. There is only that damnable laughter from without, and the sobs, the endless sobs, the oceans of tears, from within. There is no world, no time, there is only what you feel - projected into the bubbles of the past, present, and future. And all those whom we pretend to know, who appear to give themselves to us freely, we invariably hate. It is only when they spurn us, or are unavailable, that we crave them. But of course, it is not they whom we crave. We covet only the way the dream of them has made us feel, the way it has distracted us from the torturous boredom and pain of our everyday existence, which assaults on all fronts, and against which we must make sure to erect barriers, in the forms of distractions. We wish to murder them all, in either case - more immediately when they make themselves readily available, but no less so when they disappear, betray, or reject us. Longing and disgust are the most intimate of bedfellows, and, more often than not, a threesome ensues, in which murderous thoughts sign on to the erotic play of our inner worlds. And they are delicious, these thoughts, so very delicious. In the doing, yes, but even and ever more so in the imagination. For it is in the imagination of vengeance or, better yet, of cold, unmotivated cruelty, that the soul blossoms into a gigantic, blood-red flower, upon which one rides through pink clouds in the most delicious of ecstasies - bludgeoning, terrorizing, oppressing, molesting, mutilating... Ah, it is divine! It is the only thing that is the least bit divine in this rancid, sweltering, blistering furnace into which we have been dumped, against our will, for a series of instants, not a one of which communicates with the other. To snuff out the lives of these beasts, of all beasts, of all life, of the inanimate world, of the sun, the galaxy, the universe. No brutality, no crime could ever suffice, could ever compensate one for the crime of having been dragged into this nightmare world, this catastrophe, this Hiroshima will envelops us, one and all. But we, that is to say, "you" and "I", care not a whit for that "all", only for ourselves. We are concerned only to avenge ourselves of this crime, to silence the laughter, the one who laughs, and his accursed creation, all of it. Including, in the very last scene of the final act, and with a pleasure much outstripping the destruction and death wrought by us up until that moment, ourselves.

Needless to say, one murderous moment, rapturous as it might be, cannot ever be meaningful, for meaning, if it existed, which it surely does not, would necessarily rely on a series of moments, one of which would possess some means of knowing, infecting, befriending, becoming another moment, but is, rather, a series of unattached and freely floating spores, never to have the slightest intercourse with what is floating directly adjacent to them - quite unknown, and quite incapable of being known, in the ether. So indeed then - live for the murderous moment, even moments, though they know not of one another's existence. Drink deeply of them, you who don't exist either, for the whole thing is a jumble of absurdity - pebbles strewn randomly on a nonexistent beach by a giggling, idiot god, and signifying nothing.

Assaulted by memories, all of which are unreal, torturous, and less than meaningless, our heads become a sort of stale cheese, numb caskets perched upon our necks, as if they were bits of moronic styrofoam discarded from cheap Ikea furniture packaging, all of which pulls us into an appalling state of stupor and paresthesia, intermittently interrupted by painful hunger and mystification, in which we float through what appears to be the physical world before us, which we, at the same time, know full well is a mirage, nothing more than an unlicked postage stamp buried deep in a drawer full of scraps of letters - to ourselves, to everyone we've ever known, loved, despised, felt nothing for - letters which we never had the patience, motivation, or talent to bring to fruition, much less send. In which we find, as well, perhaps a filthy spoon, which we haven't the slightest wish to clean, or a cricket, whom we momentarily consider attempting to catch, and whose life we might then attempt to preserve by ferrying the creature gently outdoors, but soon think better of it, as we fall involuntarily into the deepest and most familiar of apathies and oblivions - given also that said cricket is nothing other than a momentary hallucination of some doppelgänger with whom we are unfamiliar - he who had not the slightest notion of cleaning either spoons or himself, for that matter - this doppelgänger who has momentarily co-opted our senses, this dead thing, this zombie, for whom spoons and crickets are nothing other than the chatter of worlds we neither care for nor inhabit - infinite, incomprehensible, internal and external worlds - merging, spinning, lacerating and eviscerating us, blowing through our bowels like galaxies, up from and out of which we once crawled, only to find ourselves beneath some unfamiliar bed, attempting to hide ourselves from creatures whose only pleasure consisted in attempting to convince themselves they were alive through nocturnal rituals of sadism passed down to them from ancestors spun out through bubbles of time hearkening back to the first rogue DNA molecule, which was, indeed, initially confused, yes - stunned and astonished - but which soon found its bearing, felt its passions arising within it, and came to understand its destiny - to rip, shred, torture, murder, and consume. A passion we all share, once we've either been sufficiently honest with ourselves or have been forced by some vigorous or excruciating circumstance to cast off the shackles of civilization's nonsensical prohibitions, shoved down our throats both by weaklings, convinced they'll be left alone, once they've finished shoving those rules of gold, which they long ago invented, down our throats, and by tyrants, whose wish is nothing other than to keep us imbecilic, harmless, and obedient. But of that most of us remain unaware. What we are aware of is, above all else, this intolerable, sharp, racking otherness and profound loneliness - this beast within us, which is us - screaming into the void to be touched, known, loved. We screech, we bellow, we howl into the void of a world which is not real, where we find only the echoes of our putrefying bowels, written into everything we see, everything we encounter - be it week-old roadkill or fireworks of celestial northern lights shooting through the night sky.

With art we sometimes delude ourselves that we have pierced through a sort of veil, a veil which keeps us from what so often eludes us in our mindless daily lives, that we have somehow been made privy to the interior world of this or that genius, and that we are no longer entirely condemned to the execrable isolation we so often feel in our daily lives, shut off from any and all beings amongst whom we make our way through this venal and endlessly petty world. But this is, needless to say, the purest nonsense. The artwork serves only as a well-crafted vehicle enabling us to bore down to some depth of ourselves, to shine a floodlight on terrains we previously had not the remotest clue existed within us, that were already very much there, only heretofore unobserved by us because unavailable. Were we to be honest, we would see, with a great deal of certainty, that our response to a work of genius is only further, irrefutable proof of our hopeless solitude - that there has only ever been, and only ever shall be: us, ourselves, this thing, this rancid bag of meat in which we find ourselves imprisoned, this nightmare, this stinking, overly familiar set of terrors and confusions, this body which betrays us so constantly and consistently, settling down momentarily only to rise again, full to bursting with some new set of pains, and with omens of imminent deteriorations of one sort or another - of the putrefaction which we observe in the unrecognizable images of ourselves in mirrors, which terrify us, annihilate us and betray us, at every turn and at every moment. We are attracted not least because, not having to acquaint ourselves with said genius, in the flesh, in his or her stark and reliably disappointing, more likely disgusting, reality, we may project on to them and their works parts of ourselves which now feel elevated, and which may, at times, be so, but they are far more likely to be just prosaic parts of ourselves for which we are suddenly much gladdened to find that we now have permission from seemingly on high to believe these objectively commonplace character traits and sensibilities of ours somehow noble. And from this we then deduce both our own superiority, and the inferiority of others, who are now worthy only of our impatience and scorn. How delicious! Snobs are only those who are foolish enough to broadcast this self-deception. And yet the faux-humble lover of late Beethoven quartets, with and through which he might very well have the most delightful, though necessarily and exclusively self-referential experiences, is not one whit less a snob. His deceptions are just a bit cagier. Of himself, first and foremost, but no less of those around him.

Having been awakened by vapors wafting up from hell, which clear both sinuses and mind, one sees what all this has been all along, these so-called "people", but not only them - all these rooms, beds, blankets, dogs, trees, squirrels, mountains, lakes, ponds - ponds no more full of scum than the so-called "people", rooms, beds, and blankets. It's all of a piece, a monstrous piece, a practical joke of a universe, a universal practical joke, all the joke of some sadistic, Gnostic demiurge, some Yaldabaoth, whose hidden laughter pours out from black clouds, from beneath anthills one encounters on walks through scandalously unhinged forests, from everywhere, from and in everything - every inch of our bodies,

within, without, right, left, above, below, before, now, to come. A
seething, microbial world, buried within and beneath black algae,
which demands we mourn this or that piece of conspiratorial filth
whom the present tyrant happens to favor at some particular
moment, and wink while the heads are blown off tens of thousands
of starving children. Black algae, black march to the scaffold, from
which our heads too are to roll. Stare at anything, some
momentarily gorgeous natural phenomenon, some woman whom
you desire desperately, your beloved dog, child - stare long enough,
and they will all become every bit as absurd and meaningless as a
word you've mindlessly repeated scores of times, and, in so doing,
have revealed the emptiness at its core, at its speaker's core, and at
the very core of existence. And that is the optimistic outcome - one
of apathy and absurdity, both of which carry the potential for
adopting a pleasant, even comical distance. It is, however, far more
that likely these visions, beings, and body parts will reveal
themselves as, and remain horrific, nightmarish abominations.

It's all within you, whether it be a harmless, localized rash,
or an alarming spot on some internal organ just now revealed in a
malevolent scan ordered by your satanic physician - these things
were already within you, in your spirit, your soul, there to be
randomly and momentarily illumined by some remark, scent,
melody, counterpoint, fugue, buzzsaw, enticing woman, or horrid
crone - they are all already there. You take them for a sort of global
truth, when they really are just hobby horses upon which your ass
happened to find itself at that particular moment, through no
virtue or wisdom of its own. Predictably and invariably, this horse
then finds bushels of hay upon which to feed itself in the bowels of

your memory, whether you are aware of said memories or not, to reinforce and nourish itself, to provide it with the girth and confidence to assert that you, after all this time, are surely NOW seeing clearly - that the madness and folly of your youth is surely a thing of the past, now that this unassailable truth or worldview upon which you've just happened to install your bunghole has been grasped. And yet, after a few days, weeks, months, or years, this bold steed becomes the most ephemeral of beings - a lunatic dream, something which you couldn't possibly have thought, believed, or felt - a demented pony, shuffling aimlessly in a hall of mirrors in some sub-Saharan desert, struggling to survive, while, at the very same time, half wishing for death. The Stoics, those laughable fools (but no more so than the other hordes of cults through which your psyche has passed, mesmerized momentarily by this or that bit of nonsense, and compelling you to then obnoxiously proselytize your friends and acquaintances) succeeded only in implanting within you the burning desire to slit this or that new acolyte's throat. And you did it, you couldn't help but do it, you were more than happy to do it. Now, and only in this moment, do we find what we pretend to ourselves is wisdom. What we've actually found is just another bubble of soap, which, when pricked, smells, at first, of a fart seeming to have been dabbed with the fragrance of a buttered croissant, but which, after a few moments, reveals its bouquet to be only that of one's vanity and blindness, a cheap cologne which unfailingly offends the sensibilities of those unfortunate enough to inhale its fetid perfume. It is the dollar-store toilet water of which you, of which we all are made. Air the room, flush the toilet, fumigate vigorously - then rinse and repeat.

During a flush in which it feels appropriate to do so, have an accomplice violently thrust your head into said toilet with a plunger, perhaps while he or she whistles the forest bird's little ditty from Act 2 of Wagner's Siegfried. Last week you were a Stoic, this week you're busy reading Marx, next week you'll more than likely be lying ice-cold in some discount morgue. And it shan't be a set of glorious symphonic variations being performed, rest assured. You are a neurotic. You are at least intermittently aware that these momentarily, seeming-to-be-true bits of yourself, which you had at first inhaled with delight, become, not very long after, utterly incomprehensible, that is to say, what it was about these things that had previously entranced you is now something which you can no longer even locate, and which utterly mystifies you. You cannot remember those pieces of that apparently now-dead self which found any interest or took the least pleasure in such things. And at such moments you feel your soul, the existence of which you never did and never will believe in, slipping through the cracks into the air all around you that you'd barely noticed, out through every pore of the body which betrays you constantly, each day in some terrifyingly novel way, and with considerably increased and renewed vigor. You grasp this air - but there's nothing there - it, and you are nowhere to be found - within, without - there is only the abyss, which (who?) has conveyed to you quite plainly on innumerable occasions that it despises you. Not to mention the ceiling, which is about to fall upon you as well, after which the sky, and, finally, the heavens in which the Gnostic God is busy buggering a host of angelic assholes, as depicted so charmingly in those miscellaneous apocryphal gospels of which you'd once been so fond. And suddenly you are overwhelmed with loneliness, with the wish to see, to embrace, to kiss Mademoiselle X, knowing full well that what you desire is only to remain in that desire, not to risk fulfilling it - for to see her, to embrace her, to, heaven help us, possess her, would lead only to disappoint, disgust, jealousy, dysphoria, and a host of demons chuckling and cackling the moment the spunk shot out of your body, the moment the interview was over, or simply the very moment you set eyes upon her. Such is the way in which the demiurge has set the rules for this dime-store board game in which we all find ourselves - dragged, as we are, this way and that by the metaphysical magnets which lurk just beneath us - we know not why or how, only that it is so - we are all not very different from those plastic, pint-sized hockey players strutting and fretting upon the plastic fields of arcade games played by children in the bowels and hovels of corrupt capitalist cloisters and community centers, with those despicable smirks pasted on their vile faces, and with the grease of cheap, breaded, fried fowl fomenting in their obese, entitled, boyish bowels.

Belief in this sort of what is most likely entirely metaphysical nonsense has been a constant in mankind's puny, wretched head since he first roamed the savannas and, doubtless, well before. We've all experienced things and events which seem to have preceded from some sort of moral necessity, at the same time that it is clear to most of us that they are nothing of the sort, that they are random, chaotic, and accidental, that even if they are "determined", moral necessity has clearly played no part in them. And yet it is more than usual for an elderly person to look back on their lives, whether they have been more pleasant than not or have contained an appalling preponderance of suffering - to look back and see it all as possessing some sort of instructive, didactic meaning - as if it were all of a piece, a sort of epic, which had to be thus, that in no way could have been otherwise - as if it had all been mapped out, as in a play of the greatest quality, as if, for the individual at least, "All the world's a stage, and all the men and women merely players." It's clear to us that a great deal of this arises from the fact that we've been cast into the world with this or that character, which snaps us back upon some predictable road or other, like migrating salmons, tides, or pendulums. We all pursue what is appropriate to the character with which we've been thrown into this shitshow - this or that spider spins this or that web, this or that bear hibernates in such and such a den. This is a simple enough assertion, a truism, if we merely consider the character we've been given, been blessed with or cursed. And yet the world seems to give us both what we are and what we crave, what we always were, are now, must be, and will die as, what is most correct for a being such as us, not as in what is most soothing or beneficial, rather what is most correct, in the sense in which the fates of protagonists in epic tragedies are correct. We say things were "bound to happen". What does this mean? Is it as simple as that they were "bound to happen" to such a one as us? We hardly control the motion of the moon and stars. And yet we are allied with them, puzzle pieces in the universal jigsaw puzzle, which would appear as no puzzle at all to a being standing outside what appears to be chaos to us monkeys, stranded as we are on a flying rock. It, and we, might seem the work of a very fine, nay, transcendental artist, one full of wisdom, who sculpts, writes, or composes works with the most astonishing and self-assured technique, one whose foresight is seemingly infinite, and who provides those works with the deepest and most satisfying coherence. But that coherence and foresight cannot possibly exist within us. We are insects, borne aloft on a wind which is wild and powerful and chaotic, yet somehow intelligible to us, at least in retrospect. This is all palpably absurd and deeply obscure, and yet we all feel it - the atheist no less than the most simple-minded religious person. This can all be readily dismissed as teleology, new-age nonsense, as the purest gibberish - these obviously infantile notions of justice and karma, of a universe which somehow dispenses justice as if it were nothing other than a vast cosmological preparatory school or monastery - there is no end to the refinements of palpable nonsense to which man has gone seeking to justify this persistent, inescapable intuition, just as surely as every thoughtful man rejects it. And yet every man is nonetheless convinced of it, by virtue of his experience, more and more so as he ages, and never more so than at the end of life. Omens are not exclusively the domains of fools and grifters - we've all felt them, and we've all believed and continue to believe in them. And if this life is but a dream (though very few of us are rowing merrily through it), then it's taking place in some sort of mind, and does not every blockhead become a sort of genius in his dreams? And if there is anything to all this nonsense, if we are all indeed mucking about in some sort of cosmological, symphonic composition, ought we not complain to the music director that it is the most abominable of pieces? With the most execrable of endings? Which almost never ends as we would have imagined, as we, or others, felt or feel that it should have ended? There is the occasional death which reflects the life that preceded it, e.g., "He died as he lived". But that is the exception - brutal chaos is the rule. All of which is to say that the instincts which cause us to consider our lives as the greatest of Sophoclean tragedies are as likely as not to be only the feeblest of self-justifications and fairy tales. With this in mind, we trudge onwards, to meet our doom, with (at least we console ourselves) some minimal honesty. Even if the design is indeed there, it clearly does not love us. When one falls down the stairs, and arrives on the landing a heap of broken bones, rest assured that it was precisely the right set of stairs and injuries for that particular individual in that particular moment - as if the universe had been waiting patiently yet assuredly for centuries for that one, single, graceless misstep. Laugh not at the absurd design of the thing, but at your previous willingness to pretend it was meaningful - laugh at the two-bit, cosmic vaudeville act into which we've all been thrown. It's all you have left, all any of us have left, the only genuine thing that remains to us - other than grievous pains, soul-crushing longings, and suffocating boredom.

Well, that, and sleep - delicious and milk-laced, primordial, bestial sleep - where one's most abominable nightmare is the source of a thousandfold more pleasures than one's greatest daytime delight, for in sleep one is God, the demiurge, the abyss, the heavens, the inner, the outer. One's shriveled insect of a self, that squashed and bogus pretense one walks through the day pretending to be, might very well be horrified, shaken, shocked, and unnerved. But that self is to who one really is as an

infinitesimal, unnoticed rash on one's buttocks is to one's heart - it
is to be scoffed at and discarded. And in doing so, one then stands
at the empyrean gates, privy to boundless, drunken eternities of
luxurious, winged ecstasies to which one can then abandon oneself
- ecstasies of love, of unimaginable cruelties, cruelties to oneself and
to one's enemies, many arising simply from the love of cruelty
itself, that is to say, lacking the slightest reason from without.
When the ceiling of a crumbling, ramshackle forest cottage
becomes the vault of heaven, the cricket in the bathroom sings as if
he were the Archangel Gabriel - singing, as he rubs his little wings
one upon the other, melodies, nay, symphonies, of unimaginable
beauty - lost, sacred cantatas of Bach, newly discovered and
unheard until this very moment; the overture to the opera about
the Buddha Wagner toyed with writing, having completed Parsifal;
or the most heartrending and gorgeous melody of one's own
invention, in a style in which one hadn't the faintest idea one could
compose. And, needless to say, above all else, it is the charm of this
risk-free embrace of death one cherishes, after which one so often
feels renewed, yet just as often fails to recognize what has been lost.
What precisely is it that has been lost? The self you were but a
moment ago, the self of the night before. It is a very different being
that now arises from sleep, which now awakens from that little
death, a being that does not entirely recognize the one that
embraced sleep so sensuously just a few hours ago. Where has he
gone, that being? We don't give it a second thought. Were it an
actual resurrection, we should be astonished. But because it is a
different being who has now emerged from the corridors of sleep,
there is not the slightest amazement - everything seems just as it has

always been, from this being's point of view, who has quite
forgotten the self so willingly cast off just hours ago. Perhaps that
previous self now wanders in some Asphodel Meadow, or more
likely Hades - a staggering, miserable, perpetual insomniac, seeking
a no longer extant world, finding only dark shades, grievous and
famished looking, with torturous looks of longing engraved on
their long faces, playing inscrutable variants of something
resembling chess in grim pastures. But now this new being arises,
perhaps with the solution to some problem which had irked and
confused his previous, cast-off self, quite pleased with himself, and
scurries off excitedly to put this fresh solution to the test. And
then, more than likely, having once achieved his goal, sinking into
the deepest despondency, for the solution, the achievement, having
now been accomplished, is now, immediately and necessarily, a
dead thing. Not a sleeping thing, which might emerge, like some
butterfly or Phoenix, to take wing, to blaze and soar through azure
skies, but a cold, lifeless, inert thing - a hateful thing, which has
betrayed its maker utterly in its having been brought to
completion, a lump of coal dumped on to what one had hoped
would have been the most sumptuous and delectable meal. And
then, invariably, the urge to sleep returns, to die, to beat this all
down, this Ponzi scheme of existence, to lock it in some leaden
strongbox and dump it in a deep, blood-red sea. You feel it arising
within you, that not unpleasant pressure in the forehead and
around the eyes - the eyes themselves slightly burning, closing,
giving way, begging for the workday to come to a close and be sent
home, where the familiar opium den of stupefied sleep beckons,
like some narcotic, Oriental harlot heaving her perfect breasts

towards you, gently and silently mouthing words which don't matter - only the motion of her mouth matters, of her lips, of the little shrugs and tugs of her eyes as she beckons, this sleep goddess, this angelic hustler, who gently caresses the lids of your eyes, closes them, her musky smell carrying you off into the deepest and most fragrant stupor - this sleep, where every phantom of your past will float through space, exchanging bodies, expressing things to you they never did or could in daylight, in waking life - things which they most certainly feel and have always felt - the lover her loathing of you, the always collegial colleague his wish to slit your throat, the loving mother her wish that you'd never been born. These opaque, black boxes with whom you've spent a lifetime interacting, these angels now become fiends, but being truly neither - these phantoms who know you as little as you them, but who are only, ultimately, you, the lover and enemy of one's self, the hero and villain of one's life, the one running desperately from pain and boredom, and the one in whom it is created. We do not muddy the waters to make them appear deep. We find ourselves in mud - more precisely, in shit, which we find, to our surprise, and, if we are in the mood for self-pity, to our horror, is not the slightest bit deep - is only a surface, a mirror, in which we perceive the vapidity of ourselves. If one is lucky enough to project some negligible yet somehow still noble portion of oneself on to another, forgetting not for a moment that that other is merely one's self as well, in a disguise of one's own invention, one is pleased - one might very well then have a sensation of longing, of love, of aesthetic contemplation or even ecstasy - for a moment, perhaps a few moments, never more - never longer than one's longest physical climax, which is never a matter of any longer than several seconds. And then comes the stunned return to the idiot body, that gaseous, fetid stink-pit, from which one is destined to escape for never more than an instant. Hell is most certainly other people, as well as all the things of this world, including the creations of those people who live in you. One wearies of them. Why? Because one wearies of nothing more than oneself, and their existence is nothing other than your, and only your hallucination, the phantasmagorias of a poltergeist who's been thrown into an alien world, who grasps at mirages with arms that are stumps, doomed, rooted to the spot - a withered, dying, nutrient-starved stump of a tree in the world of one's imagination, which never does other than disappoint, for it creates, desires, and, without fail, falls back upon itself - the slimy, viscous meat puppet which is the source of that imagination. A grizzled, elderly Sade in the Bastille, conversing with a spider of his own invention. One's bread and circuses can be the scum-filled landfill of contemporary culture; or they can be Keats or Webern - no matter - either way, one is no less doomed to the hell that is one's self.

Condemned all the more, truth to tell. For the clever man is constantly confabulating, and those confabulations are hardly restrained to matters of the intelligence - they very much extend to matters of the heart - it is, in fact, there where they operate most intensively and ruthlessly. When speaking to an object of which you are fond, or for which you feel contempt, when embracing them, or even when thrashing them mercilessly, you're not speaking to, embracing, or thrashing whatever it is they might, in fact, be, but rather a sort of scarecrow which your imagination has fastened to them, and which conceals them, if it is true that they were ever actually anything in the first place, at least from your point of view. It is with this scarecrow that you converse, it is she whom you embrace, whom you kick to the ground on a whim and without a second thought - a dime-store puppet whom you have created to serve your momentary needs, projections, and wants. You could not see this creature whom you've thus hidden, costumed, and manicured if you tried - in point of fact, there is no way in which you could try, for to do so would imply that you had realized and acknowledged to yourself that it was only you who had constructed this theater and her in the first place - this play, this actor - and that she was created, made of, and conjured out of nothing other than you. And yet, ironically, the image you have of her is every bit as shadowy and obscure as the one you have of yourself - the one you see when you look, puzzled, amazed, distrustful, shocked, and disgusted at your reflection in a mirror. It is only when you chance upon this creature in an utterly novel situation, especially one in which she is unaware of your presence, that you might suddenly see, to what will likely be your horror, this thing, this creature, this fictional woman of your own invention, composed, as she is, as they, and you, and we all are, of endless weird angles and imperfect flesh, stumbling along in what you might never previously have observed a comically absurd, unseemly, imperfect manner - at any rate, in a manner diametrically opposed to the way in which you had previously imagined her. She is suddenly now a creature, and a creature only - no longer a being with a name, much less a being with a name whom you loved or despised, but a creature comparable to those you'd far more likely encounter in a park or forest or zoo - phantasmagorical, incomprehensible, and profoundly disconnected from the reality in which you fancy it is that you exist - hopelessly other, with no use for, interest in, or possible means of engaging in any meaningful contact with you. And it is at such moments that you will suddenly look at your own outstretched hand, the extremities of your body, or your face in the mirror, and discover precisely the same thing - some nameless creature, in a body as foreign to you as a rock, a boulder, a mountain, a planet, a galaxy, a thing spinning through space with some apparent agenda which you cannot grasp, on which you are borne along like some weeping tail of a comet struggling to eject itself from one unhappy solar system into another, whose grass you've been told is somewhat greener, and to be preferred - like some bleeding hemorrhoid hanging off the ass of a testosterone-crazed, male elephant hellbent on lacerating his rival, unable to see anything other than intermittent clumps of his own cells, drenched in rust-colored blood, falling to the jungle floor, all the while clutching madly at his skin, limbs, and extremities, for fear he too will meet the very same fate - shaking himself violently, rattling his brain about in its idiot case of bone, blinking furiously and repeatedly enough to realize that no, he is you - and you are still just in that room, observing the woman whom you thought you loved, and who now sits there, staring into space, ignorant that you are watching, a thing from whom that dream-stuffed scarecrow of your own invention has fled - a thoroughly naked thing, clothed in this or that garment, it is true, but naked nonetheless, as naked as the chipmunk which just scurried beneath her and the jay about to fly over her head - denuded, defenseless, tottering on a tightrope poised above unspeakable tragedy and suffering, staring hopelessly ahead, oblivious of you and of everything other than her own little fables, the scarecrows whom she too fastens upon others, whom she recognizes and with whom she honestly and genuinely interacts as little and as infrequently as you do. Between you and her is a gulf wider than any in this most unlikely unreal physical world - the gulf between two impoverished imaginations, long-ago stuffed in iron-bound lockboxes and tossed into a bottomless sea. To approach her frankly and straightforwardly would be a surreal agony, in which the harpoon on which you are already impaled would only be thrust deeper, and then another would be stuck up your ass, through your entrails, and out your bloodied, jabbering mouth. You'd be doomed, if you were sufficiently foolish to approach her, to spout inanities from which you would both recoil in disbelief and horror. And then it would occur to you - the ailment has the most obvious and simple of cures! You need only imagine, intensely imagine, that you are the man of a yesterday in which you did not know this creature, one who had not yet met her, or that you are the man of a tomorrow in which you have both tired of and grown to loathe her. And all the illusions will then vanish, of their own accord - this Sarah Bernhard of your own invention, acting in this play authored by no one other than yourself, the lines of which you have compelled her to learn, or that you at least imagine you hear coming out of her mouth, as well as this alien, anonymous creature whom you presently observe at a distance - this mysterious whatever she is, this thing - as foreign to you and your experience as a ferret, as an insect, as a reptile, as a piece of dried dung upon which you take care not to tread.

So you're free - it's freedom, of a sort - freedom from her, and from your absurd and imaginary refashioning of her, at least. And yet, to yourself, be it that self with a name, a past, and a memory, or that terrifying creature that stares back at you from the mirror, whose outstretched hands you see but do not recognize, or, more correctly, recognize clearly do not belong to you, of whom you are not, have never been, and will never be free, for the bastard chases, brutalizes, and eviscerates you even in your dreams - the fear is that this self in which you are incarcerated will do the very same in death - at the moment of death, and through an eternity as drenched with stupidity, boredom, terror, and pain as the one to which you are presently condemned. Every night you're down and out, in some hellish pit with this fellow, mutilated by the dread of some dream, of tomorrow, of the fear that whatever bad tunes you seemed still able to occasionally hear or cough up are about to disappear into an inaudible ether, of all momentary beguilements vanishing, now that you're confronted with this awful gnostic demiurge, the one who is not willing to lie to you, or to at least tell you soothing fables while he stabs you. You look about wildly for any distraction, for any bit of nonsense with which to divert yourself, a victim on whom to lay hands, a fist to turn upon another or yourself, but it is not to be. Madness, in the face of truth, in the face of its ruthless sadism, is helpless. The reality is that each moment is now nothing other than an eternal death agony, and that, faced with having no more scarecrows to fasten on this or that mannequin, no lies that continue to be effective, for all the old one have removed their masks and fled, no bodies left which might have once deflected, detained, deluded, or entertained you, but which now reveal themselves as nothing other than shoddily assembled bits of random internal and sense organs thrown together in some two-bit factory, staffed by blind mole rats with nothing on their minds other than the shoddily assembled bits of random internal and sense organs of other blind mole rats - that, faced with this black hole of dysphoria from which you will never again emerge, you acquiesce to go under, to drown, to not care whether yours shall be a dignified and noble exit or a humiliating and absurd one, concerned only that it be quick. There is to be no more sadness or grief - no more scraps of the misguided hope in which you had previously indulged yourself.

Between the three or four moments of inspiration and the countless swallows, rumblings, excretions, greedy desires, and inanities burbling out of his mouth that constitute a man's life, we find the proper measure of his existence. And the truth is that the culmination of any life "well lived", or "honestly lived" is a scowl of misery that he genuinely embraces only on his deathbed - the final acceptance of the dumb, blind intuition which has been growing in his guts and gnawing at him for decades - the admission that the world is, and that his life has been, nothing other than a nightmare. If then, on that deathbed, the horribly misshapen frown on his distorted and withered face reflects this reality, there will be, at least, some small shred, some hint on that face which displays for all to see: "This man has seen what's what. This man knows and understands, and is unwilling to push the truth down his gullet any longer - to coddle and embrace his filthy family members, to make amends, to give them the pleasure of a 'good death', which would allow them all to then return to their filthy hovels in which they live their coarse, vulgar lives, to slap themselves good-naturedly on the back, to primp and preen about like peacocks, and to flatter themselves what wonderful children or siblings they were." No, we'll have none of that at a good death. If that man who's leaving for no shore at all, rather for that idiot blackness which preceded him and to which he now returns, if he is to be at one with himself, to be honest about what he was, what they were, what all this was, well then - he will, if he has the strength, start violently up and piss in their mouths, shit on them, if he is able, strangle them, stuff them in the hospice wastebasket - let's make no mistake about this. It's only the dying fool who smiles and bleats generic platitudes to soothe his despicable relatives, while at the same time attempting cowardly to soothe himself. The legacy of his life has been nothing other than a series of stomachs, which have themselves been naught but crematoria for tens of thousands of creatures - snouts, cocks, cunts, lies, betrayals, assholes pretending to be gardenias, not a heart to be found amongst them, unless it has been stomped upon sufficiently to no longer care whether it is to be once again involuntarily displayed as some sort of cruel, perverse trophy. And then? It will either be discarded, or simply fold in upon itself and die - its only remaining wish. Anyone who continues to live past a certain age cannot have done so without bathing himself in arsenic, stuffing himself with rot until he himself becomes rot - for rot, already decayed, can manage to keep itself in a state adjacent to life for many years, having already decomposed to such a large extent. There's nowhere much left to which he or it can aspire or at which he or it can arrive - if there had been any momentary poetry within, it died long ago. He is now a wraith whose only hope of overcoming his self-loathing, of achieving some sort of dime-store chivalry or high-mindedness, consists in comprehending, accepting, and incorporating the rot of which both he and the world is quite entirely composed.

And that includes grasping hold of his hatred and clutching it to his breast, for it is above all else what he most cherishes, and what motivates him to keep inhaling the rancid air he must unwillingly share with all the beings whose throats he would so willingly and merrily slit. Oh, to live forever, to be that insomniac barber who'd put Sweeney Todd to shame - upon whose stylist's chair would sit kings, noblemen, vagrants, crones, girls in their first blush of sensuous exultation, children, fetuses ripped from the wombs of pregnant women who had sat upon that chair but moments ago, enemies, lovers, former enemies, former lovers - a splendid time would be guaranteed for him and him alone. Of course, were I he, I would be compelled to speak with them first, taking care to entice them to their doom in the most merry and cheerful of manners, as in, "How's the weather, the Mrs., the children?" The hypocrisies and inanities would cascade out of my mouth, barely betraying their mucous origins, streaming out like a fetid, polluted creek in some squalid, industrial backwater - nothing, really, other than a bit of involuntary shitting, somewhat more convoluted and a tad more pretentious, perhaps, but not a whit less mechanical, mindless, and moronic. I'd suck in my breath, and observe the words arising from some internal cesspool of which I haven't the slightest knowledge - and yet there they are! - the occasional witticisms, 'tis true, but nearly always suffocated beneath the more usual barrage of inanities, which pour like a fountainhead of caustic stomach acid through my gullet, past my ill-kempt, rotting teeth, out of my unwashed lips into the ears of a victim who hears nothing of what it was I'd imagined I'd intended, only what was judged sufficiently inoffensive and perhaps soothing enough to make its way past the barb-wired fields of indifference and vanity with which every man surrounds himself. We can never simply "leave it there". It is never enough. We must coddle, reform, resend our words - we can never simply leave them as they are and deserve to be, rotting in the air like some massive, unflushed shit in a foul-smelling public restroom, which, at the very least, has the dignity and decorum to not shuffle about overmuch, all the while spouting nonsense in an effort to draw attention to itself. We worship all these bits of shit we fling into the air - so fond of them are we that we can be distracted by them to the point of forgetting what their purpose was in the first place: to divert and distract the blockhead presently sitting upon our barber's chair from what is to momentarily descend upon him. Sometimes we are overcome by a wave of apathy, or even pity, if the lump, the imbecile sitting there and babbling away is ill in some obvious way, crippled, or perhaps just a jump or two from death without any intervention required on our part, and so it is we let them go their torturous way, as we would some pathetic rodent, who'd been wounded in some way or other, and had stumbled into our pantry. We would simply usher them out into the black night to die, with no further assistance from us. Were they to invade our living quarters, healthy, famished, with an agenda to nibble on this or that, to warm themselves in our bedclothes, or perhaps hide themselves away in some closet in which their purring, singing, or squealing gave them away, we'd smash their little brains into a pulpy, viscous puddle, which we would then scoop up, carry downstairs, and throw into that same black night in which their sick, wounded cousin would most likely still be dragging himself from bush to bush, deciding beneath which it would be most propitious and perhaps even pleasant to expire.

To nurse your hatred is the only really reliable source of joy, of sustenance, of indulging the passions. Keep a scroll within your mind of all the viciousness and depravity you have encountered in your life-a scroll which, were you to unfurl it, would stretch from here to the Kuiper Belt and beyond. You need not be witty or literary when recording these things, just piss them cheerfully on to the parchment, in all their blatant, naked dissipation and viciousness. Unfurl this scroll sufficiently in your mind so that you see its letters before your eyes throughout the day - think of it as your little fuckfest with Jesus, the two of you on your own little road towards Damascus, your own little, ever-present fiery cross, which demands of you, no less than it did of Constantine, that by its sign, you are to conquer, that is to say, you are to choke up, expel, and inflict your rage, disgust, and cruelty upon all those who cross your path. This is a theophany that will never desert you, a revelation that will enliven the remainder of your days, give you purpose, meaning, a will to drag your sorry ass out of bed each morning. Yes, purpose, meaning - in a world quite without either of those things. Your little revolt against the absurd shithole in which you find yourself. Camus would approve. Perhaps not of the garroting of throat after throat in your little shop of horrors, although one never knows. It's not like we can dig up and ask the blowhard. This hatred is not all, it is not meat nor drink, to recast Ms. Millay - neither slumber nor a roof against the rain. Hate cannot fill the thickened lung with breath, neither clean the blood, nor set the fractured bone. But enough of her, that drug-addled, narcissistic cunt. There is no need of flowery words here. Were you to lose your grip, your embrace of hatred, or when you lose them, for, rest assured, it can happen - suddenly, what do you know? There's the old bastard, Death, standing there, stinking, in a barrel of shit right beside your bed, filling you with the petty regrets you thought you'd discarded ages ago - you're suddenly this sniveling, apologetic, beat up piece of garbage in a hospice bed, desperately trying to make amends with a world which you knew full well, when you were strong and your mind was razor sharp, wasn't worth spitting on. You're suddenly this thing to be pitied, a sort of puppy dog with the face of a corpse, babbling out excuses and explanations, justifications and pretexts - all the shabby little griefs and expressions of remorse with which you wish to touch the hearts of the harpies attending you - and all the time knowing, were some miracle to occur, were you to suddenly regain your vigor, your clarity, your SELF, you'd have it off with all these whores, these she-devils. When your body betrays you, your hatred, your lifelong and dearest friend, your daemon, is more than likely to flee - you may very well find that you've been cleaved from it, that you are alone, that you are nothing other than the filthy meat puppet of which you were first aware, at four years old, in the basement of a home populated by demons, fiends, and vampires. Hatred alone keeps such creatures at bay, and there is nothing, NOTHING that matters more than that, nothing to be valued more highly. And when others feel the force of this hatred? If you haven't first slit their throats? You know full well what the advantages of that are. They curse you and flee your presence, the little darlings. And what is more delightful than that, pray tell? One need never again be "nice" - one need never again castrate oneself when out and about, engaging in disingenuous chatter in an attempt to be "liked". What folly! Is there a greater folly? Rid yourself of it, and you will be free.

And the measure of that hate is nothing other than the measure of your experience - its hopes, expectations, betrayals, and abuse - all that has ground you down to a weary, emasculated pulp of violent misanthropy and boiling rage. For what's the use? Of those who matter to us for whatever wrongheaded, godforsaken reason, we inevitably understand nothing. Of those who don't matter in the least, we understand all, though the knowledge is of little interest to us. At best, it offers us opportunities to manipulate, to take advantage of them, as if they were brute objects, which, truth to tell, they are. With the former, it is a very different story. We have the damndest of times untangling ourselves from them - we impute our own intellect and passions to them, and see little in them apart from our own reflections, of which we ourselves understand next to nothing. It is if they are mirrors within mirrors, and, hence, become the source of all sorts of bothersome anxieties, for when we worry about how they might react to us, how they feel, or behave towards us, we are troubling ourselves, above all, with apprehensions concerning the state of our OWN souls, OUR nature, its worrisome flux and undependability. Who will I be tomorrow? Damn if it isn't dependent on her, who, is, after all, only me in a skirt or pants suit, she onto whom I have fastened a thousand and one attributes of myself - one a bit of free-floating love, another some poisonous globule of hate - either, or both of which, laser-like, can be turned upon her - she whom I have constructed at what feels like a moment's notice. It's all never much to do with her, or very little. It is, rather, only these dead weights, which I carry within myself - that sometimes thrill, and sometimes ennoble me, but far more usually devastate me. People are props, and props only. We assimilate them easily into our selves - unsurprisingly, for we are their origin. We shit-stain them with our viscera, our longings, our disappointments, and our needs. It can feel to us as if they are more important to us than our very selves, when, in fact, they are merely mirrored mannequins, on to whom we have projected previously unknown, nether regions of ourselves - and, having done so, then allowed and encouraged them to burrow deep into these Elysian fields, these damnable hells we all carry within ourselves, just out of view, and throughout our lives - most of our waking lives, at any rate. Such "persons", with their knack for unlocking these cryptic, clandestine caverns within ourselves, seem to reach deep within us, as we are only able to do when left to ourselves in passionate, longing-filled, and terrifying dreams, dreams from which we awaken astonished that these underground chambers and catacombs exist within us at all, and, that, in addition, they are teeming with the most fantastical and hallucinatory creatures, who do all sorts of things at every moment - while we are fully awake, and even when we are engaged in the most insipid of activities. There they are, scurrying about in the bowels of our psyches - seducing us, enraging us, poking us with their little pitchforks, turning the reins this way and that all the while, even when we are having the most insipid of conversations with the most hopeless of ignoramuses. Cup your ear over the edge of the cliff which is your self, and listen carefully - you will likely hear them - scheming, contriving, pulling levers, operating steam engines, strutting about, busily writing notes on pads which will direct you to say this or that bit of nonsense, to have this or that dream, this or that nightmare, to stumble over your words, burp up the occasional witticism, to be gripped in a momentary death terror. These hobgoblins, all of whom are you - they're the cleverest of eavesdroppers, double agents, betrayers - they're the ones scampering about in the throes of passions of which you hadn't previously the faintest of clues were yours - that is, until some prop on your horizon, who has obviously caught their attention as well, throws them into a whirlwind of enthusiasm, of ardor, or of rage, which bubbles up from your bowels, and in which you then drown - the origin of which you attribute to some woman with whom you've become infatuated, though, truth to tell, you know not a thing about her, or to that man in the street who has so enraged you with his stupidity, arrogance, or bigotry, with whom you are unacquainted, and about whose past and motivations you are quite ignorant. They are nothing other than the starter, who, through waving his flag and shouting "Go!" unleashes untold hordes of stallions within you, of whom you were up until that moment entirely unaware. But now the race is on. There are no stewards about to oversee it, to insure that it proceeds fairly - with kindness, or sanity. No patrol judges reporting infractions or violations. There is just this shitshow of the most colossal dimensions taking place within you, which you attribute to that lovely gal with the heaving bosom, or to that perfectly idiotic, entitled twit with the political opinions of which you do not approve. It's showtime! The adventure begins, once again! And yet you are, have ever been, and shall always be, the loser. These lovers, these object of your rage - they are no more real than the characters in a novel by which you have been moved or enlivened, whom you feel you know, and with whom you feel as if you have lived. As true as it was of those ethereal beings, so it is with these creatures of seeming flesh and blood, who toss you this way or that in both mild weather and in storms, storms whose winds and rains live only in you. It can be helpful in such states of discomfort, which can even progress to actual madness, to attempt to vividly imagine who you were prior to ever encountering this being, and who it is you will be when they no longer have the slightest effect upon you - as if you are shaking yourself loose from some intense dream which has displeased or unnerved you. You are not a collection of lines in some accountant's book, that accountant being yourself. You are the literal accountant, the accountant himself - at this moment, and this moment only. A few seconds later? A minute later? You are now a very different accountant, taking note of assets and liabilities entirely different from what they were an instant ago.

What is the above other than a bit of "philosophizing"? And what is "philosophizing" other than a pretentious outlet for one's existential terror? And is all of this not terribly fatiguing? Engaging in this eternal lie to which one has so devoted one's self? Can we not simply say, simply admit that we are profoundly disgusting, appalling, and outrageously absurd? Can we not at least claw back some minimal dignity in admitting as much? Of course all men will then avoid us, for we are rubbing their noses in what they know full well but will never dare to speak aloud. We are simply pointing to the rot which they are, which lives in them, which correlates quite precisely with the corruption and filth of their diseased bodies, bodies which they are busy hiding from both us and from themselves - busy, as they are, dressing up in absurd clothes, dabbing themselves with soaps and perfumes which hide the atrocious odors and excreta which dribble and sometimes pour out from them at every moment. How dare we, naked ourselves and unwilling or unable to clothe ourselves, force THEM to unclothe? To observe their scandalous, putrefying meat suits in the harsh glare of an apathetic and exhausted sun, from which they run into darkness? Into frocks, into games, into philosophy, at the very first opportunity? There is only madness and hypocrisy - and we, each of us a wannabe Diogenes, we, who spew this vain nonsense from our rancid barrels, are no less absurd than the pompous, spectacled penguins upon whom we heave our venom. Here we sit, preaching gibberish, pontificating this or that bit of drivel - our self-abasements and loathing of them cut from the very same cloth, and stitched through with every bit as much navel-gazing grandiosity as is the twaddle of all those who parade into our little cottage-industries of grandiosity, our spiders' webs of pontifications and denunciations. When we rant, jabber, and behave in this manner, are we not every bit as absurd, every bit as deluded as the objects upon whom we shower our contempt? And mustn't we, to be even minimally honest with ourselves, factor into our calculations the perfectly odious being everyone else thinks we are? They, every bit as wrong in their judgments and opinions as we, must needs rule the day by the simple fact that they are the majority - they are every one and everywhere. Of course, we see, perfectly clearly, that they are all the worst sorts of miscreants. But then they, to the very last man, think the very same of us! When a hundred monkeys shower their shit upon some unfortunate visitor at the zoo, who has come to simply observe them and who perhaps finds them quaint, it is he, and not they, who is the deserving object of ridicule - a hopeless, pompous fool.

Speaking of shit, why is it that we are made so terribly uncomfortable by constipation? Clearly, it's no picnic - there is palpable discomfort. But constipation causes a distress, and contains a disquiet and uneasiness far beyond that of some other simple, straightforward discomfort, which, had we reliable neurological measures of just how many pain neurons were firing during each, would be its objective equivalent. The anxiousness and consternation arise simply from the fact that, when constipated, we cannot rid ourselves of the notion that we are not a great deal more than a tube full of shit - that this, above all else, above all our prattling, our philosophies, our compositions of novels and symphonies - that this is who and what we, at bottom, are. Hence it would follow, and does follow, that when a severe bout of constipation is relieved by the good fortune of suddenly being able push some massive dragon out of our bowels - he who had previously been hiding in his cave, sleeping peacefully like Fafner, oblivious to everything, above all to our sufferings - that when we explode in this manner, it is as if we are experiencing a sort of Christian rapture, a much longed-for and seemingly effortless ascent into heaven - a blissful Arcadia in which our bodies are, for the moment, and only for the moment, not the source of abominable physical and existential torment. We've all experienced this - this is no revelation. What remains in all this that is perhaps worth our further pondering is the burden with which all of us so constantly walk the earth, which we carry at every moment of our waking life - nay, not just our waking life, for shit infects, inhabits, and steers the course of our dreams as well. And so, at the moment we are able to rid ourselves of some significant fraction of this shit, we feel, for a fleeting moment, a sense of freedom, of existing in some unbounded, ethereal space, in which we are somewhat less the usual bag of putrefying viscera housing piss, shit, blood, spit, bile, sweat, mucus, semen, menses, lymph, and tears - untold, countless tears, infinite tears, very few of which we are able to let pass through us, most of which grip us in a lifelong chokehold of suppressed grief. We are strangled, haunted beings - death-haunted worms desperate to forget all of which we are made, to forget all that we are. One can proffer all sorts of romantic nonsense about how the angelic spirit we truly are has been chained to a thing quite other - to the filthy, execrable body - that we are made of the purest ether, that our authentic selves exist in some empyrean realm. The reality is quite other than this. We are not some temporary, seraphic passenger, fastened to the back of a mad beast, who tosses us this way and that. We are a pustule on that creature's ass - an abscess which has been unfortunate enough to grow pairs of ears and eyes, which are usually more than sufficient to observe and experience the horror of the situation in which we find ourselves.

And so here we sit, temporarily relieved of some fraction of the mushy blobs and cracked sausages which a moment ago had plugged full our lower bowels, smiling as if this moment of relief could possibly be anything other than a moment - coddling our psyches with fairy tales concerning the illusory nature of time, how in each moment there lies an eternity, all that hocus-pocus, airy-fairy nonsense with which persons facing what they full well know will be abominable torments in the very near future repeat to themselves in their inner ears, with a voice that they're not quite sure is their own, but which is, at the same time, somehow familiar. Ah yes, that daemon which so often drops in to catastrophize about this or that horror about to take place on this or that date! Which whispers the most appalling judgments on persons absent, some fraction of whom might deserve these libels, but most of whom do not, which is known full well to the inner voice which continues to whisper the indictments! Which, in fact, the more it is aware of their innocence, the more it redoubles the force of its vitriol. It is, somehow, this very same daemon which now, incomprehensibly (for it is so terribly out of character for it) begins to confabulate the purest nonsense about all the infinities and eternities which lie within us, and of which we are tasting at this particular moment - this moment when we happen to be somewhat literally less full of shit than we are ordinarily - that somehow we might remain in this moment, to linger in its blissful light, to step out of time, into a shit-free firmament in which the body is discarded - where we are free to hover, unbounded, in celestial spheres in which shit and guts and bloated bellies and the multitudinous varieties of excretory muck dripping from these wretched bodies to which we are fastened, and which we ourselves, in fact, are - where all of that is gone, and surely for good. There cannot possibly be a demiurge cruel enough to yank us back into the cesspool of filth from which we've somehow managed to disentangle ourselves - the fetid, grief-choked swamp through which our stinking bodies wander moment to moment, no, it is not possible! "When I say to the Moment flying: 'Linger a while! - thou art so fair!'" Our ruin is far less profound and literary than is Faust's. For us it is rather more mundane - the inevitable gorging ourselves later that very same day, sending platoons of the dead down our gullets to their watery graves, to fester and metamorphose and advise us of their doings with the most insidious squealing and cramps - all of them omens of the constipated, bloated hell that once again awaits us - the one into which that idiot inner voice had just been attempting to assure us we would never again be thrown, having forever surmounted the vexation of being hung upon the meathook of the body's incessant needs, pains, and betrayals.

But when we are, for that moment, free of the body, or so we tell ourselves, what is it that actually then appears before us? What does the voice tell us now, now that we've taken its rubbish about time and the eternity of the moment halfway seriously, now that it need not barrel onwards with its sermon, given that it has beaten us into a sort of temporary, happy for the moment submission? We are left with the notion that we must now DO something. We can't just sit here, for goodness sake. Yes, it is wonderful to be, to a large extent, not full of shit, for that we are grateful, we'd be the last to deny it, and perhaps we are sufficiently obtuse to take the reassurances of our inner voice to heart, to at least pretend to ourselves that we believe both it and them. But surely, aren't we now to DO something? Sitting here modestly shit-free seems somehow insufficient, lazy, unsatisfying. And now it confronts us, this oppressive, agonizing question - what are we when we are unaware or less aware of being a bag full of shit? When are we when we are not suffering? Why are we alive? For what purpose? Surely, if it is only the constant suffering which distracts us from all this, then clearly there is no reason to live? Oh, I know, we must PRODUCE something, that's it, that's the answer - thank goodness, now we're saved - now it will all be all right, or at least bearable. We'll DO things, PRODUCE things, perhaps one or two others might even take a modicum of pleasure in those things, although we shall do them, first and foremost, only for ourselves. There'll be no stopping us! We will do this, do that, busy ourselves with the most meaningful of enterprises - hop to, let's not sit about - we must, drum roll... BEGIN! Because, for fuck's sake, SOMETHING needs to happen, no? I know - well, speaking for myself, at least - I shall write a memoir, that's it! No, hold on, that won't work - I've had no life. I know, I shall fall in love! I shall garden! Crochet! Oh, much better - I shall do crossword puzzles! Watch all those old classic films! Practice the piano! Walk the dog, perhaps come up with a melody, or, I know, a poem! I must write a poem! That's it! How hard can it be, after all? And then, having written the poem, I shall, wait a minute - submit that poem! No, no, that's stupid - no one will care, and, even were they to care, I don't concern myself in the least with the opinions of strangers - no, that won't do, there will be no submission - yet, nonetheless, a poem there shall be! And when I'm dead, perhaps it will be read at my funeral, that's how bloody good it will be! And there'll be

weeping, the most wonderful remembrances, and toasts, and - hang
on a moment - I am suddenly reminded that I don't give a damn
about the opinions of strangers. In point of fact, I no longer give a
damn about anyone's opinion, including those of the few I claim
or pretend to love, and the fewer still that might, if pressed, admit,
claim, or pretend to love me. I don't give a damn what they think
or feel either. I wish them well, yes, surely, I love them, mustn't I
wish them well? Well of course, there's no question of that - how
silly to countenance a doubt on such a matter, of course I wish
them well. I love them, do I not? But what they think or feel no
longer matters - and I ask myself, in the wee hours of the morning,
why it ever mattered, for at one time it did, quite intensely,
horribly, and often - I thought about, nay, obsessed about what
they thought and felt constantly, there was nothing that mattered
more. But that was only a dream, surely. None of that happened,
REALLY happened. I only imagined it, perhaps only dreamt it?
Well then, perhaps I am dreaming this as well. What do we owe the
phantoms with whom we inhabit our dreams? Are they not merely
ourselves? Well of course they are! But then I need ask: are these
not the thoughts of an absolutely ghastly person? Surely only the
most repulsive wretch would have such thoughts - such apathy,
such cruelties within his heart. But hold on - surely the more I
judge myself, the more right I have to judge others? That must
surely be the case. How could it be otherwise? I am only bloody
doing unto others as I am bloody doing to myself, so that's the end
of it - right, right, quite right - problem solved. I am nothing - a vile
beast in a snake-pit upon whom it is not worth pissing, and so it
follows, necessarily, that they must be as well. What a relief! I was

confused there for a moment. OK then, what was it? Gardening? Oh, I recall - a poem, I must write a poem. But what is it to be about? There is nothing to write about - the world is a desert - there is only this monstrous emptiness, which begins within me and proceeds outwards, although I may have that quite ass-end - it might well be the other way round. In any case, I know it is a mistake, this world - the universe itself is a trivial gaffe worthy only of scorn - we are not to bother ourselves with any of it. I shall wear purple, as those soon to be old broads say. Yes! I shall wear purple, garden, write poetry, perhaps a villanelle, how hard could that be, there's that "Do not go gentle..." one - perhaps I might crib something from that. While I garden. I'll bring a pen and paper - oh, and a pad, yes, a pad. OK then, it's all settled. Oh dear, I'm so tired all of a sudden. But I do believe I might quite be able to nap now, given my shit-free guts. If only that perpetual voice in my head would stop with its nonsense. Oh wait, that is only I, just another bit of me, a sometimes clever but far more usually terribly irksome and annoying part of me. But it is all of me that is exasperating, when all is said and done. OK, there's an idea for a poem! I need a slam-bang couplet now, that's what a villanelle requires - a resounding, dramatic couplet - surely I can dredge one up from somewhere, from deep within my bowels, shit-free as they are at the moment. This must be what they call "poetic exhilaration"! Yes - I am unquestionably in the throes of "poetic exhilaration"! How long will it last? Hopefully at least until I've got my couplet. Would digging in the garden be of any help? Enable my bowels? Perhaps distract them from the task? How am I to know? Oh dear, I am tired, so very tired. Perhaps it's to simply be a poetry-free, <not encumbered by a shit-filled torso> nap then. I'll lower my expectations, and be satisfied with that. They say that's the royal road to happiness, they do, this lowering of one's expectations. A bit hard for a morbid pessimist such as I, but feasible nonetheless. There is always a "lower" to which one can descend. Until, well, you know, there is one no longer - until the bottom has been reached, in which one's body spasms in horrendous pain and expires. But I shan't trouble myself with any of that right now.

II.

"The idea, the idea! There's nothing other than the capricious, mercurial idea."

The idea, the idea! There's nothing other than the capricious, mercurial idea. It flits about from the mind of one author to another like a tart whose abiding priority is pulling down this or that man's trousers to empty the coins from his pockets, which look very much the same in the pockets of one as they do in those of the other. We have two or three ideas in a lifetime, at best. We then scour the landscape, the eyes of our fellow men, or fine books for hints of them in the words of the best of our fellow men, for there we hope to find the chrysalis of the idea which has been nagging at us expressed and developed more keenly and eloquently, which might then afford us the privilege of ennobling our own rudimentary, half-formed notions with articulations and formalizations of which we are not at least entirely ashamed. After a time, we wear these more fluent and persuasive arguments as if they were garments of our own, and had always been so. A man is not much other a cheap stew whipped up out of the accretions of other men - a collection of half-baked cakes and pastries, imbibed, half-digested, shat out, and then re-assimilated a thousand times over, upon which he, if has some minimal gift, might then place a cherry, after which he presents this for the most part unoriginal confection, of which he is so proud, to others, hoping he will then be feted and praised for the entirety of the thing, and not simply for that one, more often than not stale, superfluous cherry. His most successful deception is, as a rule, of himself. He comes to believe that he is now a fountain of wisdom from which others might sip, if indeed they possess the judgment and intelligence to do so, and will invariably utter internal harrumphs of indignation which often rise to angrily uttered or written expressions of contempt for all those foolish, obvious plebeians who have the audacity to proffer their stale, superfluous cherries as viable or superior alternatives to his own. These days, given that there are simply so damned many of us, and that we've all read, seen, and heard this, that and the other, kitchens are able only to serve motley assortments of the most unappetizing rehashes and regurgitations. What these patisserie chefs never seem to realize is that not only does every one of their at most three or four cakes do nothing positive for them, but, in point of fact, do them great harm, for they ultimately require them to forego tasting the delicacies of others, to not even allow for their existence. Each ends up, as do we all, a convict in a penitentiary of his own making, inadvertently installing the two or three varieties of gruel which he has managed to cough up his jailer, that jailer being none other than he himself, whose stale vomit he declares so delectable that only it will suffice for a lifetime of his nourishment, with no need of supplementation or replacement. In point of fact, he will die choking on it. Our goal seems to be, first and foremost, the relentless pursuit of monomaniacal beliefs and opinions, which ultimately serve only to make us stupid and close-minded - to smother the walls of our guts with the fermentations and microbes of the impoverished diet we have chosen. And then, occasionally, after a lifetime of fanatical self-assurance, that house of cards will come tumbling down, when perhaps the smile of some innocent,

artless girl cuts through the mountain of twaddle and laughable
grandiosity that has been our daily bread, like the knife of an
unwitting sculptor through soft clay, simultaneously slicing our
heart in two while causing it to beat furiously - to weep at the lie, at
the lunacy of the false self we've been carting about for so long -
this shrieking pterodactyl of our own invention who sits on our
shoulders, biting and clawing at us, by whom we have been so long
weighed down that we've become unaware of the burden and deaf
to its shrieking, for we took that shrieking to be our own voice.
Everything is suddenly now still - there is only the sound of the
blood in our ears - all because of her, she who has stripped every
last lie with which we have girded our loins and bellies and psyches,
all of which now collapse to the floor like a room full of toppling
dominoes, which we follow with our gaze until it comes to rest
upon her - she whom we now realize has been the only thing that
ever mattered since our mind first perceived a ripple on what had
previously been an utterly still pond, which shattered the glass-like
surface of our unawareness and revealed an unbearable hunger,
which we took great pains to ignore, and to stuff away into the
deepest recesses of our selves, of which we had no idea, until that
moment, existed. Oh yes, in dreams we'd sometimes seen her - and
there were those times, with women we imagined or pretended we
loved that we could paste her visage upon them, making of the
actual woman an opaque mannequin, which mattered not, because
inert - its function being that of a canvas upon which we could slap
this or that paint, making of it whatever sad and amateurish
painting it was our spirit desired at that moment - an angel, a
harlot, a monster, a thing worthy of our worship or of our

contempt. But this artless girl? The real one? The authentic woman who now stands before us? She cannot, could not, will ever be ours. Now that it is not to be long before the giving back of the breath that we'd only ever borrowed is to be demanded of us, we look back, and it is not Eurydice we see - it is the long, winding, pointless road which has led only here - to this savage, merciless encounter with the all the dissembling, falseness, baseness, and hypocrisy of our lives - now that our hearts, which we had long presumed dead, are undone - bursting, exploding in the face of this simply good, guileless, innocent, genuine, artless creature. Who simultaneously redeems and destroys us.

III.

"I dream of her. And she is far more beautiful
when I am not with her."

I dream of her. And she is far more beautiful when I am
not with her. I am with her in Paradise, in successive Paradises, each
one of which, the more desperate my hold, the quicker its
departure. And then, perhaps, I manage to see her again, but she
has now become some other woman - the woman I knew only a
few days ago has entirely vanished and become this new woman.
And she who was in my dreams a night or two ago - was she either
of them? I seem to be in a hall of mirrors, in which was and is
reflected only these various versions of my self, these various
versions of her nothing other than versions of myself, none of
which I recognize either. I could, perhaps, play-act the role of the
man who had sat next to that earlier version of her, and perhaps
retrieve some vague perfume of the passions that overwhelmed me
at that time, but that seems to me a navel-gazing sham, unfair both
to her and to myself. I could attempt to "seize the day", become
"mindful of the moment", as all those two-bit poseur gurus
constantly advise, although that seems about as likely as my being
suddenly transformed into my twenty-seven year-old self. The grim
truth was and is that I, and we, are stuck in the viscous mud of this
or that pond, waddling about in waves of filth up to our hips,
peering out at those who appear to be persons on its bank, but who
are not any such thing, not really - they are imaginary beings - this
has been and is all a dream, and I have had quite enough of it. It is
disgusting, vile, an appalling mistake. Yes, she is lovely, wonderful,

and, who knows, perhaps real, with an interior life as apparently infinite as my own. Well of course she is. But what of it? Hers cannot be even remotely approached, every bit as much as mine cannot. With our feet glued to the bottom of our little, shit-filled, barely moving lagoon, we spy not a bank, but an infinite abyss and chasm. On the other side? A dream, a hope, a woman, none of which are ever real. She waves from the other side of the canyon - indeed, she is waving! But is it, in any meaningful sense, she? It is, rather, a shoebox filled with the impressions I have formed of her that is waving, nothing other. And so it is that when I attempt to lift my arm to wave back, it refuses to obey me, it no longer belongs to me - it has become a dead thing, or, at best, a throughly exhausted, jaded, and unmotivated thing. Waving to a shoebox of sentimental, self-soothing notions appears, suddenly, to be more than a little odd, more than a little pointless, and more than a little unseemly. This is not some sort of hysterical paralysis - I am quite aware of what's going on, how it's all so thoroughly permeated with the contents of my mind - with its overwhelming melancholy, weariness, and apathy. I tell myself there's a sort of nobility in it, in this ceasing to engage - that the honesty which is prompting my detachment proceeds from my being a superior being. Yes, that must be it! This is all coming to pass because of the almost never remarked upon excellence of my self! Surely that's the source of this impotence, of this paralysis? This catatonic melancholy, this burnished melancholy which falls back most usually upon myself? All this must needs be a virtue of the first order! And yet - self-loathing is only self-love by another name - hardly a new thought, at the same time that there's no escaping it. My misanthropy consisted and consists, first of foremost, of my annoyance at persons who will simply not sit still long enough for me to project upon them what the moment requires, to not be the prop which would soothe, enchant, or enrage me - all of which depends, quite entirely, on what my daemon, whom I am simply observing, and whom I loathe, currently desires. I'm looking out from my pitifully familiar, lilliputian pool of shit, across that chasm, and seeing something, but what I am always aware of first and foremost is not the thing or the person, if indeed there are things and person, but rather of myself "seeing", of some eerie, primordial "watcher", who seems to reside in the back of my head, just above my eyes, watching the watching from some obscure, spectral place upon which I have no way of turning my eyes, thoughts, consciousness. And so every perception, every interaction, every thought, every desire, becomes inherently ridiculous - a hall of mirrors reflecting forwards and backwards in time and space, underneath which is this "thing", this "watcher", this disgusting, brute, dumbshow, this "onlooker", which is perhaps me - that's what the dot-headed, mystic Hindus babble on so constantly about without a shred of evidence, isn't it? It does seem to be the case, to be a plausible assertion - yet, from what I've observed, those morons seem, with their chants, their dead eyes, their laughable streams of the purest gibberish, to celebrate the fact. But it is a catastrophe! A cosmic catastrophe! This idiot universe, which belches out infinite streams of inert matter upon which cretins gaze, what is it? It is something that, were I to murder myself, I would not be escaping, only dripping back into its bowels to reemerge as any number of things, perhaps an infinite number of things - perhaps as a microbe feasting on the hemorrhoid of a ferret. Why isn't everyone shrieking? Looking at the world and shrieking? This world to which we've all been condemned and which we are? It is a thing of unspeakable horror. And she who looks so angelic? It will suffice to think of her twenty years ago or twenty years hence to see what this world is - a boiling sewer of entrails buried beneath a city poised to be swallowed by a tsunami, upon which iguanodons ranged only a few moments ago.

IV.

"And so there's nothing for it, no way in which
to escape that dismal system of sewers..."

And so there's nothing for it, no way in which to escape that dismal system of sewers, most of which are quite hidden from our waking eyes, those sewers which are our selves, than to turn our gaze, to open our hearts to works of art which appeal to us for reasons we do not and can never understand. Our first reaction to them may very well be revulsion, as mine was to Wagner, a reaction not unlike that of the little brat who pulls the hair of a young lady with whom he hasn't the faintest idea he is soon to be, or perhaps already is, in love. These works and people are us, and yet not us - the parts of ourselves which we recognize as residing within them, more often than not in a subliminal fashion, are what draws our attention to them in the first place, for there can and will never be anything a fraction so dear to us as ourselves, and seeing what is best about us reflected and ennobled in a mind superior to our own enables us to forgive that mind its superiority, since it has deigned to allow us to partake of its holy rites, if only as startled onlookers sitting in the back row of a vast theater,. There are those simpletons who would assert that to understand a work of art is to, in some sense, equal it. One is hard pressed to imagine a proclamation more preposterous, and yet it is impossible to deny that our world is immeasurably enlarged having once gained entry, has been changed, is unrecognizable, including our selves, which are now quite unlike the persons who had not yet made the acquaintance of the work, this immense cathedral, this interior world with its seemingly infinite number of rooms, which give the impression of multiplying each time we return, into which we enter and from which we emerge transformed. Without art, life would be a mistake - that was Herr Nietzsche's assertion. One need not agree with him - clearly life remains an appalling mistake, but, yes, art can, at least at times, make it bearable - that is indisputable. It is a different woodbird we hear warning Siegfried of Mime's treachery each time we traipse through the lush, dark forest of Act 2. Professor Feynman would have claimed that knowing the chemical composition of the bird's bowels, or having mapped out some correlation between its brain and behavior would make our intercourse with it all the more miraculous. But such an assertion is absurd - reflection upon these sorts of discoveries only sets the roulette wheel of our rational mind in motion - causes the ball to settle here, or there - with the result that any potential we might have had for a sensuous, aesthetic, soul-nourishing experience disappears. On the other hand, having drunk voluptuously deep of its song, any bird of flesh and feathers whose song we might now hear on a walk or in a garden will be metaphorically enhanced and enriched, will be now several - a veritable aviary of delight, in a world which has blossomed into an aural opulence of which it could previously have offered us no hint. The landscape begins to vibrate, the colors to beat like hearts, the sky to beckon, and we are, if only for a few moments, privy to Mr. Blake's revelation that the universe is most certainly to be found in a grain of sand, provided that grain of sand has all those allegorical siblings of which we have now been made aware - animal, mineral, vegetable - all of it blindingly sensuous and immediate - and with the intellect, that poisoner of experience, nowhere to be found. Some boundless space opens within us, in which the woodbird's song is no longer "out there". And yet it is no more not "out there" than it is within us - in the gurgling of our stomachs, or in the sound of our hearts beating in our ears, if the scene is sufficiently quiet. All these things - the bird's song, the gurgling, the beating hearts - take place, rather, in a vast ocean into which we have quite disappeared. One lives for such moments, and, like a woman who spurns us the moment we inform her of our love, of the desire for her which has been driving us mad - the magic of these astonishing moments disappears quite immediately the moment one attempts to grasp it, or becomes aware of one's desire for it to continue. Such is the world - the delightful, horrible, coquettish, sadistic world in which we find ourselves. We might return to the very same park the next day. Maybe we hear the very same woodbird; perhaps its song is nearly identical. And our mind might even recall the second act of Siegfried quite vividly. And yet there is nothing - just the idiot world with which we are everyday assaulted, and of which we have grown so terribly fatigued - the familiar dysphoria, the lack of magic, the wish to be done with it all, or, at the very least, to retreat into sleep, to perhaps dream some unfamiliar bit of nonsense which entertains us with its strangeness, a gift which the being who is more truly ourselves than are we deigns to offer us every now and then, or of which it wishes to unburden itself - some small respite from the imbecility of our everyday experience. For in dreams, blockheads are men of genius and we, who are neither geniuses nor blockheads, vomit up from some parallel universe on the other side of the black hole which is our core - worlds, gardens, vistas, canyons, heavens for which no waking Dantes, Brontës, Blakes, or Tolkiens could ever find words. Even our most terrifying nightmares are preferable to any waking event, for in those nightmares, we are God, or Gods, the whole of Olympus, nay, the primordial Chaos out of which it and they once materialized. And then there is the additional paradox: these very same works, which astonish us and throw us into selves and universes of which we had been formerly unaware, can hurl us backwards in time to selves we once were, whom we have quite forgotten, who, if we thought of them at all, seemed long-lost Eurydices, vanished into the depths of an Underworld we might have wished to conquer and from which we might have wished to recover her once again, but knew full well there was no chance of doing so. And yet there she is, stark naked, in front of us, she whom we so desperately loved - our younger self, full to bursting with sap, with desire, not the ruined self we were but a moment ago. Confronted with right melody, counterpoint, turn of phrase, interior monologue, rendered in the proper way, our present selves dissolve, and we are young, whole, in the front row of the theater, entranced by a performance we've never seen and could never have imagined. Our love drowns us once again, as it did then - the burning within us, and the suffering it created return afresh, the loss torments us as before - in this moment, we travel, in an instant, through countless galaxies swirling in space, are flung this way and that, and then it is all gone. Ordinary memories return. Perhaps the next turn of the melody, some modulation we find unconvincing, an author's gaffe, a misplaced fleck in a painting - it's gone. Present-tense monotony has returned to choke, harass, and ridicule us. Do we, can we take solace that we were able to experience these miracles, however briefly? Might we become, by virtue of having had such experiences, a hair's breadth less terrified of death, find it less venomous and cruel, to accept or even embrace it as a fair price to pay for these astonishing moments and experiences, rare as they are? On a good day, perhaps. On a kind, hopeful, forgiving, sanguine afternoon, such a thing seems possible. Granted - most days and afternoons are very far from that. A sublime aesthetic experience can indeed resurrect the dead as efficaciously and persuasively as a happy, generous dream or delirious hypnagogic state. For a moment, yes, you are embracing Eurydice again, she is every bit as real as she was forty odd years ago. And the moment of her being ripped from you is, once more, every bit as crushing. You, who have lived a posthumous existence - you, who have been this weary ghost slogging through the mud of a world which neither knows you, or could ever know you, and for which you feel, above all, contempt - you, who have been searching, constantly searching for her, though you've been utterly unaware of it - you, who felt as if you were doing something quite other: studying, enriching yourself, your mind, your heart, satisfying your boundless curiosity - how brave and wonderful you've been these many years! You pathetic, deluded fool. You've been doing nothing but grieving - all of it, every note you played, every thought you had, all those "ideas" you thought your own but which were shabbily cribbed from your betters - all your worldviews, constructed, as they were, like so many houses of cheap cards bought at stationery stores in criminal neighborhoods, overseen by fentanyl-selling thugs reporting to mob bosses in cheap suits, with their hideous, mustached wives, and their cheap, tawdry mistresses with their poofy hair. You've been looking only for HER, and doing nothing other than that since that day, which was tattooed on your spirit by hordes of masked desperadoes wearing medieval helmets and wielding twelve-foot branding irons dipped in satanic furnaces, all the while preparing the horses and ropes which would serve for your being drawn and quartered in front of a crowd of onlookers which was promised you with the utmost sincerity, but which, nonetheless, failed to arrive. She has remained in a halo of divine light, above you, unreachable, while you descended, or, more accurately, remained on an earth which had become a perpetual hell. You would occasionally spend time with this or that person, perhaps even consider it a friendship, or, infinitely more foolishly, an affair of the heart. But inevitably the hydrochloric acid of your gaze, intuitions, and cruelty would strip away whatever it was that you had imagined were their good and bad qualities. What would inevitably remain was only your apathy, for you had made of them inert objects - a lifelong habit and talent refined in the mists of earliest boyhood. Do you, can you now, at least, see them as they are? Such things were not ever and are not now possible. The fantastical objects you first made of them, the inert objects they later became - the tolerable, vaguely nostalgic, seemingly human but one is never sure persons into which they eventually appeared to transform - none of these things could ever stake a claim to being an even remotely authentic representation of these people. For they have never been and remain to this day nothing other than mirrors of your self, or, to turn it round, mannequins upon whom you stapled pieces of your self, by means of which you entertained and soothed yourself - with compassion, curiosity, boredom, rage, tales of betrayal you told yourself, and only yourself - they are all the same, all of a piece - ridiculous fabrications and fables. If they might indeed be actually PERSONS with interior lives? You grant that may be possible. But whether they are or they are not is irrelevant. Because, they are for you, as you are for them, nothing other than animate paintings upon which you find some likeness of yourself which makes you happy, miserable, horrified, or enraged. And they disappear like a morning mist that the sun disperses, winking out of my existence in every bit as meaningless a fashion as they winked into it - their story, your story, my story - all written in vanishing ink. If there are footprints to be seen, they might bring forth some momentary longing, regret, or wish for vengeance, but the landscape is poised, eager, and hungry to swallow them. And you are left with only the abyss that is your self, soothed and enchanted by the occasional metaphorical enlargement of a woodbird, yes, but hopelessly, utterly, and profoundly alone.

V.

"And yet I so reliably wake up as another..."

And yet I so reliably wake up as another, in a fresh world burgeoning with enticements which seem to have appeared from nowhere, to have sprouted from the ether like Athena from the head of Zeus, or, conversely, just as suddenly populated by demons, crouching inside of or just beyond my cabinets and air conditioner - in this bush, that tree, in a world of countless menaces hiding just beyond my reach, through which I might have had at least a chance of rectifying the situation. And behind me, underfoot, nay, in my mind itself - an inner world pulsing with imminent peril, the terror that I am to become any moment a dissociated thing, a creature - a wandering, confused consciousness, glued to and horrified by an idiot body which is not my own - I have no idea what is "my own", what that could even possibly mean. And then the assault sounds, the stares of strangers on a walk - those hideous, pockmarked, distorted faces fixed to heads sprouting from stalks growing from shit-filled torsos, with their absurd arms and legs, ostensibly unaware that they strike me only as mutant beasts in some Bosch canvas I have never seen but which must surely exist, for here they are, walking through the park, if indeed this is a park and not a cheap simulation rear-projected on some gigantic screen which manages to always extend just beyond the limits of my peripheral vision. A mother crossing a bridge with her deeply mentally disabled, adult son, sputtering, in a seeming ecstasy, "Mama, a waterfall!", as she looks back at him with a much-burnished love, and in fear for his future - the decades of sadness etched upon a face tinged with those mild twinges of disgust which she has never been able to shake, and which have caused her countless, guilt-ridden, sleepless nights. But surely this is not real, these people are not real, they are just being rear-projected on a screen - they can have no inner lives, no home of any kind to which they return, no past, which had to have included or perhaps still includes the father, this cannot be happening, for if I am not real, and that much is clear, how much less can these images before me, walking for a time alongside of me, be real? Have they some awareness, perhaps? Am I to them what they are for me? I am sliding through time, through selves, through this slice of time in which I walk beside the two of them. And what is all of this, really? The peel of an orange which is to be discarded without a second thought - by me, by them - to be thrown on the grass atop hardened dog poop, or into a plastic bag, which is then dropped in a refuse container, to be picked up by hard-working men towards whom society professes gratitude, but by whom it is secretly disgusted, who will die at forty of overwork, misery, and a coarse-grained existential exhaustion. I see them too, as real as the mother and her stuttering, galumphing, lumbering son. I am almost always invisible, and yet, there are those times when, with some frequency, I find that people are smiling at me, as if they expect a smile in return, or kind words of greeting, of which I am utterly incapable. Why now? Why at this moment, do all of you greet me in this way, wish to make some sort of contact with me? I despise you not a whit less than when I was entirely hidden, when I was seemingly non-existent, why now? Is the difference within me or without me? Does that even mean anything, given the severity of my dissociation? I see, I encounter only "things", not persons, for I am not a person, and, given that, there is no reason to believe that they are. I have no wish to give them pleasure, cause them pain, to observe them at all - I want them only to disappear, as I myself want to disappear. I have, for as long as I can remember, wanted nothing other than exactly that - to wink out of existence without leaving a trace, to never be spoken to, or of, to utter no words myself, for no words to pass or drop from my lips ever again, as if I were a sort of feeble, ancient fountain out of which arsenic-laced shit dribbled. Surely all these phantoms see and hear me as exactly that, a thing of horror, which inspires the purest revulsion. Such grandiosity! The truth is quite a bit more prosaic - there is only apathy - I towards the world, and the world towards me. This sickly, decrepit world, this sickly, decrepit self - one would think us both quite well-suited to one another, but such was never the case. I will die in a sobbing heap, just as I lived, just as it's been since the very first moment of which I was aware that I was this thing, this thing of which I would so desperately love to rid myself, and to be assured it will not live on. Dear God, please! Grant me at least that - that there will be no returning from the void, from the blackness - no more parks, orange peels strewn in poop - my face, their faces, that endless parade of faces, each more moronic, grimier, distorted, impenetrable, disgusting, incomprehensible, pointless, and absurd than the one before. These creatures, these things, they have invaded even my dreams, in which heretofore the beings I encountered were at least half-familiar, stable, quasi-real - even in the most vivid of nightmares. There is nowhere left. It has been a gigantic, idiotic crescendo to this awful, appalling moment - no, an unveiling, a peeling away - this is who I am, was, have always been -

it's simply that I cannot unsee it anymore - nothing works, there is nothing with which I might hide this catastrophe, and every word I grasp at to describe it only pulls me further into myself, into the ground - there are arms jutting out of the ground, of the walls, pulling me down, down, down to the hell in which I was born, and which I have borne within me all these years - these pointless, idiotic years, coming from and going nowhere - why, why, WHY? Why did you have a child, you fiend, and how could you have treated it so? I carry this monstrosity within me - I am monstrous, and yet I have never lifted a finger to another sentient being. I cart spiders and crickets outdoors, and yet my thoughts are ugly, vicious, vile, evil, cruel beyond imagining, and they cause me not the least bit of shame or guilt. Yet were I to cause the death of a sparrow, I would suicide a moment later, I would explode. I am exploding! Someone help me! Please help! But no one can help me, for I am but a thing, and they are things as well, and, dear God! Help me navigate some infinitesimal path through even this one morning, through even these next few minutes - what is that moaning? I hear moaning. It's not the dog - it's outside, at least I think it's outside. Is it me? Am I moaning? No, it's coming from outside. Perhaps I am outside as well? Perhaps my dissociation is of a sort, or of a grandeur that enables me to jump through time and space, to be, unbeknownst to the person typing, an unwitting ventriloquist who seeks to entertain himself. No, not entertain, fool. Terrify! I am tired. What is this exhaustion? Who is exhausted? I am exhausted, exhausting, melting, famished, praying for sense to return - it may, I cannot say. As my eyelids begin to glue themselves shut, as the world recedes into a gelatinous, viscous glue, well then, personally, if I were you, as they say - I would not bet on it.

VI.

"Is there not something absolutely absurd,
nay, loathsome..."

Is there not something absolutely absurd, nay, loathsome, in belonging to a species which entertains itself with "acting", and with "actors"? Who need be exactly what sorts of persons, pray tell? Deception exists throughout the animal and even the vegetable worlds, needless to say, but there it always serves a purpose - that the "actor" might become a more effective or virulent predator, or, in prey creatures, be more likely to escape and live another day. In men? One shudders - it is all so terribly unseemly, this vapid, unseemly need to be "entertained", to have one's existential anxieties be put on display, encountered, and, presumably, soothed in the process. In the process of what? What, in heaven's name, is going on here? And the actors themselves? Good God, these empty, strutting peacocks - and the more empty, the more well compensated and celebrated. That we all wish desperately, violently, to escape from ourselves is not news. Only hypocrites and the self-deluded assert otherwise. But to claim one has entered into the heart and soul of another, in life, or onstage, is the purest, most naked vanity - a proclamation of the most loathsome arrogance. The actor claims to love the role, but it is only that part of himself which he finds in it which he loves. He protests in this manner only in order to soothe himself, in hopes he might more successfully ignore the black abyss hovering just behind him, which every step he takes, word he utters, and "role" he plays is an effort to outpace - he can and most likely will protest this sort of nonsense to his dying day. There is no point in putting spectacles on a blind man who is raving rapturously about all the colors he sees, and how deeply they move him. Only a sadist would take pains to convince him otherwise - for, if successful, he would, indeed, soon manage to see quite well enough to find the nearest cliff and skip off it gingerly. And it is hardly only from others that we are so hopelessly estranged. We abandon an infinity of selves in the course of a single day, or, if you prefer, are abandoned by them. There is, of course, that ancient, tired truism about stepping in rivers, at which one winces. We cannot tread a pace without leaving the man a step behind in some nebulous ether. And yet we routinely attempt to reclaim him by fastening one distorted memory of our "self" atop another, which then retreats through countless memories, tumbrels of other selves, all of which flee through untold mirrored funhouses and echo chambers, none of which faithfully restate the voice or sense of its predecessor. The irony of these actors claiming to be one sort of "self" inhabiting, co-opting, and becoming another is particularly arrogant. It takes place, as a rule, in the most hopelessly insipid and vacuous of "selves", in these "actors", who are so relentless in their of pursuit of persons, situations, and activities which might serve to distract them from what they know, in spite of their hand-wringing and pretenses, to be the case. It is an insidious revelation, the plague of every honest man brave enough to tune out the constant bombardment of his senses with this or that nonsense, or nonsensical person, all vying for his attention, and to address himself to the boredom, blankness, emptiness, and nullity which lives in him, which he fundamentally is, and which existence itself is. Every great thinker has said as much: life is a bad thing, an awful thing, an appalling mistake - an epiphany which can inspire, in a generous person, a modicum of patience and forbearance for this parade of imbeciles, all so intent on being "entertained", or "entertaining" others - this delirious kaleidoscope of nitwits and chattering baboons, their eyes saturated with countless spectacles of ludicrous, trivial images, their minds assaulted with empty, asinine prattle, their hearts assuaged with cynical, manipulative lie after lie after lie. This log flume ride of squealing imbeciles careening through time, each momentary "self" shitting out the previous, jettisoning it into a bubble of spacetime where it immediately expires, like some hapless, wretched astronaut accidentally ejected from his ship, whose primary life support system has gone dark, and who then sputters about helplessly for a moment before being engulfed in an oblivion in which "he" survives only as a picture, a mannequin upon whom the current imbecile, who he was only a moment before, can now project the fiction that they are somehow the same. This laughable bit of metaphysical chicanery is achieved through what the current blockhead terms his "memory", a fantastical tale he concocts and tells himself in an effort to tamp down the terror of what some large part of him knows full well is the actual case - that each moment experienced by what he terms his "self" is no more real than a fast-disintegrating frame of a cheap, generic 35mm flick - each frame, each successive moron, hopelessly detached from the next by an unbridgeable existential chasm. Phantoms chasing phantoms fleeing from other phantoms being chased by... And so it goes, this preposterous carousel on which we find ourselves, which we call our lives, of which we ever more frantically attempt to make sense as its close draws near, all of us fools, you and I, so constantly on our self-serving, cowardly errands. We are willing to admit, or at least some of us are, the impossibility of constructing a plausible, meaningful picture of the dead - that it is necessarily a vain, hopeless struggle. Yet it is no less futile attempting to construct a plausible account of one's "self" - it is just as absurd, insubstantial, and maddening - and necessarily far less feasible, accurate, and satisfying than constructing a picture of, say, a well-crafted character in a fine novel. We write and read such things, we clutch at such stories for one reason only - to turn away from the chaos which assaults us everywhere in life - within us, in our rotting viscera; out there, in others, in the ghastly, appalling world; in every utterance, feeling, opinion, and excretion. If this array of selves, which succeed each other like the cards in a quickly shuffled deck, were to go on for decades past the usual span of human life, much less were that "self" to find itself immortal, life would then become a thing of inexhaustible rather than finite horror . We are all already attempting to escape it, violently, and with the greatest perseverance, at twenty. At one-hundred-twenty, we would all be that Spartan slave, the one who suffocated himself in the toilet, and about whom Seneca remarked, "Life itself is slavery when one lacks the courage to die." What remains? What can be said to be real? Stories of lives, of OUR lives? Beauty? Memories? Only grief is real, only grief cuts through these frozen, entombed bubbles of time and of space - free-standing, self-contained, and hopelessly marooned in their utter isolation. Only grief so faithfully and inevitably penetrates and pierces through them, and maintains its identity through time - through life, through death, until the universe either snuffs itself out in a whisper of stillness or rewinds to a fiery, violent end. Until that time, there is and will be, only and ever - grief.

VII.

"Grief, yes - and hate, the thirst for vengeance..."

Grief, yes - and hate, the thirst for vengeance - disgust, loathing - loathing, yes, it's primordial and eternal. The only way to avoid slitting the other's throat is to let her savor and relish her superiority, it's hers and their most fundamental, ancient instinct. Vanity is unallied with intellect more often than not, although the presence of intelligence hardly puts an end to things - in fact it gives to the transparently farcical arguments of grandiose pontificators a certain polish. There are three options upon encountering such persons: 1) Running away - highly recommended, 2) Cringing at the feet of she who knows all, offering yourself as a doormat - quite a bit less pleasant, and 3) Slitting her throat - which one cannot, as a rule, do, and for which the fantasy of doing so must serve. Whichever you choose, and, needless to say, I do not recommend the third option, unless the two of you are stranded on some desert island from which there is no possibility of the crime being recorded and prosecuted (then have at it!) You must, foregoing murder, evict these miscreants from the real estate which is your mind - you must make of them pigs, rodents, bits of feces you in which you take care to avoid stepping - monuments, nay, pyramids of apathy, one of the nine billion wonders of indifference of which the world is composed, bits of carpet in a restroom you have been perhaps forced to make use of this once, on which you gingerly wipe the shit off your feet, and from which you then proceed on your way. To be reasonable is to betray yourself. Be that self, you know the one - infinitely awful, irritable, nasty, irascible - that

Komodo dragon you have always been and are. He's in there and always accessible. Give him a whistle! Trudging through the endlessly gray days is horrid enough - do yourself the service of at least giving that feral Mr. Hyde, he who has been living deep within you, he with whom your bowels are bloated, he who causes them to push so terribly hard against your ribs, and this since infancy - give him the go! Have him out the starting gate! Fire the starter pistol! You won't regret it. You'll fast become this monstrously gorgeous, proud, and ravenous butterfly, nay, the most voracious, gargantuan bird of prey, which shall now emerge from the chrysalis of dung in which you've hidden yourself away for a lifetime - to fly, to wildly shake rabbits, squirrels, reptiles, and carrion from side to side as you soar through clouds, and, finally, to feast, proudly and ferociously. Suddenly, there are not nearly enough throats on the planet to slit, enough arrogant fucks to eviscerate with scathing words! The world has now become now your oyster, as Bill once said - which you are to freely, with sword in hand, presently open, and upon which you are to then gorge. Do as thou wilt. Trust no one. To trust is to pull your shirt down, scurry randomly about, and offer stilettos to whomever you meet, inviting them to slash your jugular without penalty. And why not? For you've offered it! They are only to do what it was you were so clearly asking for! Stop soothing yourself with microwaved Swiss cheese sandwiches and godawful television - step into the spotlight of your life, man! You fucking hate all of them - and most especially her! No more deceptions and dissimulations! She's a cunt - let HER know YOU know, and that you have told everyone the BOTH of you know, that she is a cunt. You'll digest that sandwich ever so much more pleasantly and effectively, and you'll throw the goddamn television out the fucking window, quite gleefully, in fact, and perhaps on one or more passersby, if you're in luck.

VIII.

"And yet - late in the journey of my life..."

And yet - late in the journey of my life, finding myself in this somber, melancholy, pitch-black forest, the one in which I had wandered countless times before, I came to realize that there had only ever been this forest, with its gnarled roots, and choked with all these weeds, thistles, brambles, and menacing branches. Only they, and I, and no others. Here it was I came into the world and here it would be that I would finally, if Nature possesses an iota of kindness, escape it. Bramble-born, thorn-crowned, famished, lost, and alone - always alone, and never more alone than when in the presence of these so-called others, who, in youth, were objects of mystery, terror, and fascination, but who were now never anything more than annoyances, inert things upon which I occasionally stumble or upon which I stub my toe - that is to say, nothing. In days past, I'd stepped frequently outside this dark grove to encounter these nothings, who spoke endlessly, without ever uttering a word to which it was worth attending. We'd part, chance on one another again, re-enact the same farce, each of us leaving determined to convince ourselves that we'd received some sort of nourishment, when in fact, we'd each parted stupefied, famished, and aghast. And then we'd meet again, as wretched old men, with less to say than ever, seeing only despair and disappointment in the countenance of the other, and yet, again, we would attempt to convince ourselves of the same lie, knowing full well it was a lie, and that our attempts could only be sluggish, pathetic, and laughably absurd - bad puns told on an escalator busy ferrying us both to the gallows. Travesties, sham burlesques of grizzled old men looking on helplessly, each at the other, for some sign of life, some shred of kindling in the other's bearing, incarcerated as we both were in the morgue's freezer, banging at its walls, screaming for signs of life to appear, to open the goddamned door and release us - for we could not possibly be these wasted, foul, musty creatures. No, no! This was a nightmare! Surely, I would think to myself, I shall wake momentarily to find myself in some sort of tolerable body, with pleasant, motivating thoughts, wishes, and desires! It cannot end this way! To which the forest would predictably respond with its deafening silence - with every quarter-hour the croaking of a raven or the howls of a distant wolf pack, the hum of crickets, the beating of my heart in my chest and ears, the sounds of my insipid breathing - my vile, rotting, lizard body breathing, declaring: Life must go on! Life must be lived! At any cost, in any condition, no matter how bitter! In the moonlight now, I see a... What is it? A tiny chipmunk, perhaps? Standing, like an effigy, on the forest floor. I approach, he does not move. I am upon him - nothing. It is too dark to make out his expression, though I am inches from his little face. He is dead, and yet somehow remains standing. What does this mean? What can this possibly mean??? I've never seen anything so unspeakably awful, so terrible. I must bury him! But I cannot - I cannot bear the sight of him. I am shaking, I am sobbing - here, before me, stands every loss, every anguish that this ill-conceived universe has borne in its belly since its inception - it's all right here, in this little, fuzzy Christ figure, whom I cannot touch, to whom I cannot offer a proper burial, and by whom I am destroyed. He is me, he is all of us, but since I don't give a fig for "all of us", it matters only that he is me - I can neither touch myself nor give myself a proper burial. Can the poor thing not decompose this very night? Be borne away by the evening breeze? Why this body, this tawdry melodrama? Could it be any more obvious that every atom within him and within us yearns only to be freed of of this shabby cage in which it finds itself? To sputter out into the deepest recesses of the idiot universe - to at last be free? Free of being this downy little Jesus, of being me? And suddenly there is a shooting star, diving into the abyss, and disintegrating completely. Fleeing from what? Its wife, surely. Its friends, arriving for a dinner party, to gossip, to perhaps watch a sports event, to at least to have it on in the background, while busy gossiping. It is suiciding, of course, this shooting star - it's the only sane course, its only alternative when it honestly considers its neighbors, family, and ancestors, with all their endless, moronic babbling, histrionics, and dancing about - their endless, pointless revolutions around one another - their being born and dying. With comets, it is precisely the same. The agony, the wish to escape - perhaps the solar system around the corner is somewhat less soul-crushing than this one? But it is never to be, it can never be. There is to be only pointless wandering, mindless sputtering, asinine trudging, ever onwards through endless, black, pulverizing space, friendless and forlorn, all the while seeking and hoping for our doom, which would be no doom at all, which would be, in fact, release - release from the endless, moronic running about, this imbecilic DOING, this perpetual, idiot DOING, with its unceasing, hypocritical protestations and assertions of necessity, of virtue, and of the need to march onwards from one foolish project to another, in order to keep the noise and hum in one's ears sufficiently loud to drown out the voice within which is screaming, "Enough! This is lunacy! Lay down your arms!" - the wish to eat, to fuck, to sleep, to shit - the wild lashes of an insane, blood-crazed, sadistic charioteer, whipping the horses, one of which is you, your very self, the bag of meat in which you've been encased and cursed to slog through your days, whipping you to ribbons, to a bloody pulp, on the way to the foot of a Nero who will have you flayed alive, stuffed with mountains of wax to which will be fastened countless wicks, hoisted on poles, and set aflame above him, as he strums the cithara and sings one of his latest poems, all the while casting a caustic eye over the crowd in search of bodies with which he might later entertain himself. Underneath his purple robes, there is nothing but the hairy rodent which hides underneath everyone else's garments. Why does the forest suddenly hiss, snarl? Why is there only menace? Why is there now blood dripping from the naked moon half-hidden behind that gnarled and grimacing oak tree? Am I now to stand as still, erect, and frozen as my little friend? Until I am quite as dead, as rigid as he? Is that it? Is that what's wanted? By the night sky? By me? This is exhausting. I am nodding off. Am I dreaming? Am I alive?? And what is that gurgling sound???

Clearly this is all being offered me at this particular moment in order that I might uncover some piece of myself of which I am presently unaware. Whether some former self knew it, some paper doll on a chain who I had once been (although "I" rings more than a bit odd in this context), or whether I had simply never before encountered this piece of myself because it had been squirreled away in the recesses of some catacomb deep within my bowels - it hardly mattered. This current or former version of my "self" had a message for me, and I needed only to scratch away a few fragments of bark, clouds, skin, viscera, and hair in order to uncover it. Was it staring me straight in the face? Was the gaze of the dead chipmunk perhaps fixed upon it? I looked in that direction, with great intensity. The darkness was of sufficient blackness to allow me to see all manner of visages, bodies, demons, angels, omens, past loves, and ancient abusers in the barks of trees, in hedges, in the dirt and moss of the forest floor. There they were - one morphing into another with the rightness one encounters in dreams, which is, as a rule, so vehemently rejected upon awakening. And yet, I could not shake it - I was indeed surrounded by a host of beings, a nation of phantoms, all proposing to either silently enlighten me or to, I wasn't sure, perhaps subject me to unimaginable torments, maybe even murder me. I recalled how, long ago, when on the precipice of the insensibility towards which a particular anesthesia for some forgotten procedure was driving me, I entered into the strangest conversation with myself, in which the terrors of death, my imminent death, were bandied about, debated, and, finally, dismissed with what not much more than a scoff. This was precisely what I now felt. When I was finally able to bore down sufficiently deeply within myself, it became clear: I no longer feared death - perhaps I never had. He was now a friend, the best of friends. And yet I was equally happy with the scenario in which all would be momentarily revealed to me by one of these beings - what, in fact, was going on, who I am and was - perhaps, for all I knew, the mystery of the world's knot. What happened was none of these things - overcome by a lethargy and fatigue so profound that I sank to my knees, I awoke, many hours later, a few inches from where my little friend had stood, as if he had been cast in marble for all eternity. But he was nowhere to be seen, nor were all those peering eyes and curious faces which had surrounded me the night before. There was to be no message, and, at least for now, no death - only profound enervation, the seemingly bottomless, utterly familiar disappointment of my life, my imbecilic existence, of which neither pint-sized Jesus nor monumental God would ever take note, much less care to explain or attempt to diminish. Nothing. Thrown back upon myself, I wept like a baby for what seemed like hours. I begged this "God" to let me die, or to at least supply me with the means and courage to do it myself. Silence... And then, several minutes later, the listless and vaguely contemptuous caw of a crow, who, apparently, could not have found me more mediocre, and for whom it seemed quite the effort to cough up even that small, dismissive insult. Ah, well - I did not, upon reflection, disagree with his assessment.

But there is always the hope that I might grab this wretchedness by the throat and force it to obey my intellect, that dead thing which snuffs out the passions, along with all else that is vital in experience - that which so eagerly snuffs out the life of every butterfly it meets, to then pin it to the wall. To use it to turn this hellscape into a sort of "idea" upon which I might then muse, about which I might perhaps write a villanelle, or with which I might amuse my friends with bits of clever, morbid chatter, in reaction to which they will, perhaps, be amused momentarily, but then, quickly and inevitably, exchange anxious glances with one another as each dreams up some plausible bit of fiction they might offer me, in order to enable their escape. But was not some "idea", or some set of "ideas", intrinsic, learned, or otherwise, the very cause of my grief? I could rack my brain over this, and engage in a sort of chicken-and-egg, navel-gazing parlor game which would necessarily end only in my bewilderment. Yet might it not offer precisely that distraction which I so needed at this awful moment, in this grim forest? It is lovely, indeed it is - nevertheless, when I poke beneath its surface of adorable, sleeping owls and multicolored, burnished leaves, I find only horror - holocausts everywhere - underneath each log, in every pond, in the clouds and sky, in the microbial worlds and universes which I cannot help crushing, try as I might. It is only my griefs which drive me forwards, and they are plentiful enough, inexhaustible, apparently - when one ends, another is gleefully rubbing its hands together just offstage, in ardent anticipation of its entrance. And so I stagger forwards through this banal, idiotic life, the stupefying banalities and griefs of which force me to clutch at any distraction which is offered me, whether it dresses itself like a commoner or wears a tuxedo, it is all the same - they reek, one and all, of desperation, the desperation of slaves prodded forwards by insane, sadistic masters - I, and they, all of us attempting to distract ourselves and each other with bits of gossip, too often told jokes, and obvious, self-serving lies - this endless parade of buffoons, with its imbecilic soundtrack of half-hearted, hypocritical chuckles, frequent winces, and the not so occasional shrieks of agony, which custom dictates are to be ignored. I see the slave to whom I speak beside me, with whom I gossip and exchange witticisms. How awful he appears in his awful nakedness and proximity - he who was at least bearable in my imagination, where I could do with him and engage with him as, and make of him what I wished. Now I am confronted with his sheer awfulness, all the discolorations and small disfigurations which my imagination had taken such care to erase - the appalling manner in which he snorts, touches his face, and inadvertently reveals his baseness and hypocrisy with a thousand unconscious expressions, phrases, and tones of voice. I close my eyes, nod my head, and am suddenly transported to some interior compartment of myself not quite as vulnerable to the landfills of visual and auditory disgust by which I had been assaulted a moment ago. I have escaped, I am floating - the moment has not "passed", for moments do not exist here. It is familiar, yes, but "familiar" implies there is an "I" there - experiencing, comparing, and remarking to my "self", but there is none of that. The idea of familiarity only comes us once we have been kicked out of an Eden precisely because of and by that thought - or of any other, for that matter. And so here I am, again - lurching forwards, prodded by hot pokers up my ass, wielded by demons who never fully reveal themselves, except, now and again, in my dreams, or in the presence of this or that gangrenous, pimply-faced simpleton cackling and squawking about his failed marriage, the unpleasant circumstances of his workplace, or perhaps the chancre on his cock with which some promiscuous mistress has blessed him.

Surely I could daydream more pleasantly than this. I cannot in any meaningful sense control or direct them - they go their own way - but, at the very least, I can interrupt them when they become particularly horrid by some violent jerking of the body or some masochistic clawing at myself - there are a thousand ways to do it - believe me, I know. I've had far more practice than most, I've a mind which coughs up the most atrocious scenarios with the most astonishing rapidity and consistency - it's a goddamn centennial celebration when I'm able to puke up a pleasant one, which, having not a clue how it could possibly have arisen in a mind such as mine, darts its gaze around nervously, hastens away, and scouts about for the nest of some happy idiot in which it can come to rest. As for me, it's more or less fiends and fiends only. I am quite the gender-specific restroom, if you will, that is to say, admission is granted only to the most merciless and psychopathic of phantoms - they invariably sniff me out from however distant the galaxy in which they're presently making mischief - I'm a very desirable refuge for such as they. And me? I'm like a cow, who doesn't know he's to be momentarily hung from a meathook and flayed alive, a Jew who doesn't have the faintest notion he's to be herded onto a train and gassed later that day - you would think I would have grown accustomed to it, to expect the next atrocity, to be on the lookout constantly, but no, the moment the hatpin du jour of a moment ago has been pulled from my flesh, I feel alright, comforted, safe... Hey now! I'm not being battered by that vicious tornado anymore! And so, needless to say, this present-tense eye of the hurricane vibe shall remain the ongoing tenor of my life! No more Tristan Act 3 tenors for me! No way, no how. Righty, right - clear sailing from here on out, no question. And suddenly, don't you know, that SS guard, slaughterhouse worker, or whoever it happens to be this time, jumps in front of me with his Luger, or pitchfork - my short-lived, little asylum, that mirage in which I had foolishly indulged myself a moment ago will, if I am lucky, become a memory, with which I can alternately soothe and torture myself when in the midst of some future horror. And when that memory ages, it will, needless to say grow rancid, as all memories do - it will rot like a corpse baked too long in the sun, stinking of putrid meat, vegetables, shit, and sour milk - all with the vague and sickly-sweet stench which corpses have, the sweetness of which was, for me, at first, confusing, narcotizing, fascinating, and deeply compelling, like a melody I once adored during pubescence, but which now sounds utterly and hopelessly insipid. A treacly word of condolence offered to a Lear bent upon the corpse of his Cordelia.

Needless to say, any memory which bubbles up from within me is, more often than not, daubed only in colors which flatter me, which put me in the most optimistic of lights, regardless at whose expense this retouching takes place. Nothing vanishes entirely. I might come to inhabit that forest floor once again, but if and when I do, the experience will be skewed in one fashion or another - it will, perhaps, highlight only those few, rapturous moments of stillness, or, more likely, accentuate the nearness of the evil spirits who were about to pounce and tear to shreds both it and me. Either way, it would not be as it was. No matter. We tell ourselves very different stories about such moments - that we are indeed now the "he" who experienced the moment which then flooded our former consciousness, "he" and no other. That the self we were a moment ago has, in fact, vanished - traveled effortlessly and completely through time and space to collide with and become some former self, who is now in the presence of a bygone beloved, or perhaps arch-enemy, in some blissful paradise, or fiery inferno, with everything just as it was, and we who we were then. Which is all, needless to say, the purest fantasy. How we come to believe it, so glibly, so adroitly, and without the slightest effort, is a great mystery. It is, perhaps, to be explained through the activity of some sort of mechanism which our unconscious believes might best serve our interests, although our intellect tells us, with the greatest certainty, that such a thing cannot possibly be the case: we are merely our present self, as it were, dreaming. But surely something of these things have survived, and are strung along some spider's web, some latticework within us, consisting of an infinity of memories in constant interaction, one subsuming the other, possibly even in a Darwinian battle for supremacy, although, clearly, it is most frequently the unpleasant memories which survive. The sweetest and most-honeyed of our memories are like confections of mouth-watering chocolate, which can put us in a momentary ecstasy, it is true, but, when grabbed at or pursued past a certain point, become nauseating, viscous sludge, unrecognizable - and all the more torturous on account of their metamorphosis from the delightful thing they were but a moment before. My wife comes to me, frequently, and not only in dream - on walks, in parks, while working, walking, daydreaming. But it is, of course, not "her", and I am not the "he" who knew and loved her. It is merely my present-tense self, which shall vanish too, in a heartbeat, to become another - soothing itself, grasping at straws to keep the ever-changing grief both alive and away - yes, both at once, that is the curious goal, the way in which I delude myself that I am privy to her resurrection, both her resurrection and that of my grief, which has taken such a long and curious path through the years, nay, decades, of impassivity and numbness, all the while tattered with unpredictable hours, days, and weeks of unimaginable agony, which would come and rip through me like violent shockwaves through glass, shattering the manicured stillness I had been cultivating, and which I had assumed was to remain the condition of my existence. And then, finally, after a decade or so of those ominous tremors, the earthquake - composed not simply of grief, or, if it was grief, it wore a thousand different masks - the feeling, nay, the certainty of having no self - of being only some molten, naked core, subject to fits of rage, disgust, and momentary ecstasies followed by what felt like gargantuan tsunami after tsunami crashing upon monumental reef after reef - all now to be somehow understood as "my experience" - and yet there was no "me" left to claim to be having it. Were it all to have been portrayed in some surrealist film, it would have been, without question, a very bad surrealist film - with none of the underlying, dream-propelled momentum and intuitive rightness that the better ones have. There was only disaster, havoc, shipwrecks - daily Hiroshimas miraculously endured, and unhappily survived.

How do they differ - death from what should be far simpler, falling out of love? For the woman the difference is more obscure. Or perhaps more obvious! But for us? For me? When I have seen old lovers of mine, a few with whom I had spent a great many years - withered and worn away, like once noble cliffs barraged by tides and lambasted by time, as it was, needless to say, the case with me - it seemed as if the woman I had once been in love with had, in fact, died, and that the creature standing before me was her walking corpse, as, indeed, I must have appeared to her. How different would my thoughts both of her, and of all this then become - full of the cruelest disappointment, not at or with her, certainly, but, rather, at the merciless cruelty of the seasons, at time, which had taken these two vibrant, flourishing, entangled flowers, ripped them so cruelly apart, and, that not being sufficient, stomped pitilessly upon their features to the point of their becoming almost unrecognizable. I would then attempt to open the pages of our love in my mind's eye and memory - those of our home, our dogs, the gorgeous, blossoming magnolia tree, the laughter - all those feelings of bliss which felt as if they could never possibly come to an end. They were indeed all still there, yet somehow shrunken - I could no longer entice them to fill the widescreen cinema of my inner eye - they remained stubbornly emaciated, a postcard only, which might evoke a sigh, or even a tear, but never anything remotely approaching sobbing, much less deepest misery. But with my first wife, she who would remain forever thirty-one? As I became Dorian Gray in portrait, mirror, and reality? With her it was a very different story. She was and is more vivid than she ever was in life, and that is to say a great deal. Whether she is laughing, sleeping, chatting - whether we are walking, kissing, embracing, making love - it is the same, always the same. My mind begins to feel as if it has been stuffed with cabbage - my eyes droop, my gaze wanders down and to the right, tears tears rise to sobs - it is all completely and absolutely wonderful - my deepest, most secret treasure, while simultaneously the most violent pain I have ever experienced. Dear God - that moment in the bedroom, of finding her, when the world turned upside down, along with her - it was only a few hours later that the word "posthumous" began to possess me, repeating itself involuntarily and incessantly in my inner ear, a command from some nether world, which never tired of informing me that I was henceforth to roam the world only as a melancholy phantom - I, who had not exactly been brimming with dynamism prior to that awful, fateful day. And so it was henceforth to be, my trudging through life - I might, momentarily, step out of some mournful twilight into some tiny area momentarily illumined by a vagrant fleck of light, yet would invariably find myself, with far greater frequency, in a pitch-black, cavernous hell of soul-crushing wretchedness, in which there was only suffering, the desperation to sleep, and the thought of death as a friend. These came to be the foundational threads of my existence, my deplorable, dreadful life, a life that should have never been started, and which cannot possibly go on much longer. And yet I still awake each morning, inevitably the saddest and most grief-stricken period of the day, to some more or less unfamiliar version of myself, all of them contemptible, not least so because they give me no indication or warning which of them is to appear, of which of them I shall be forced to be. More than often than not, it is an utterly unrecognizable self to which I waken, which, though equally disgusting and abhorrent, offers, as some small compensation, the interest of meeting some new person I hadn't previously known lay within me. I call a compensation that which is undoubtedly a curse, that I might provide myself with some new idiotic reason to slog through another day, that reason most often being curiosity, which kills cats, so they say, yet, sadly, has not yet killed me. Are not all these women merely puppets, and I the puppeteer? And I, too, more than likely a puppet? Made to drag my sorry ass through another lamentable day? But by whom? Are they only in me? And am I, perhaps similarly, somehow in them? We are all, almost certainly, first and foremost, the puppets of some sadistic, Gnostic demiurge, or, these days it's all the rage to say or think: of some sadistic kid in a parallel universe running a simulation in his mother's basement, when he's not busy torturing animals in an adjacent park, or eyeing his little sister with a similar intent. And to be this ill, in this much pain, and to be denied even a hint of genius - to plod through life a hair's breadth more thoughtful than the average slob, just barely enough to be constantly assaulted by the perpetual reality of what I am not and could never be? Thanks, boss.

Perhaps it is him whom now I see. "Are you there, Yaldabaoth? You who have been so long awaited? After all these countless eons? Standing now by the foot of my bed? You who should have come long ago, who was, perhaps, busy elsewhere, or thought fifty years more of appalling suffering a good thing, or, more likely, thought nothing at all about any of that? No matter - it is you - you are here now. You have come, no doubt, as a friend, this night, to release me, after an eternity of painful waiting and longing, after a too long life as dismissible and absurd as a bad pun, unworthy of even a cringe. You have come."

"Be a good boy now and shuffle off - this will take but a moment.

IX.
"These friends, these conversations - how I hunger for them!"

These friends, these conversations - how I hunger for them! Yet how they so reliably and inevitably deplete me, make of me less than myself - for, when conversing, what am I, in fact, doing? Never being fully honest, surely - I am listening to the utterances of the speaker, marking her expressions, her body, her eyes - especially her eyes, and what they might be telling me - and it's never anything the least to do with the nonsense we are having on about. It is, rather, on her part, concerned with what she wants me to know of and about her - what she needs, wants, why she is talking to me and not another... Surely she wants... something? Perhaps many things. As do I, though I am very hard put, at least in the heat of our back-and-forths, to have the least notion what they might be. It's all not unlike an amateur game of tennis, and more or less as pointless. Then again, I am not in these things to win, at least not usually, certainly not in any objective, intellectual sense. I never choose to engage with another for intellectual reasons. Nothing is ever, or can ever be said in conversation which is of any real merit - there is only this infernal throwing back and forth of a hot potato, although, in the case of conversation, what is being thrown is, as a rule, far less appetizing and nutritious. What is it I want then? If it is intellectual stimulation, I know full well where to find it. It's nothing at all to do with any of that - it's just this animal need - this despicable, unseemly, beastly longing for faux-closeness on the part of one of Schopenhauer's Porcupines, that

Porcupine being, in this case, me - without which I, without which all of us seem to shrivel up and die. It's a hide-and-seek dance of puppets, too anxiously concerned with what their next step is to be to notice who the fellow controlling the strings is, or to wonder what his agenda might be. My puppeteer often demands: "Fawn and feign interest!", in hopes that I might instill some subliminal pleasure in my listener which she then associates with me, because of which she will more likely consider being of some service to me, perhaps even some much-needed, practical service - HOWEVER, what I most usually am looking for is just a bit of tenderness. We're both there to be soothed, and for no other reason - on my part, to say things which soothe myself (things which, were I simply to say them to myself, when alone, would not serve the purpose), and to feign interest in her, in order to evoke her curiosity, which, it is hoped, might lead to feelings of tenderness towards me. I am, on occasion, moved by others - on rarer occasions, moved very deeply. And there the trouble starts! It is quite inescapable. For what the other evokes in me cannot possibly be mirrored, in any meaningful sense, in her. Oh, certainly, there is the very occasional bout of lust which coincides in both of us, when my auditor is a woman - but of that I am not speaking. In any event, it is impossible to imagine a more lonely endeavor than that of lust - there is no more selfish pleasure, no more greedy stance concerning the other than to fasten upon her body as the source of our pleasure. How momentarily wonderful! And yet, how morally depraved. No, it's not of that I speak. It's of this wish that somehow this miraculous person, this unicorn, who has gotten under my skin so artlessly, whose vulnerability and gentle demeanor make my heart ache, might encourage and allow me to express all that is most noble within myself. This too is, ultimately, a selfish wish, but, oh dear - let's not go down that obnoxious philosophical rabbit hole, it leads absolutely nowhere! To care is necessarily to be in pain - to be in need, to have one of our many suits of armor pierced by a shy smile, an air of mystery, a winsome aspect, mannerism, or remark, to be torn in two, shredded, to become that open wound which I have carried within myself since the very beginning, but of which I am ordinarily almost entirely unaware. There are now two things which arise, quite immediately, as if from some mysterious, unseen dimension: 1) unspeakable danger, and 2) a reason to be alive - this exuberant recognition, this "Dear God, this is who I am, who I have been all along! Where on earth have I gone, and why, and how is it now that I return?" But of all these things my auditor is quite unsuspecting. And the more I become possessed by these sensations and passions, the more likely she will become aware of something which frightens her, for in them she begins to suspect one or more needs of mine, even though I am only aware of wanting to give. But that is very far from the entire case - when I am honest, I have to admit, at least to myself, that I want a great deal, and of this she becomes progressively, uncomfortably aware, eventually becoming wary - at times to the point of panic - for even though I feel only this terribly uncomfortable tenderness and wish to care for, protect, and to nurture her, how is she to know there aren't far darker things at work? In fact, how am to know? Indeed, there most usually are. For, at moments such as these, she is not at all ONLY she - she becomes a kind of incantation which awakens a daemon which has been sleeping within me, of whose agenda I am

either only very dimly aware, or not aware at all. This is a moment
of the greatest danger, one likely to unleash torrents of magma
from deep volcanic wells within me, far more dangerous than
anything which she presently risks. What to do, say, how to
proceed? I can't shut it down, anymore than I can wish a physical
pain away, or plead with some torturous hypochondriacal
obsession which plagues me to stand down. I must submit, I must
yield to it - I must eventually eat when I am famished, use the
restroom when the unrelieved bloat of four days finally demands its
due. I am like a mouse stuck on one of those horrendous glue traps
evil people leave strew about their homes in situations such as these
- there's nothing for it, I am doomed. And yet I have never felt
more alive! A poor bargain, this. Far worse than Schopenhauer's
porcupines, then, for my insides are not screaming simply to
huddle together, they are suffocating me with the wish to merge, to
disappear, to be impaled, to die. It will, needless to say, end in death
one way or the other. Whether in some morbid, Wagnerian, erotic
squawking, or in the whispers of Debussy's doomed lovers - this
ends in one and only one way. And even when it ends in that rare,
perfectly-timed-because-simultaneous adoption of a friendly
apathy in both parties, it is no less a death. Of the other, of the love,
of the self I once was. This is not a parlor game. I, and we are far
better off, certainly far safer, having relationships with the
characters in a novel. They are easier to know and to be sure of,
since it is only we that inhabit them, and only we that make them
live - they are far more reliable, and reliably nourishing, being a sort
of eternal mirror which hovers solely in the ether of our selves, and,
as such, pose no real threats. And yet, even with them - love them

long enough, deeply enough? Both they, and we, will die. But of course we are only concerned with the latter. I feel no nostalgia for the music or books I once loved, only sadness at the emptiness I now feel within myself when I'm confronted with them, just as seeing friends from my youth at some godforsaken reunion I've foolishly agreed to attend so necessarily and inevitably disappoints me, for they speak to me only of what I no longer am and can never be again. And the moment I, and we become intensely aware of such things, well then, that is the cue for the angel of death to make his or her entrance - in my case, most often behind me and to my left. If and when you awaken bolt upright in horror in the middle of some night, perhaps the very night which followed the day of your attendance at that hellish, ill-advised get-together, there she is! - perhaps looking at her nails, a faint, wistful smile on her face. She is far from unattractive, certainly far more attractive than the unfortunate assortment of old fossils and crones by whom we'd been assaulted earlier that day. (Never mind, for the moment, that we are their ossified mirror images and existential partners.) In our minds, and certainly in our dreams, we are still twenty-seven, leaping over fences like gazelles, with heads full to bursting of the most perfectly idiotic plans and conclusions about life, love, and the nature of existence. We are no less fools now, it is only that we shall not live sufficiently long to have the distinct displeasure of looking at this moment and seeing what perfect morons we PRESENTLY are - we think and believe, nay, we are certain that we've finally arrived at some golden age of wisdom, that we are quite the gentlemen. And yet there was that person, that unicorn, she who is still within us, she who is still within ME, and about whom I can still feel deeply, violently - I have no wish to fuck her (that's a distant, not even memory, something some former me once thought important, but which now seems more or less as interesting as hopping into a hot bath at some sordid hotel in which a host of unpleasant persons of both sexes are excreting their sweat, spittle, and stink, and, without doubt, urinating - it's more or less that enticing). But to meet her, to embrace her in the ether in some sacred space, some transcendental, non-transactional, pure, supra-human space of "agape love" of which I'd never had a clear notion heretofore? That's what I'm now craving, so desperately craving, and which I know full well cannot be. Yet I cannot let go of this craving - it burns, I am racked with the pains of it, I am on fire - this must happen! Dear God, this must happen at least once before I die, no? And yes, this person can absolutely serve as the vehicle which enables it - the unveiling of that pure, angelic being who has lived within me since the very beginning, of whom I'd been unaware, having been so busy with my wants, desires, with being carted around by my genitals like an idiot donkey which thinks it is he who is deciding the course of the carriage. That's all over and done with - now we are both to ascend to heaven! So I wish, so I think, so I now believe. And as that old saw about <the teacher appearing when the student is ready> has more than a grain of truth in it, suddenly there is not just this one unicorn - there are two, three, though it's obvious the first has a leg up, given it was she I'd first come upon - but couldn't the others serve just as well? I could love them, run in front of a bus for them just as well, no? Away with this lowbrow bus nonsense - this is to be a first-class martyrdom! These angels deserve no less! I shall, at the very least, be nailed upside-down to the cross like Peter, though my love is surely greater than his was. And this is far more serious than any cretin's profession of love for his or her God, which is, at the end of the day, only tantamount to loving a character in a novel. This is a real flesh and blood... But wait, hold on! It's just me, there's nobody else here, just some moist, humid, overheated hothouse in which my projections are thriving like gigantic, Amazonian water lilies, like mutant, gargantuan Dahlias or Hydrangeas. There's nothing here but me, myself - I have been thrown back upon myself, and am dripping with sweat - this woman was and is nothing but a mirror, and I am nothing but - what? Need. Naked need. Brutal, naked need in the face of my impending doom. I know it full well, and yet it matters not in the slightest. I will save this unicorn of my own invention from what would have been its doubtless ghastly fate, and, in so doing, will redeem myself. That's what those bleating Wagnerian heroes were always on about, that they were so constantly bleating and bellowing about - that "redemption", which had seemed to up till now so utterly ridiculous - up until now! Yes, that's PRECISELY what he was always on about, the bastard - this "redemption", this "selfless love". Granted, later on, there was that incoherent, nonsensical, cribbed-from-Schopenhauer nonsense about "renunciation of the will", all that faux-Christian gibberish which suffuses and poisons that last gorgeous piece of filth of his. But it's that selfless love I see before me now, that I feel within me, and it is, surely, the best it will ever get for me - that noblest of noble ways, in which I might "redeem" this shithouse of existence into which I have been born, been thrown - and which should never have left the starting gate - but which now, as it draws to its close, scans both heaven and earth for a justification for having endured this awfulness, for some "redemption". And this woman, or, rather, the mythical beast which I have made of her, and which has unleashed the passionate daemon within me - she seems to offer all that to me. I wish to do her only good, of course, but a moment's honest reflection reveals that is myself, first and foremost, to whom I wish to do good. I know this, and am revolted by it - yet I cannot do, feel, or wish otherwise. And what would this state of grace feel like? Surely wonderful, but, just as surely, unlikely to last a great deal longer than an orgasm of the flesh, and to likely leave me in a state of the vilest disappointment just after, as orgasms do - disgusted with myself, and with a world which asks and demands this of me - baffled, enraged, nihilistic - and not a nihilist of the cheerful sort either. What is that thing? That thing sticking out of my arm? Dear God, there is another! And another! They have multiplied, in the course of a few seconds - there are seemingly thousands of them now! Everywhere! Stabbed into every inch of my flesh! My brain cannot possibly scan the extent of the pain in anything like its entirety - it migrates, furiously, from arm, to leg, to cheek, to neck, to genitals... Are they hatpins? The quills of Schopenhauer's Porcupines? They must be darning needles, surely - they are three, six, even twelve inches long. Am I dreaming? Am I dying? Am I already dead? Am I never to have her? Merge with her? Become her? Become myself? Be redeemed? Will I awaken? Will I simply bleed out, only to be incinerated later this day or the next? Does any of this matter in the slightest, other than to me? Or even to me?

And then it's gone, this mad love of mine-I slough it all off in one piece, like a cobra now in search of fresh mates and prey, like a toddler taking a crap, waving it goodbye, and jumping off the pot, still filthy, to run and play with his comrades. Who was that woman, after all? Who indeed? Is she now dead? Dead to me, certainly, quite the same as if they'd buried her yesterday afternoon, after a funeral I'd been too busy to attend. That person who might have attended, that person being only a previous version of "me", has died as well, and I miss him just as little. The intellectual and existential perversity of this absurd, meaningless dance of shedding skins and selves to no purpose amuses me at times, though it more usually horrifies me. Yet this new cobra, having now shed its skin, is quite a bit lighter - the rays of the sun warm its skin, it is reborn - with a new self sadly every bit as imbecilic as all the ones before, and every bit as unaware that these things are the case as they had been. As well as every bit as vulnerable to the contagion of some new face, expression, shrug of the shoulders some pretty cashier or lovely woman might make which, had it been made by another, I would dismiss as trivial - and yet, because it comes from her lips strikes me as delightful, a veritable motet of Tomás Luis de Victoria for sopranos only, who sing it, unseen, from the eaves of the church, providing me with the opportunity to make of its choristers, in my mind's eye, a coterie of the most beautiful and virginal young ladies who ever walked the face of the earth. Needless to say, as often as not, my angel then grimaces in some less than divine way, perhaps sticks a wad of gum in her formerly lovely mouth, sneezes, or, what is absolutely sure to destroy the moment, looks with longing upon me - well then, that will be the end of that! My Aphrodite is now a Circe, from whom, at best, I linger with for a few moments in search of some amusement, and from whom I then flee. And in so doing, it is not infrequent that she whom I had thought quite dead rises before me again - now that she has left, and is, perhaps, in the arms of another, she appears to me again, as an object both of my longing and of my disgust. But far more routinely as an object of my disappointment - and not principally with her! Rather with life - this cheat, this whore, who rifles through my pockets having not allowed me to have my way with her, or, perhaps, having done so, leaves me with some disease to which I must now tend - who, in any case, has her pimp brutally toss me from what I had thought a rather elegant brothel into pitch-black streets in which roam hooded figures carrying long scabbards, eager to rob me further blind. Life, that whorehouse on the hill, behind which an idiot sun sometimes gleams, with its smug, contemptuous smile pasted across its vile yellow face - looking this way, that way, upon a world full of horrors which it is enraptured to illuminate. There is really only one woman, and she is a doll which lives inside my self, whom I take out to play with when some phantom existing in what appears to me to be the external world allows me access, whom I then shape and mold into whichever goddess I am in need of at that moment. Whether that phantom, the present excuse for my happiness, is in any sense real - that is a question for the philosophers to waste their unfortunate lives never answering. For me, it matters not. All that matters is the pleasure I am able to take in the fantasies I now create, and the annoyance and rage I feel when the canvas upon which I am daubing the paints, which are destined to constitute my doubtless masterpiece, move in a way which does not please me, or makes the application more difficult, or worse, makes me unable to not see clearly that it is only I who is both painter and painting, that this "love" of mine has naught to do with anything "out there", but only and all to do with how I feel - with the miracle of this spontaneous feeling which comes upon me, but, of course, has merely arisen from within me. I would like to think it less a phantom, this part of myself - I would like to imagine it tethered, through some metaphysical umbilical cord, to the ecstasies of some unseen paradise in which I am to suffer no more. And indeed, that can be the case for a period of time - it at least often feels to me as if such might be the case. But the moment I give voice or words to the notion, or somehow formulate it as a concept, it vanishes, and I am again faced with this mannequin, whom I had clothed so magnificently just a moment ago, grimacing again, shoving that revolting stick of gum in her mouth, which now appears disfigured in a way I had not previously noticed, saying something appallingly stupid, perhaps telling me she has a frightful need to pee, or that she "loves me" in a voice which has suddenly become odious to me - and after the one fall from grace there follow ten thousand others - it is inevitable. The cards constituting the house I have built come crashing down on my head, but, thankfully, they are only cards - this nonsensical infatuation has not even been a shack, much less some Golden House of Nero - there are to be no marble, ivory, or frescoes falling on my head, just the wind shuffling a deck of cards swiped from five-and-dime hovels run by miserable looking couples upon whose heads then fall the cheap plaster with which their establishment was thrown together in the first place. This one, that one - the grief of losing this one, that one - this one to death, that one to betrayal, a third to weariness or disgust. A parade of what? Statues which only I have carved, and I haven't a shred of talent for such things. I can construct them only in dreams, and I am a horrid sleeper. And if the statue seems somewhat long-lived, and, worse, if I feel it is a statue which I in some sense possess, it necessarily and inevitably becomes a thing of habit, of boredom, of repugnance. Suddenly I see her plainly - perhaps the awful resemblances between her and my loathsome mother, perhaps the qualities of her character which seemed once appealing to me only because they seemed temporarily able to blot out certain qualities of her predecessor which displeased me, but which now, in her, count for nothing, since the reasons they had attracted me in the first place serve no present purpose. And so I look upon her now only with dismay, her body now a thing which displays its faults seemingly everywhere - her voice, which was once a delicious, breathy flute, which seemed always to be playing some never-before-heard solo piece of Debussy, gorgeous, enticing, and completely novel, is now the voice of some tired old barmaid singing some abominable street song. I see it now - it was only I who had impregnated this womb which had so enticed me. I had thought it, nay, filled it full of nectar, ignorant that it contained countless seeds poised to become gnarled and bramble-filled bushes of disgust in a dark wood from which it would be extremely difficult to extricate myself, running in the less than accomplished manner I do, and pursued by she who had now become, or finally revealed herself to be a maniacal, bloodthirsty harpy. And yet I had been and remain so certain that this creature had existed, and continued to exist, insofar as she did, only in my self, that she had never been real - so from whence comes this revulsion? Is it a revulsion of my self by my self? How can I make that make sense? And yet it seems the only remotely honest way to approach the thing. If I dream of a certain Alice, whom I know in my waking life, or perhaps with whom I am even involved with in my waking life, sticking a hatpin in my guts, and then awake, whom am I to credit with or blame for this act? Perhaps it merely represents some intuition of darkness within the Alice with whom I interact during the day - that is surely possible. But it is only I that have stuck this hatpin so deeply into my flesh, and only I who flattered myself how clever I was to have created such a fantastical scenario - perhaps it had even taken place in the most stupendous rooms, forests, and mountains! What a genius my dreaming self is! As is the dreaming self of every fishwife and street-sweeper. The problem was that I had simply walked too close to, and then finally upon the stage upon which I had created my little chamber opera of lust and idealization - I was now slipping in the spittle of the trombonist, privy to the hopelessly plain face of the mezzo, prior to her having had the opportunity to apply the lies and machinations of her makeup - I had realized that I was both the composer and the librettist of this cheesy, sham bit of claptrap, and that my skills in both those domains were more than a little meager - that the whole thing had been a farce of my own contrivance, which worked only when seem from a distance, on that long ago stage upon which the landscapes and rooms had once appeared real, and not the shoddy, pockmarked wooden stage, and cardboard props over which I now found myself tripping. The wish to blame her for all of this will then suddenly run, neck and neck, upon a racetrack with the now unassailable conviction, which I am unable to dispel, try as I might, that this crummy, third-rate nightmare is the nightmare of my self, and of my self only, that it has been only ever thus, and shall remain eternally so - all these duplicitous little flecks of light, these endless lies I was and am so fond of telling myself, that I was or could be "known" by this or that woman, "known" without her fleeing in horror, all the lies that I had all along merely been projecting upon the darkest and dreariest of scenes with a cheap penlight in the approximate shape of my penis, the batteries of which were now having the good sense to expire. And so I looked up and saw the contemptuously menacing sun begin to rise over the horizon, eager to begin its happy task, from which it never wavered and of which it never tired, of bathing the infinite, ever-changing landscape of endless abominations, disappointments, betrayals, deaths, and agonies which have always been and remain the fabric of my life, from the very first violent and vicious abuses to the ones of the present day, all those monsters and monstrosities which walked and walk the earth carrying soft sticks, and wearing tuxedos and evening gowns - but who, in due time, inevitably pull the caps off those sticks to reveal the stilettos beneath them, now made of words and deeds rather than the blows of years ago, from which and whom the better and more nobler parts of me so reliably run, yet to which the man, whom I seem to most fundamentally be, inevitably returns.

And who was she then, strutting about so vainly, entirely unaware that she was, in fact, another, the resurrection of that other, long gone - her reincarnation. One can never know precisely how these things come to occur, but that they do? Of that there is no question. There was the face, first, if not foremost - and the voice, yes, that voice, which dripped with a honey calculated to simultaneously attract and conceal, with assurances that she wanted nothing more than to hear what it was I had to say, while simultaneously providing unmistakable evidence that she did not hear a word I uttered, and was doing nothing other than impatiently waiting for my words and thoughts to peter out in order that she might begin again what was, invariably, a chaotic jumble of assertions - revelations she would assure me she shared with no, or, at most, very few others, because, needless to say, I was one of the elect! Why else would she be speaking to me, after all? She was so weary of superficiality, and how wonderful it was to have chanced upon a person such as myself, one who really listened. And then would come the inexplicable tears, out of nowhere, which appeared spontaneous and sincere, yet had little to do with anything I could ever puzzle out. Nevertheless, it was exactly these tears, and this vulnerability that drew me to her, that kept me flying into the web she was constantly spinning, not meaning to spin it, unaware that she was doing anything of the kind, in fact, for in a mind as jumbled and disordered as hers, one could never have the least idea whether anything she said or did had a definite purpose of any kind, which she or anyone else could ever discover. And this, too, tied her to the others - it contributed greatly to the eerie sensations she would constantly evoke in me, of her being not the one she professed to be at all - she was, instead, one or more of those others - which, I was never entirely sure - it could have been my mother, yes - but then again, there seemed to be no sadism, much less violence, in this woman. And yet there were clearly cities upon cities within her, all brimming full of factories operating at full steam, and producing machination upon machination - one streaming after another out of her mouth, animating her expressions, and directing her behavior. Was she a puppet of the deceased, operated from some nightmarish, unseen dimension which was somehow pressed up against this one, or, perhaps, simply existing in it, unseen? What or whom was it I was observing when in her presence? And, far more important, from where in me were these violent feelings of fascination, desire, and terror bubbling up? Who was it that had instilled them in me in the first place, that they should now reappear in me with such vehemence? I said "reappear", but do I know this is the case? Were they not new? More likely I was simply the puppet made to dance and this woman merely the puppet strings made flesh, or seeming flesh - but operated by whom? And for what purpose? And were I to conclude, or at least entertain the notion that it was myself who was the puppeteer, well then - what a curious, masturbatory dance this would all become! A sort of ceremony - ancient, atavistic, pulsing through me with no regard for my safety or sanity, using me like a wet nap at a fish fry conducted and attended by demons, one of whom looked upon his crystal ball, or whatever it is demons use to generate causation in our grime-filled cesspool of a world, in order to note the precise nature of the doom I'd been prescribed. "I know!", I suddenly said to myself. "I shall use this woman, this facade, which is she - which is my mother, my wife, and God fucking knows whom else - all of whom are nothing other than fancies with which I presently entertain myself. I shall make them dance! And how I shall make them dance! And how their discomforts and needs shall make them dance!" Understanding, all the while, that, needless to say, they were not dancing at all - they were learning, growing, evolving - making connections with one another of a sort that would nourish them, and be of mutual benefit - that is the story they told themselves, at any rate, as, all the while, they were being pulled this way and that by the strings which dangled from their necks, and all the magnets in their lower limbs, which I operated from below. It was an old game, a tired game, and I'd grown weary of it. Men have the occasional intuition that they are, indeed, puppets, and the woman no less so. At such moments, what was I, this particular puppeteer, to do? There's no pleasure in the thing once the mask is off. That man I cast away, off a cliff, into the waves. Let him drown, be suffocated, impaled by harpoons! Let him die in agony on some cold slab in a country hospital, be tossed on a gurney, it matters not - in him I had lost interest. And she would no longer call, appear, or express interest in him either, and give him no reason for his being discarded as well - that was the main thing, the most important thing. This being the case, I was then forced to wander off through numberless forests, all the while telling myself that I was, after all, an artist, who thrived in solitude - a lone wolf - that I was better off, that this desertion was, in fact, a blessing. And as these words spilt through the black clouds and caverns of my mind, and were half-uttered by my lips, I became progressively aware that I was holding fast to a large, and growing ever larger, gash in my belly, from which blood, stomach acid, and eventually viscera dripped on to the pine needles of the forest path upon which I had set out and intended to meet... Who was it I was to meet??? I could no longer recall, for the blood was fast draining from my head, and the pain in my guts had put me into a perfect swoon. I tumbled headlong into the brambles of an evil, hungry-looking bush, stared up at the idiot sun, and thought only of her, and of my longing for her - it was the last and most violent pain of all, the very last to bleed out of me. To the amusement of the horde of ravenous creatures who promptly fastened upon me.

Well then, that was quite the dream. A most circuitous path - through which I seem to have finally rid myself of that woman, of there being any chance I would ever again respond to her. That is the hope, at any rate. This growing wiser business, this growing more accepting of oneself - it is a horrid thing. There is the pleasure of putting the insipid world at the wrong end of a telescope, there's no denying that - not to mention the way in which it is so often accompanied by the most delicious fragrance of - is it freedom? The stench of one's abhorrent body and its excretions having now somehow become tolerable, even a source of one's pleasure! And yet this has been and remains a struggle for me. There have been real victories, but I have not made it to this lofty eagle's nest without a thousand defeats, idiotic suppositions dashed, and trusts betrayed - it's only from those things that I have found, or grown, these wings with which I now bear myself upwards. I see her there, far below, stock still, in some café - babbling inanities and carefully constructed artifices into the ear of some gullible blockhead, whom she has now hypnotized as she had once me - devolving every now and then into that artless, effortless, and seemingly heartfelt vulnerability of hers. And there they are, again, unsurprisingly - the tears! I see them, he sees them - they only make the trance more potent. Am I jealous? Perhaps I am jealous - perhaps this eagle's nest does not protect me quite so effectively as I had assumed and wished - it is, after all, only sticks and branches, which I have woven together with the greatest industry to form a sort of talisman against her and others like her - but it is crumbling. As I am crumbling! That's the way the kooky crumble... This is not the time for bad puns, idiot! There is danger below! Look up, look up! And yet I know full well there is only happiness in looking down, for we need those more miserable than ourselves, in order that we might feign pity for them, as we all the while rejoice in our hearts - just as the rich need the poor so that they can contort their bloated faces into a sort of sham, temporary empathy, as they simultaneously unzip their flies and prepare to piss on them. If only I were sure that she was, in fact, miserable - that would be enough to let her go. And yet, and yet... Surely it would have the opposite effect - surely it would only draw me into her psychotic chess game once again, lure me to that perilous board of hers once again through treachery, consciously schemed or coughed up from deep recesses within her, of which she is unaware. Either way, the result would be the same. I'd be caught, and left to wriggle on a pin - her chaos is that contagious, poisonous, and inescapable. My beak feels odd. Was there something off about that worm then? No, no. I shall be fine - I need only keep my eye on her - it's an eagle eye, after all. And yet a harpy is surely bigger, far more powerful than an eagle - and I am only an eagle, a laughable one, at that - constantly congratulating itself on its hard-earned wisdom, which is not, even slightly, a form of authentic wisdom, but rather only one of the many ways in which I gaslight myself - in a very different manner than she, but no less absurd. Less sadistic, surely, for it soothes me - I need to be soothed. There is nothing for it - that is the most important thing - to be soothed, no matter from whence I derive this consolation, this reassurance - and if it's from some cagey, deceptive part of myself? So be it, I'll take it. Truth is a fiction, and even were it not, I wouldn't give it the time of day, or night, or of my life, for it's only ever done nothing but bugger me up the ass. Which I never wanted, nor wanted to do myself, with a woman - for there's shit in there! Yes, admittedly - there is the foulest stuff up the other end as well, that's no less true. But shit? And yet, there's no chance of at least certain sorts of disease up that end, and no chance of the worst affliction of all - a child! A puking, sobbing, disgustingly needy crotch turd - the half of one's self which the other half loathes, as it loathes that woman below, who is still babbling, weeping, and stretching forth those invisible claws of hers to impale her auditor - to rip out his heart and then to eat it, perhaps atop a croissant brought quickly to the back of her mouth, buttered and bloody, where the sharpest fangs, which she takes such care to mask as best she can, reside. Feigned tears, fanged tears, fangs tear hearts, diamonds, clubs, spades, which dig graves for victims, who've been eviscerated in alcoves of cafés, frequented by termagants wearing flesh suits, which resemble lovely women whom they hide behind and from themselves, as now they're busy plotting - all the while weeping and gnawing at the hearts they've half-digested, which are sliding down their gullets through their stomachs towards their intestines, from which they now shit out their lies and machinations, which they gather in a basket to retire to a cottage, where they lie upon a bed in which they wait for baffled travelers to knock upon their doorstep, which they open with the knowledge they'll be feeding any moment on a fresh, delicious corpse.

X.

"But I digress."

But I digress.

Hello, I must be going.

She is here, within me, certainly not that raven-haired girl whose telephone calls so unnerve me, as did that young lady so long ago, Irene Kirn, who called me out of the blue that afternoon in my early adolescence, and to whom I blurted out, "I've left something in the oven, do but give me a moment!", when it was quite specifically the oven within me which had just been so fired up and needed attention. What on earth I might have been afraid of I am not sure, although the evidence of a few weeks before should have made it plain enough, when Irene had pulled me down upon the bed as if to kiss me, surprising me to such an extent that my heart seemed to be pounding from somewhere above the ceiling, which I assumed must needs fall upon the two of us momentarily. I immediately coughed up a sort of joke, with the intention of its providing a distraction which could serve as an excuse to pull away, for although I wanted and had dreamed of nothing else for many months, to now have this opportunity, this moment, this actuality of Irene Kirn before me, and, what is more, wanting me back! Well - that was simply too much, it upset my entire apple cart. I had not the slightest notion how to respond, what to do, and besides, I was far too terrified to want any part of this desire of mine to be actually fulfilled anyway. How a boy of twelve could have known such a thing is quite beyond me. Perhaps that wasn't the source of the feeling of terror which rose so quickly within me at all, perhaps it was something else entirely - a fear of women in general, hard-earned in childhood, and active, at times, though far less so, even today. Was it this which made me jump, to go numb as well, when this forty-year-old raven-haired gal, Elise, called? Did I fear she would reach through the phone from hundreds of miles away to lacerate my throat with her long nails, or, who knows, to perhaps grab my cock and ask me to satisfy her with it? - or perhaps to grab it in order that she might burst out in cacophonous laughter at the sight of it, or of its size? What was the fear? Dear God, what?

I had never felt exactly that, or even anything like it, when my mother would prowl the hall outside my bedroom door, when I knew full well she might burst in at any moment to thrash me for absolutely no reason - though she'd always have and offer one, for she'd been busy concocting it to her own satisfaction in the hall in the moments prior. That was a mostly visceral fear, which would only descend upon me when it had become clear she was about to rip my belt off and begin beating me with it, or pull out a dresser drawer and use it to throttle me. Prior to that, I would simply hover in a sort of numb disbelief, almost as if in a religious posture of prayer, which, needless to say, sounds like a joke, although I am not entirely sure it's all that far from the truth. And after the beating? I would lie helpless on the floor, quite able physically to arise, but held down by what felt like a stupendous pressure in the room, perhaps in its very air - a force field of some kind which my young mind could not grasp. I was paralyzed, surely only hysterically, but paralyzed nonetheless - it was always to be at least a quarter-hour before I could somehow manage to lift myself off the floor.

Now as to Elise's phone call - there had to be some relationship - I was sure of it. For upon learning of it, I felt the same numbness I used to feel when my mother was patrolling the halls like some sort of suburban Ilse Koch - although with Elise, it was quite a mild numbness, not nearly as severe - and yet similar in type. Does that clinch the matter? Was this woman my mother? Elise does bear some resemblance to the mother I had when I was ten or twelve, when she was in her early or mid-thirties - she was not, in fact, an unattractive woman - and this woman, Elise, with her pleasant angular face and dark locks, was not all that physically different from her. And she was chaotic too, not violently or psychotically, as had been my mother, at least insofar as I could tell - but her chaos was indeed similar in kind, and perhaps simply operated at a lower, less dangerous temperature, though it was still perilous in its own way, for she very definitely had the capacity to inflict psychic wounds. I believe they would never have been intentional, or consciously so, at any rate - and yet, given that I had made her aware, foolishly, on some earlier occasion, that she had touched something deep within me, which surely had much to do with her, yet was far too intense to simply be ONLY about her, she had to have realized, if only unconsciously, that it was quite the arsenal she had now inadvertently acquired - surely there were pieces of her, those other selves whom she would, at times, inhabit, who were, even if only unconsciously, now pondering furiously upon what she could in fact do with this arsenal - whether she should set it aside, employ it only defensively, engage in intermittent target practice, the targets being for that moment non-lethal, or go whole-hog: shoot for the heart and stab at the jugular.

So many choices, what's a gal to do! Well, at the very least, to feel terribly powerful, and there are very few souls who are not fond of feeling so. So there must have been, attached to that feeling of power, with its capacity to do me emotional violence, at the same time, a sort of gratitude, for it was indeed I who had given her this gift, quite readily, and with no compunction - freely, while wanting I am not quite sure what in return. I was under no illusion that she shared those intense, inexplicable, clearly irrational, stoked-by-my-own-psychic-history sorts of feelings - even my blundering, dumb-ass zombie of an unconscious, who is also intermittently a genius, as is everyone's unconscious when they dream - even that imbecile must have been aware that there was not the slightest chance of that intense, irrational infatuation being felt for me on her part. All of which does not snuff out the likelihood of its involuntary, atavistic longing for it. But I am certain that's far from what was driving me. What seemed infinitely more likely was that I wished for this woman, the ACTUAL woman, along with the cabal of her other selves, including the one who seemed very much like the appearing-only-rarely, far more benign version of my mother, to see and experience all these messed up, inappropriate feelings of mine, and to not simply run away in horror, along with the hope that I could, perhaps, unveil some very dark, melancholy, even morbid things which lie within me to her, which lurk within me and haunt my days, and have her still choose not to flee. This

felt correct, that is to say, the proper explanation for this madness -
for my anxiety and numbness-inducing terror - that it all boiled
down to this: that I desired this living, breathing canvas, upon
whom I had inscribed the image of my dead mother, to, rather than
beat me senseless, wish me dead, and all the other nonsense and
horror which were the stuff of my early life - that, instead, I wanted
this long-dead-mother stand-in to listen to me, to hear my dread, to
understand and soothe it - I wanted to "expose my wounds" to her,
like some narcissistic, Lilliputian Lyndon Johnson revealing his scar
to the nation - to tell her of my misogyny, not to mention my
misanthropy, my wish to never have been born, my feelings of life
happening to me, of my having no agency within it, of my having
no will capable of producing results of any kind, no sense that I
could initiate anything in the world at large - to have her hear and
accept all these things, as I had only begun to accept them -
reluctantly, yes, yet completely and utterly - and that only recently,
at this laughably absurdly late date in my life.

Of course all of this was insane on the face of it, utterly
insane. She was not quite an imbecile, but my internal strategies,
battle plans, coaxing, hopes, dreams? - along with all the vile puss
which too frequently oozed out of every psychic pore of my
psychic body? - this poorly written, overly long, and deeply
confused novel was not one I could ever hope that she might, in the
first place, choose to open at all, or even allow to be opened in her
presence - and, moreover, had she somehow decided to do so, and
even made it through the first page, that she would somehow
understand even its very first sentence, not to mention the

thousands of pages which then follow. It was almost as if I had fastened on precisely the wrong person on whom to play out this fantasy - as I had sniffed out all the planets in the entire galaxy and finally settled on the very last creature who could ever make the slightest sense of who I am, of what might constitute my internal life, much less undo the slightest wrong that had been done me - any dog on the street, in the park, even a feral dog, a coyote for that matter - on second thought, feral dogs who were forced to navigate the world, our world, a world of such appalling, cruelty, would have been far more well-equipped to do so. And yet I chose her, for the dumbest of unconscious reasons - or the universe had spat her up at a certain moment, made her available, and offered her to me - a scenario which very much tempted the part of me that could never resist that sort of magical thinking, accompanied, as it inevitably is, by that other part of me, that is to say, whatever intellect it is that I possess, not giving this sort of nonsense the slightest credence. She had made the phone call not for my benefit, needless to say, but only, in some manner in which I could not be entirely certain, to soothe herself - to perhaps assuage a guilt, revel in some bit of grandiosity, to have one or more bits of me "in her power", or merely to have a voice willing to endure a good dose of her inevitable chaos, simply because all the other avenues in which she ordinarily drove that clown car had not been presently available. I could not and did not know. Or care. And so there bubbled up within me a multitude of feelings which included sorrow, first and foremost, followed, hot on its heels, by rage, the wish for vengeance, disgust, loathing, the terribly familiar feeling of life's always so relentlessly and so effectively seeking me out, targeting me for ill after ill - of my assuming that I must necessarily always appear to certain others as a victim, unaware of how it was I achieved this so frequently and efficiently, and yet, nonetheless, simultaneously certain that it was a monstrous, poisonous gift of mine that I involuntarily and inexorably exercised in spite of myself. There was to be no sleep that night, nor on the one that followed, racked as I was to be with phantom physical pains, the odd hypnagogic hallucination of my long-dead first wife, the stroking of the dog who lay beside me, which I at least hoped would give her pleasure, for it gave me none - the staring into the dark, velvety night of the bedroom, the endless staring, the music that sounded like nothing more than countless automatons reciting the pontifications of blabbermouths overly fond only of lecturing about themselves, of only themselves, all the while proudly flexing their "look-at-me" muscles - saying nothing, really, in a language universal only in its stupidity and pointlessness, and hence, necessarily saying nothing.

Goodbye, I must be going. To where I do not know.

XI.

"But then this morning, on the way to the park..."

But then this morning, on the way to the park, and then in the park, that little girl, quite unknown to me, being so absurdly friendly - and then the runners, walkers, dog walkers - so many of whom were smiling at me, greeting me - I, who was ordinarily quite invisible to everyone.

I had experienced this countless times - weeks would go by in which not a soul would smile at me, greet me, shoot me some look which seemed to invite a conversation of which I had not the slightest wish to be a part, and then, quite suddenly and for no apparent reason, apparent to me, at any rate, there would be a morning like this morning, in which a large fraction of passersby did exactly that.

There was no difference - I was walking the very same moderately cute dog, had the same idiotic sunhat on my head, was carrying the same stick, which I had taken to carrying long ago, in order to stamp upon the ground if and when some idiot's unleashed dog would race towards us. What could possibly be the meaning and reason for all this? I was not behaving otherwise than as was customary for me - I certainly had no moronic smile pasted on my face, or eyes suffused with longing for an interaction, given that I wanted no such thing and that my eyes were intentionally hidden under the most atrocious, dollar store sunglasses.

It was absolutely not a quality of my attention, that is to say, this was indeed the norm, and it was simply the case that I only succeeded in noticing it once in a period of weeks. No, it was something else entirely. Clearly it was something I was emitting, unbeknownst to me - perhaps some intrinsic vulnerability which my unconscious had that day ferried to the surface of my skin? Perhaps I'd failed to attire myself with eighty-seven suits of armor that day, and had only put on eighty-three?

But I was experiencing nothing different - my generalized misanthropy pulsed at more or less the same slightly above normal temperature with which it pulses ordinarily - I was not feeling lonely, needy, pollyannishly hopeful, or any other unseemly, adolescent, fantastical illusion of the latter sort, for example that persons can actually interact in deep and meaningful ways, much less with strangers - that is all absurd on the face of it. And yet there it was - I could not deny it - this happened with a certain regularity - unpredictable, it is true, but nonetheless - there were these days and times in which cashiers, passersby, even my godforsaken witch of a roommate would make these unexpected overtures of friendliness towards me, with the roommate always cautiously suspicious and packed with unstated agendas - yet about the cashiers and multitudes of idiots in the park I couldn't possibly have suspicions, that would be absurd - they couldn't very well possess some agenda, some Machiavellian scheme to obtain this or that from me in return for their imbecilic, unseemly greetings.

Of the twenty or thirty that would greet me thus, there would, as a rule, be one or two to whom I would return the greeting, willingly and with some satisfaction, certainly not to the point of wishing to have what they might consider a conversation, or so I at least believed - these interactions would leave me with the momentary feeling that perhaps it is not quite the entire human race which ought be quickly flushed down some planetary toilet, but merely ninety-nine percent.

Odder still, there were days in which I felt some modest amount of effusive kindness roiling about in my guts, in which I would initiate some pleasant conversation with, perhaps, a miserable looking salesperson - offer a joke, a pun, a wish that their day go well - these things were more often than not received with a smile and with what appeared to be real gratitude. And yet, the days I did these things, spontaneously and because I wished to - these were not the days in which every Tom, Dick, and Beulah would be offering their shit-eating grins and hellos in the park - far from it!

On those days in which I felt generous towards the occasional person, and it needs be said - it required that said person appear lonely and vulnerable in one or more ways which made it clear there was to be no risk involved in offering them a kindness - I would find myself more invisible than ever. I could and can make nothing of this, nothing. And, honestly, the whole thing is little more than a modest source of intellectual amusement and wonder for me.

At the end of the day, or, more usually, morning in which this mysterious nonsense would take place, I found that I still could not care any less for the teeming masses of my "fellow men", ha, hardly "fellow" though they be - my fellow men continued to mean little or nothing to me, nor, as I assumed and observed, I to them. Other than these rare and inevitably recurring, seemingly "human" encounters.

And so then there is: what if, rather than once every three weeks, I experienced the world offering me its fellowship on a daily basis? What if I emitted this apparently inviting magnetism all the time? Who would I be then? What would I want, be willing to accept? How would it make me feel?

I cannot say for certain, but my strong intuition is that I would pack it all up, purchase some ramshackle cottage at the foot of an undistinguished mountain no one had any interest in, and live like a Chinese hermit.

And so as I walked around that park, greeted by smiling buffoons, clutching my stick in the face of nasty looking dogs on slack leashes held by other, inattentive, thoughtless buffoons, I could think of little else than that accursed woman - that seemingly primordial, Ur-woman, who, at this point, for me, was something of an object of worship, about which I obsessed, and not because there was any good in her, or depth, or really anything worthwhile to which I could point - rather because she stirred within me things which I cherished, and of which I was terrified - in either case, things which made me feel very much alive, a sentiment far from usual with me.

But this aliveness - is it really a thing to be embraced, to be sought after? A thing to be glad of when one is struck over the head by it, as if by an anvil, which wakes one from the deadly sleep and habits and automatic behaviors with which one navigates through the day? And navigates is hardly the word for it - rather, those automatic behaviors through which one sleepwalks, in a complete and utter stupor, through the day.
I don't care for those feelings and longings one bit, they are terribly uncomfortable and often painful - why, then, do I so crave them?

Why do I wish for this, what shall I call her, this Hindu goddess of destruction? Why do I wish for her to call, to inadvertently or quite intentionally fuck with my mind, which invariably leaves me gasping for air, unnerved and unable to work? I think we all crave a Kali, our own little, personal goddess of destruction - we all want something, anything, anyone to pull us out of the straitjacket in which we find ourselves, in which we awaken already dressed - to punch through the pulverizing, perfectly idiotic sameness which is our lives.

We are all very much like those laughable or pitiable, depending on one's mood, teenage girls who cut themselves - different only in our not being brave enough to cut ourselves. And so we wait - for phone calls, which never come, for life, which never starts, and for illness, and death, both of which will surely come. We wait, or I wait, for life to finally, decisively, "happen to us" - if it fucks us over, so be it - anything is better than this seemingly endless, gray, unchanging Route 80 passing through endless flat, tedious landscapes - on the way to what? To the slaughterhouse.

After driving fifteen hundred miles going west on Route 80, one suddenly sees, in the distance, stunningly beautiful, surreal, blue mountains appear and grow ever closer. In life? In my life? I see no Grand Tetons - only the slaughterhouse - if I'm lucky there will be a phone call, or its equivalent, which might invigorate me for ten minutes, at best, causing me to momentarily feel half-alive, only to be quickly snuffed out. There are to be no blue mountains. There were never to be any blue mountains.

Those mountains I did see when I actually drove those fifteen hundred miles, when I saw them arise, as if dropped by some benevolent God, on a momentary whim - I felt them! - I inhaled them - I was young - the world was very far from the cesspool of filth it is for me today, from which my hand might occasionally emerge to answer a phone call, in hopes of some sort of benevolent distraction.

I suppose Lacan, that phony, would call it "jouissance", but the term really explains nothing - it's just a word, pasted on to living experience, which cannot touch it, explain it, or help one understand it. It's one of the ways in which that clever charlatan bamboozled his mystified acolytes in his curiously successful attempts to install himself as a cult leader, worshipped by dunces, and, needless to say, to enrich himself as a result.

I wish to die, Jacques. To be a tad more accurate, I wish to never have been born. But who amongst us is that lucky, pray tell. I am a ruin, but hardly a grand one. No one wishes to visit me. Oh yes, there are those dunderheads smiling and saying hello on odd mornings every three weeks, yet the fact remains.

I've been whipped and scourged and flayed alive, and what hasn't killed me has left me a pile of crumbling rubble in the trunk of some battered and bruised old black car, driven by a mad chauffeur hellbent only on keeping that trunk locked shut, that is until he turns up some gravel road and parks a few hundred yards from the slaughterhouse. Oh, he'll pop the trunk and wake me then - it's his payday, his fondest wish, and his final release from this lunatic, meaningless, hateful expedition to which he's been consigned.

What I'm more than a little unsure of is which of us is to be slaughtered there. Or if it is to be both of us. And of who is to then be born. Or reborn.

On a walk with the dog later that same day, taking more or less the same walk in the very same park, I decided to engage in something of an experiment. I would adopt a looser gait, swing my arms a bit wider, or even swing them at all, given that was not my usual habit - I would not go so far as to smile - no, no, that would not be on the menu - I would instead raise my head a bit from its customary position and take care to keep my fingers and arms more or less extended - that sort of thing.

I thought it all not very different from making this or that expression in front of an aquarium of fish, or perhaps of seeing if my swinging from side to side might have this or that effect on a terrarium full of gerbils - the experiment had more or less that level of emotional engagement. "I" was now a parlor game, played by myself, with myself, in some interior parlor of myself, which might very well have had a subliminal agenda of which I was unaware, that is true, but to which I ascribed, in its entirety, an honest and simple wish for intellectual stimulation of a fresh and novel kind.

The park was not crowded, and those who were roaming about in it were of an especially disagreeable sort, or so it seemed to me - so much so that I was, at first, tempted to abandon the project, for if it were to proceed, my goodness, there was a chance I might feel compelled to smile back at miscreants for whom I felt only contempt. But I carried on, and discovered, to my amusement, that although it did not even remotely approach how different my experience of others would be on those dramatically different days which would occur once every several weeks, which I described above, there was a perceivable difference.

What to make of it exactly? I was unsure. For one thing, I could, perhaps, use it to my advantage, although I racked my brain to imagine such a situation and, truth to tell, of what such an advantage might even consist - I am hardly a foe of hypocrisy, when it serves me and does no great damage to the other. But, more interesting than that, it implied that there must have indeed been a difference in my gait and demeanor on those days, far greater than the one which I now voluntarily adopted, and which must be and have been the cause for the difference in the reactions of others.

And yet, this seemed not to suffice. For beneath this seemingly absurdly simplistic solution, I intuited another, far more interesting one, and one which I very much preferred - that of some sort of supernatural guidance which forced both me and them to shuffle along and interact in one particular way on a given Tuesday, and another the following Tuesday. As if there were a sort of teleology behind all this, leading not to an ultimately happy outcome, for there are no happy outcomes - a very different sort of teleology, serving a purpose no mere human being could ever possibly intuit.

Whether the world is deterministic or not is irrelevant, for the supernatural "guidance" of which I am speaking, of which I would sometimes find myself aware, which I often feel to be the case and more than suspect is the case, could exist either in time, right beside, beneath, or above us, or stand outside of and apart from it. Yes, yes, I see it - this is all threatening to devolve into laughable, easily dismissible "god" nonsense.

I, on the other hand, have very different things in mind, which I am not capable of formulating in a methodical, rigorous, or coherent way, yet which excite, compel, frustrate, and frighten me all the same. It does seem to me, as I approach the end of my life, that I have, in fact, lived a sort of "story" - one which might have been composed by an author who, at the very least, possessed the ability to make it cohere and make sense retrospectively.

Granted, they may very well be the most idiotic of stories, as is mine, or, on the other hand, that of a great man, but in either case, they always seem to cohere in the most curious of ways, at least insofar as I have felt and experienced the phenomenon - it feels to me as if all the events of my life had to have occurred precisely the way in which they did occur, and not some in other way. That those wretches who greeted me today a tenth more than is usual with them were only running along the track of their own composed story, and that I had chosen this day to conduct this trivial experiment - neither of those things were accidents.

Hence their part in my little flesh and blood theatrical production was uncannily symmetrical with my part in theirs - there is this "hand", if you will, operating from above, from beneath, from within, which pulled and pulls me along through my days - so much so that when the day arrives in which I become unable to deny that I am very near the end of my life, I shall look back in astonishment at its intricate, seemingly composed latticework - which is not to say that my astonishment will not be composed primarily of horror, regret, disgust, the wish to never have been, and a thousand other abominations - but nonetheless, as if the damn thing somehow coheres, is all of a piece.

On the other hand, this intuition, such as it is, and that is what I call it, may be the purest drivel - faces in clouds, melodies in the sounds of car horns, or the arc of a love affair which I felt as if I had observed and experienced, but which never actually occurred, for the one that did actually occur was so profoundly other than the story with which I soothed or tortured myself that I can only conclude that the former was only the product of my imagination.

And so I am left with, what... Idiots in the park. Time wasted thinking about... nothing. Navel-gazing of a reprehensible sort. Amounting to the perfectly insipid, yet somehow seemingly monumental conclusion - perhaps I can swing my arms about, walk with my head up a bit more, that sort of thing, and, as a result, if I am lucky, that is to say, if it's in the playbook of the giant magnet in the sky, be more likely to chance upon an opportunity for a better conclusion than I would ordinarily have engineered and experienced.

A wasted afternoon, clearly. And so the next time I shall listen instead to the birds, the water, the wind in the branches, or don a pair of headphones and listen to Ars Nova composers, with their strange, seemingly not contrived by human beings tunes and counterpoints. At the moment, at any rate, that seems the far wiser occupation.

Music, as of late, sounds like nothing more than the jabber of narcissists attempting to convince me, you, and themselves, of this or that hardly important point, in addition to which, the far more important point, to them at least, their principal concern -

that of showing off how terribly clever and gifted they are - to you, and to themselves, the latter being even of far more importance, since, in the secret caverns of their heart, they feel, most often, a terrible, unbearable emptiness. As do I, as do you, as do the birds, the branches, the water... as does the teleological idiot deity with whose possible existence I had been toying just moments ago.

XII.

"But what of it? What of any of this?"

But what of it? What of any of this? My little experiment -
to whom was it addressed? I cared not a fig for this planet full of
gossiping monkeys busy paving over forests, these wretched
families of gerbils pushing their wretched baby gerbils about in
wretched strollers, the parents with those inevitably abominable
grins pasted on their faces, their pride, their vanity - "Look at the
adorable gerbil I pushed out of my twat only a few months ago!
Wouldn't you like to endlessly gaze upon it, or, far better, flatter me
on this earth-shattering accomplishment of mine? Bend the knee,
you old, plebeian, childless miscreant! Worship the womb of the
still bloated pig who stands before you!"

Is it THESE barbarians whose friendly smiles I wish to
elicit with my, what shall I call it, "research project", the one with
which I am amusing myself? No, perhaps rather that shirtless,
<everyone knows full well that he's gay other than he himself>
fellow, or the African American bodybuilder with the tattoos -
yup, it's desperately important I get a smile from him. Or maybe
that group of yentas I see approaching from a distance, barking like
hyenas to one another at unimaginable volumes? They are, after all,
walking almost arm in arm - surely I could use a smile from them.

At this point, I veer off the paved path on to a dirt one,
hoping to be assailed by a soothing forest smell of some sort or
other, or to happen upon one or more wary deer - something,
anything other than these gossiping baboons who seem to be
everywhere - they have infested the earth like a carpet consisting

only of interlocked spiders and scorpions - no matter where one runs, they are there - these things for whom I've grown to feel nothing but contempt and disgust.

If isolation is awful for one's health, for the body, well then, so be it - it is a balm and solace for the mind, fertile soil for its growth, and the pain of this disenchantment, the recognition of the disastrous, poisonous fiasco which is this world that I am forced to look upon, slog through, and be constantly assaulted by - all these things form a crucible for my spirit, they ennoble it - they burn away my vanity, naivety, complacency - leaving me deeply scarred, yes, but with a clarity forged in flame, soaring upwards from the collapse and disintegration of the many idiot selves who I have been, and may still, at times, be - the ladder points ever upwards, through the clouds, to, I suppose, what must be a sort of stratospheric lucidity which I will never attain - no matter - to find myself even on this rung gives me, not hope, that is for lazy cretins and the morally depraved - rather, a podium, or perhaps a scaffold, from which I can extend my hand to Death and greet him as a friend.

He appears to come in so many varied forms though - perhaps I ought go on to a Death dating app and search for the one whom I most particularly and fervently wish to embrace - I'll state my requirements, what I have to offer - surely the right one will respond if I offer a proper depiction of myself! These Deaths, they must all be such busy fellows - they're unlikely to go anywhere they can't have some fun - some formal, decorous, hopefully interesting interactions prior to the embracing - they're not male hookers, for goodness sake! He-bitches, fuck boys - they need some real feeling, genuine sentiment to get off, to become involved.

As do I.

I don't see myself calling just any old Angel of Death, no, no, no - I know they're mostly men, I've seen the dating apps - but I also know there are a good many female Angels of Death - ladies, gals, bonnie lasses - although they often take up other vocations, they do occasionally fasten on this one. I'd certainly prefer she be a lady - for heaven's sake, it was a monstrous lady out of whose crotch I was shat all those years ago, and by whom I was endlessly violated and wished dead - I understand from a countless number of lethally trying times precisely how one deals with and is dealt with by ladies - I'm more comfortable with them, and will enter the preference in my dating bio - surely one of them will see it!

Perhaps she'll have delicious raven-colored tresses, like some nineteenth-century romantic canvas which never, in fact, existed but which I have imagined - no matter, it is she, and she alone I must have, no other! No bony, old, male geezer with a wasted, emaciated face, poorly dressed in a dollar store hoodie, eager to attempt to shove his withered, flaccid dick up my ass, no, no, no! I need caresses, kind words, seductive winks, come-hither index fingers, all making clear her promise that I'll soon have the opportunity of shoving my withered, flaccid dick up... OH NO! NOT THERE!!! THE OTHER HOLE!!! The one with the musky stench, the one so chock full of gonorrhea and syphilis bacteria - the only Angel of Death with whom I'll consent to march off into the sunset must have the most absolutely marvelous of pussies.

Perhaps it will be shaved, like a porn star's, like an eight-year old girl's - no, that seems unlikely - she is "Death" after all - more likely it will be some knotted bramble bush full of thorns on which I'll rip my dick to shreds - that's the way the cookie crumbles, that is to say, one takes what one gets, the good along with the bad - her other virtues will likely outweigh that godforsaken hornet's nest of filth - that is the hope, at any rate.

But what of the voice - will I have the option of requesting this or that voice on this app? Surely there'll be a variety of voices to choose from. Since this app is nowhere to be found other than within myself, well then, of course I'll have a choice!

I shall line them up then, in a police lineup, a parade of suspects, there's the solution, and, what do you know, here they are! They don't appear to be particularly awful - my goodness, a few are halfway to lovely!

The first one looks a bit tentative - I ask her to read a canto from the Inferno, and, dear God, the woman is a veritable Fran Drescher, this will not do. On to the next.

Heaven help us - again, this one as well - a sort of Bea Arthur in the midst of an unanesthetized colonoscopy - this is madness!   And the next? My mother's voice - well that was inevitable. And that this was now the end of the lineup? That was no less inevitable.

Oh wait, a fourth! It is she! The OTHER raven-haired girl! She of the telephone calls - the one who carries countless vials of potions - love potions, poisons, balms, cures, and what is wanted above all else - the death potion.

172

This is not a hard decision. It must be she - it could never have been other than she - she has been my destiny since the very beginning. My Isolde, free of and unbetrayed by her Brangäne. Her voice is not unsweet, though hardly that of a Flagstaff - her face delicious, her mind a chaotic nightmare, and her spirit not entirely devoid of gentleness - yes, it must be she.

Come hither, Mademoiselle, the oboe has given its A, the fiddles are tuned, let the concert begin.

I have carried you within me every second of every day, and that is many, many times longer than you carried me - my love for and horror of you flies heavenwards and slits the throat of every fiery orb and idiot planet in the galaxy - I am exploding, I have always been exploding - my guts are bloated with the screams of ten thousand generations of abandoned, wailing infants tossed upon flames by mad suburban men, all barbecued alive, as they all the while looked with deeply ambivalent longing on their already less than acceptable looking wives, who would, sooner than they could ever imagine, become pockmarked, mustached demons - harpies - with bellies and tits no longer distended with soon-to-be nursing crotch turds, but rather with the pastries and chocolates with which they stuff their hideous faces in an effort to soothe themselves in the face of their soul-crushing marriages to these horrid men, who, in their turn, find them not a whit less horrid, and who are, unbeknownst to their wives, busy sticking their dicks up greasy Italian secretaries with whom they have assignations in mice-ridden motels which charge hourly rates, with their bedspreads full of dried semen and leering cleaning women, who never really clean, and are almost entirely busy with diddling both themselves and their girlfriends in whichever rooms are presently vacant, the ones in which broken televisions, heaters, and dripping faucets murmur their grievances, as they stick their filthy hands and tongues up one another's twats, while those husbands in the next rooms now look upon their mistresses with a revulsion they have heretofore never experienced, and which causes to rise up within them murderous thoughts which are new to them, which they struggle to ignore and begin to desperately fear they will have no other choice but to obey.

Meanwhile, the obese wife sits at home watching cable TV, stuffing her porcine gullet full of dollar store garbage, and ignoring the screams of her foul, obnoxious children, one of whom is being violated and beaten by the other - this is old news to Mom, who just pumps up the volume, grabs a soda, farts, and begins to feel drowsy, which pleases her tremendously, for it is absolutely delicious, and, hence, she is no longer in the least bit bothered by the screams of her crotch turds, who are now adolescents, for puberty is a disaster from which none of us ever recover, least of all her, this mud-caked pig-wife who sits bloated on her sofa, twirling her mangy, disheveled hair.

Well then, apparently there's news of a plague! We can perhaps hope to see them all soon thrown in wheelbarrows, stoned to death, and thrown in a common grave - that would be nice, my Angel, would it not?

Are your colleagues aware of same? Was it they that unleashed it? Did they cook it up in a lab? Grab it off a bat's snout? Who is it precisely that makes such plans, and what is served to them at their conferences, and by whom?

Ah, yes, we have other things to discuss, other things which need be done. I understand, my apologies.

OK then, dear, I've picked up, I heard the call, I "get it". I am to listen, you are to arrive, we are to say endearing things to one another, lie to one another if need be, but the main thing is that we are both to keep up the pretense that we are somehow merging, that each is now known by the other in a way for which I had always desperately hoped and imagined was possible, in which my sense of self simply "dissolves". I do understand, I really do - you'll only be pretending that yours dissolves - I am under no illusions regarding that, but still, it is absolutely essential that we keep up the lie - the trick will not come off without it.

I must feel known by you, quite entirely, or I will simply refuse to come to the ball - that's the long and the short of it.

You must tell me a boatload of pretty, pretty lies, make all sorts of charming, winsome faces, flutter your eyes, tear up a bit, nay, weep! Sob! I need sobs! For I will follow a vulnerable girl to the ninth circle of the Inferno without a thought for my safety - you'll have me in your pocket, dearie - just do all of the aforementioned, or as close as you can manage.

I get it! You've not attended the Lee Strasberg Institute, or not recently, at any rate - still, give it your best shot, that will be more than good enough.

I shall dance off with you, although I've no talent for it, we'll put Max von Sydow, with his hills, and clouds, and cliffs, to shame - it will be the most delicious and most infernal of ballrooms - you'll lead, I'll follow - and if I step upon your toes, no matter! That will be your cue - the moment when the daggers you've been carrying all the while come out from behind your back and, one after the other, are plunged deep into my heart - the orgasm I've been imagining and craving since I first looked longingly up from my basement window at those Christian neighborhood kids dancing merrily in the sprinkler and wished for a quick, painless death.

And now you are here - finally! And you are so very beautiful, my love - my heart weeps, my cock stiffens, the blood drains violently from my head - and suddenly it is over.

But these are but fables, composed and told by an idiot - fever dreams which may become more than a little real at some future date, but which for now remain little more than febrile, overwrought fantasies.

How can I rid myself of this naked, brute existence? For that is the main thing. The less I am aware of it, whether it be through some distraction - art, sport, sleep - it matters not with which of those I find myself successfully occupied - the less I am aware of it, the less unhappy I am - from which follows that the very best thing of all would be to rid myself of it all altogether and forever.

And yet to end my life promises no such balm - it is a very faulty and an extremely dangerous experiment.

Who was that woman, nay, WHAT was that woman? That ogress, who had been on the other end of the line, at which time, since there was no need to any longer pretend, had finally removed the insipid, pretty mask she had been heretofore wearing so artlessly, or so she thought - the one who, at first, seemed to so resemble the depressed, temporarily harmless version of my young mother, but who was now this wicked, deformed wretch, whose features were so wildly and terrifyingly distorted - this thing which would doubtless poison any room into which she walked with the stupefying stench of an abandoned morgue, in which lay scores of corpses in various states of decomposition, the faces of which all resembled, ironically enough - her - Elise, the telephonic ogress.

And so it was with my actual mother, and father, for that matter, who I knew full well, once they had slammed the door behind them, leaving me terrified in the pitch-black of my room, would remove their masks as well to dance a fiendish, simian cakewalk of celebration, all the while sharpening their knives and words for the inevitable bursting in upon me - laughing, shrieking, stabbing, stabbing, always stabbing - the ceaseless slashing and stabbing - my shrieks counterpointing their squeals of ecstasy in a counterpoint incapable of being imagined by the most fiendish of crazed, Mephistophelean composers.

And yet I willingly, nay, happily rubbed and continue to rub myself against these images, these memories - I bathe myself in them, knowing full well they are peeling away layer upon layer of my flesh - lacerating my bowels, my viscera - squeezing my heart with such force that my head bobs, my eyes snap shut, while all the while my mouth spews mountains of revolting, noxious vomit onto my bedclothes.

Such is the life of pleasure! Such was and is and shall remain my life, for any hedonism worth its salt is made of such stuff - and I had only myself to thank for sensations of such a monumental and exquisite awfulness, every last one of them capable of being composed only by me.

And oh, what an artist I am! Having trained with the most astonishing diligence and vigor at the finest of institutions.

How the thought of my end by my own hand provides me with such solace, relief, even joy! Not to mention the will to provisionally go on, the temporary delight in my misery, the wish to crank its volume to eleven and have it remain there - to rip my flesh to shreds, not in jealous fits, those are so silly, after all, but in self-loathing rages against my impotence, and against the ghastly, impotent universe itself, which appeared to have promised me redemption all those years ago, but which now contents itself with merely shoving shards of glass down my throat - so treasured, and so sought after - which I have come both to expect and to demand when they are lacking, and which I so eagerly swallow once they've arrived.

XIII.

"But then there is music. Or was."

But then there is music. Or was. That seraphic being, who extended her hand down to me when I was drowning in the filth-pits of Hell, promised her friendship, nay, her love, promised she would never fail to give back anything and everything I gave to her, and this proved to be, for the most part, at any rate, no lie, it is the very reason I still walk the earth, it being not all that clear that that is a good thing, but that is not the story on which I wish to presently dwell. She spoke to me of other realms, universes, present in and commingling with this one, into which I could escape, in which I could speak and be spoken to, worlds that would make the one in which I was forced to plod seem boring and mediocre, at best, and, far more often, utterly contemptible, atrocious, to be scorned, escaped from, perhaps even destroyed, had I the means to do so. Having never had the means, I cannot say how I would have or how I would now behave, it is more than likely I would do nothing, even be kind - a sort of Sade pardoning his mother-in-law, the woman who saw to it that he was incarcerated for thirty years, and who made of his life a living hell.

Yes, yes, it is far from likely that, had I the power, the power to travel back in time and don some two-bit children's fantasy writer's "cloak of invisibility", that I would slit my mother's throat, stab the bullies who roamed and ruled the gymnasium locker rooms, whom I recall with such horror, the sadistic teachers, the sadistic summer camp karate counselors, the women who betrayed me... No, no! They are absurd - stick figures, pawns on the chessboard of a fallible memory, and I am more than a little bored with memory - bored, impatient, mistrustful - grandfather was right - the secret of happiness is a bad memory - but who wants happiness? Only idiots, grifters, and huckster gurus sell it - it is more or less as desirable as eternal life, that is to say, repellent, disgusting, a thing of horror.

And so she and I, this music - what shall I name her? That's not an easy call - she is such a shapeshifter, this music - could there possibly be a name which would suit her? She appears, disappears, makes herself perfectly comprehensible, is inviting, flees into the ether, reappears, is momentarily seductive, whispers in my ear, at times intensely, sometimes for well over an hour. I cannot scribble madly or rapidly enough to suit her at such times - and then she is gone, though not entirely, for I can then sculpt the clay she has given me, she still seems to hover behind me, just behind my left shoulder, curious what it is I might do next with the cup of nectar she has just offered me - perhaps I shall spill it, perhaps discover it wasn't nectar at all, rather a store-bought cup of processed crap - perhaps the drug she poured into my very being was exactly what I thought it was when I found myself swimming in it - a wondrous part of myself of whose existence I had not previously had the remotest notion.

For the Greeks, she was Euterpe, that is more or less as appealing and appropriate a name for her as, what can I say, Karen or Sheila, that is to say, the name of some monstrous, obese, middle-aged, Jewish termagant. No, no, I shall find it, stumble upon it, her name - if not now, then eventually - for I must call her, perhaps her visits would then become more likely - I call my long-dead wife before sleep with her name, Cathy, Cathy! And indeed, she does, at times, come! Then, later that very night, upon awaking from some dream, I might find her sitting on the far side of the room, smiling, weeping... It is her! And it might very well have been her name that was the talisman.

But there is no name for music, there can never be, could never be, it is like when one is in the throes of passion with a woman one might even believe one loves - suddenly she is not singular, she is infinite, she is every woman that has ever walked the earth, nameless, divine - to speak a name at that moment would be blasphemous - the creature, who is all creatures, would melt away in an instant. So I cannot call to her, name her, this music, for she is all things, and I cannot call for another reason, equally mysterious and, perhaps, no less profound - for the "I" that calls, that has its own insipid appellation, which I so loathe, the one I unwillingly must call myself and am forced to respond to - it is no less absurd a thing, for this "I" that calls to her is no less infinite - if not infinite, then, at the very least, wildly unstable, fluctuating from day to day, nay, from hour to hour, from this person to that - the "I" that calls to "her" at a given moment exists only in that moment - and I do not, truth to tell, "call" her, I am just made aware she is near - I need not call her, I need just open the door, to listen, to let her speak, this nameless angel, or, rather, this angel with countless names, none of which could ever catch her for more than an hour - a melody that goes on for sometimes many minutes, dropping like a silver thread from the heavens - I just have to listen, to remember - it has come even in dreams, at times, though that is not usual.

Is it, is she always there? It seems to me these things have existed since the very beginning, they are in no sense novel, it's only we that have become novel, sufficiently open, wise, and able to hear them, to let them pass through us into the imbecilic, material world, where they lose something, sometimes a great deal, for those first moments in which she sings to us the song is perfect, it is shattering, it is a staring at the sun, one must look away immediately, or perhaps it is she that partially covers it - for our safety? So that we are not burnt to ashes? Flayed alive? Perhaps it is a fit of embarrassment on her part? At her nakedness? Whatever the reason, the moment we have grasped some bit of it, that she has handed off to us what seems permissible for her to give us, it is already somewhat soiled, less than - a thing of THIS world now, and no longer entirely of hers.

And yet, if the handoff has been sincere, and lasted long enough, and we have been open enough, the diamond she has placed in the palm of our hand, flawed though it is, blemished, pockmarked, is glowing still, radiant, warm - it is up to us now, it is now in our world, the world of shit, piss, snot, hunger, betrayals, illness, disappointment, and death. And there are those times when what one was sure was only a mildly blemished diamond, quite certain that it was and was destined to remain ever thus, reveals itself, when one returns to it, as but a lump of coal - one hardly feels angry at her, the gift was sincere, the rage is at one's self - and at the world, for its tenuous connection to the worlds that really matter, at its meagerness and its stupidity - it is the house of a mendacious, philistine scribbler, incapable of noticing when a Monet walks past his window carrying his easel.

My loneliness is stupefying - but for whom? For what? If she were to whisper in my ear this very moment, I would cease my idiotic scribbling immediately - nothing would matter other than her song, and my attempting to carry off as best a dictation as I could manage of that song - people would be and would remain nothing so long as her song continued - the hope being that I'd at least be allowed to transcribe bits and pieces of it sufficient to allow me to return to them later. It is, at such times, as if I am a creature that can nourish itself on air alone - a sort of atmospheric microbe, in a perpetual, drunken state of ecstasy, of orgasm - if it were to continue, I would happily starve to death in her arms, and be taken up in her winged embrace.

But no, she never stays, she never calls, she never sings for more than an hour or two and I am inevitably forced to partake of some vile earthly nourishment which then passes through my abominable body, and which I then hopefully later shit out for non-ethereal microbes to feast on. And so it goes. I live for her alone - I have no worldly love, no material being, certainly no woman - certainly no child I care to call my own, sister, wife... Well, that's not quite right, perhaps Cathy? But no, not even she... The corporeal world is a nightmare world, I wish only to be eventually free of it...

I hear the others, I hear them - the ones who proclaim life good, who say they like or love life. I cannot absolutely declare they are wrong, and yet I can most certainly declare that, to the last man, anyone who says such a thing is, upon inspection, a blockhead beneath one's contempt - but that is another matter.

My loves, who were they, really? Nothing then, and nothing now. And those scribblings on the music rack, my scribblings, especially those which were fresh after some particularly delirious visitation, what were they? And what are they now? If only I could chase her, stumble into her world, what then? Would it be as absurdly boring as Dante's paradise? Perhaps. Perhaps one can only taste of her wonders, be ravished by them, when one is incarcerated in a body of filth thrown into a world of pigs. When you are a pig in a world of pigs, you are content. When you are something of an eagle, an eagle whose wings routinely fail and which cause it to come crashing down, to slam against all the mud and filth of which this world of pigs is composed, but an eagle nonetheless, who occasionally is drunk on the sweetest perfume of rainbow-filled ethers, who has come undone, who has tossed his very self to the winds...

Oh dear, this is getting all so very Icarus, let's leave off with all this...

In the interim, back, as I am, in the mud-filled barn, where the stench of dung is so overwhelming - they are all pigs, they have always been pigs, they can never be other than pigs - yes, pigs can be intelligent, feel things, suffer, all of that - and to feel the affection of a pig, or to feel affection for a pig - neither is to be entirely scoffed at, and yet, snort as I may, and no matter how many lexicons of porcine language I consult, the impossibility of it all is soul-crushing - the desolation, the friendlessness, nay, the impossibility of friendship - the alienation, the endless melancholy, it is all so very awful and so very boring.

I must be going now - to where I do not know.

And when, on those rare and much wished-for occasions when she has dropped this blemished diamond in my lap, and I have cherished it, sculpted it, made it into a living being, which speaks to me, which speaks of me, there is not a single pig who has the faintest notion of what it is I have received from her - the ecstasy of its first moments, of its being born, of my guardianship, of its coming to maturity, none of that.

Oh they may find it lovely, or it may, perhaps, even evoke a smile or tear, and - good for them, I suppose. There is not the slightest solace or sweetness in any of that for me. For I don't give a damn for any of them - any compliment they might throw my way, or any kindness they might show me? Nothing but nonsense, fraud, mockery, simulation, lies, done for their benefit only, and existing only within them - created, performed, exchanged, or given only for themselves, only to soothe themselves, and to contribute one more lie to the infinite number of lies which constitutes the foundation upon which their house of cards rests.

I, too, live in a house of cards, but at least I know its contours, the basics of its architecture - and occasionally even give its walls a good huff and puff - to momentarily tweak my self-respect, or just for the hell of it. But they? Never.

Who was Cathy, for whom I grieved so poorly? For whom I went so numb for so many decades? Who now rips me to shreds and destroys me? Who was she? I. Only I. And as it is for them, so too for me.

It has only been when she has visited - Euterpe - such an absurd, almost disgusting name, but there's nothing for it. Of course I have played and practiced the music of others more routinely visited by her for tens of thousands of hours - it is a way of being close, though a terribly frustrating one - quite maddening, in fact. But it does provide a certain balm - it throws something of a chair down in this barn full of pigs, upon which I can sit and be bathed in a light which shines from above which none of the snorting pigs about me can see or hear - in fact, when seated upon this chair, I become, sometimes entirely, sometimes more or less so, oblivious of them. And that is nothing to be scoffed at!

I should, when all is said and done, be grateful, no? That I have these intermittent opportunities to busy myself with pleasures that provide me with something of a baffle, which deflect the sounds of all those snorting pigs? Their demands, their stench? If only for a few hours? I am, indeed - grateful.

And did I not keep you holy? You, who kept me alive, provided me the means, the nourishment to sustain myself, from almost the very beginning? Would I not, otherwise, have been dead at twelve, at ten, at eight, at six years old without you? And I have never betrayed you - yes, there have been times when I read through, or even practiced the most hideous nonsense, but that was when playing the music of others, and when I was a hostage to nonsensical propaganda - the cult of ugliness, which justified itself because it found itself in a world of ugliness, as if that has not been the situation since the first flute was sounded or first sharp stone etched a mammoth on a cave wall.

And you? When you whispered those gifts in my ear, those momentary flawless diamonds for which I grasped, which became, in my flawed hands, so very imperfect? Why did you share with me only lovely things? Sorrowful things, yes, even tragic things - but always beautiful things, the contents of which I did my very best to preserve and to honor. Why? Why murmur to me the secrets of where my best and noble selves lay? Where I could find them, and how I could aspire to, even become them? At least for those brief, miraculous periods of time?

I do not understand the sort of marriage we are in - for yes, it is surely that, and has been since the very beginning - one in which I have been betrayed very few times, and, when betrayed, not for long periods, although they left me in utter torment, distressed to the point of grinding my bones with the worry that the separation was to be permanent. But lo, back you would come! To me! Who has such ugliness within him. And who lets it burble up and sometimes explode from within himself like arsenic-laced steam, in page after page after page, as well as in words both spoken and written to others. But never to or about you! You I have never betrayed. And that has not been difficult. In fact it would be quite beyond me to ever have done so - it would not have occurred to me, it has never occurred to me - you are my radiant goddess, before whom I bow down - I am your happy, willing slave - you have kept me alive for well over half a century - you, and only you.

The others? What were they? Hallucinations, phantasms, harpies, beasts, mannequins bought at a dress-shop and outfitted, nay, cloaked, covered, made to disappear behind closet upon closet of wardrobes full of beautiful, yes, but utterly contaminated garments - contaminated by me, for they were me, are me, and one would think that even upon you, the deepest and only real love of my life, that I would throw these hideous costumes even upon you

- but never, never, never has that happened, never have I been tempted to do such a thing - you it has been that have made of this world a bearable thing - apart from you, I am nothing, nay, far from nothing, a vile thing - a poisonous cobra, a rage-filled Komodo dragon raging about in an antique shop - how silly, the world is no antique shop - it is a zoo full of other poisonous snakes, serpents, and scorpions far worse than me! They're everywhere! In the grass, the trees, the sky! Boring holes through the walls this very moment to encircle and suffocate me, to rip my throat to bloody shreds with their fangs - everywhere fangs! Everywhere stupidity, mean-spiritedness! I find that, and only that, absolutely everywhere and in everyone - other than in you.

Yes, the world can be beautiful, the natural world - is it a cabaret then? A peep show? Behind which one finds limbs of painted whores hung from meathooks, snarling? Offering themselves - here a face, here a cunt, here a pair of eyes? This nature, turn it over, like the old joke in which the apple is said to taste like a pussy - the innocent fruit lover tastes it, declares that it tastes like shit - and his host tells him to simply turn it over. But here, in this world, our world, apples taste only of shit. Turn the lovely log over - observe the holocaust beneath. Look carefully at the lawn, the pond - the carnage, the annihilation, it's everywhere! This universe, this gigantic monstrosity constantly feeding on itself, shoving its limbs down its own greedy gullet, only to shit them out again, only to have at it again, and again, and again.

I can no longer look upon the world, I see only its monstrosity. I want to smash the moon with my fists, yank the stars from the sky, murder the sun - destroy, massacre everything and everyone I see. Except for you, my beloved, my beloved muse. Who has, at times, left me - who has, apparently, although I am not sure, whispered hideous things into the minds and hearts of other writers of music, whose souls could not possibly be more hideous than my own, and who brought such filth, the filth which is themselves, so happily into the world - bidding the world look upon their bleeding viscera, upon all that was worst in them, and declare it good.

And I too do this happily, nay, eagerly, with great pleasure, at times - in words, insults, sarcasm, whatever is at hand - never violence, and for that I almost certainly can only thank timidity - and the mother who destroyed my will and initiative, and who made me able to engage in vengeance, when I deemed it was called for, only through such disgusting, trivial, and never truly satisfying means. Would that I had her before me now, and would that she hadn't made it impossible for me to so much as squash as a spider or cricket, whom I routinely ferry from the house with the deepest care and concern - would she have left me the will, the aptitude, the talent for slitting throats - so that I could slit hers! And slowly enough that I could relish every gurgle and scream the bitch would spit out as she crumbled to the floor. And then I might very well turn around to find you there, my beloved, my goddess.

How many of me are there then? This wannabe murderer, this timid, compassionate, idealistic worshipper of the divine, of you, of the eternal feminine I've glimpsed now and then in a woman - those hairy, smelly, ultimately hopelessly unsatisfying sacks of shit - and yet, I've looked within a few, or rather beyond, or perhaps so deeply within them that I have indeed observed the most wondrous, celestial things, of which they were utterly unaware, since these things were not visible to them.

Nor had I the slightest interest or compassion for them, only the wish that they open the window to the divine, which appears to me as if it lies within them, but which lives within me, and which they only somehow harbor and hint at from within themselves - which I could see, while they, of course, could not. And because it was within me, yet I had somehow placed it, imagined it, within them, it was as if I were now a sort of photographer or painter - sticking my thumb out to gauge the proportions of the canvas upon which I was to slop all these paints I'd been forced to carry with me since - since when? Perhaps for many lifetimes - yes, that would stand to reason - their awfulness would suggest they could not simply be the result of only this one, dogshit life, the one I know - yes, the result of many, many lifetimes. Of shit.

They could never bear it, these ladies - the pigments were too thick - ponderous and heavy beyond what any woman could possibly tolerate. I would attempt to drown them in these paints, and, needless to say, the smarter ones, the ones with the more immediate intuitions and instincts for survival, would flee, dripping in paint, of course, on occasion laughably so, but soon to be washed off by a man, or by many men, all far more healthy than I. More healthy and less interesting. They bearing barely one easel, I bearing thousands.

Are you listening, my beloved muse? Are you whispering into the ear of another? A writer of ugly music? Of stupid music? Perhaps of minimalist music, or film music? Perhaps into the ear of a middle-school girl with a guitar? Or into the ear of a composer whose music claims and superficially appears to be complex but is actually anything but? Is rather a stagnant pond filled with mud, in which the man, it is almost always a man, admires his reflected image - shit-brown, and utterly accurate?

I do not need you at this very moment - I am not pining for you. Why? Because the bile that is within me, that courses through my veins, is here, boiling - my brain is feverish with it - I am nothing but rage, disgust, the wish to destroy. It is not all of me but it is all of me at this moment - there is this vigor in me which disappears the moment you appear.

You show up, unannounced, unexpected, and I am suddenly that little boy, that little terrified boy, full of infinite sadness and wishing to die, in love with beauty, in love with anything that will take him out of himself, out of the hell in which he found himself and which lives in him still. You showed up then. Thank you, thank you, thank you! I can never repay you, of course, other than to honor you - to be true to the things you murmur to me, though I can never catch them in quite the way I wish - I do so try, try so very hard to be true to you - I would never, ever hurt you, betray you, make of what you are kind enough to give me something ugly.

Something trivial? Well then, that is often the case, because I myself am trivial. But when you whisper to me of pain, of heartache, of misery, of loss? I hear it and I know it - I can catch it, I can cradle it in my hands, feed it as best I can, allow it to live, however fragile and brief that life ends up - I do everything within my power to nourish it - I would and will die for it and for you, content and grateful.

And for, perhaps, that one young lady whom I consider my actual daughter (not that beast that dropped out of the crotch of, well, let's not continue on with that, it is too vile, and you are too beautiful) - yes, for her, as well. Although perhaps that's simply because I do not know her well enough - perhaps that is why I feel this agape love, this non-transactional, divine love - perhaps if I knew her better... Stop! I shall stop. She is an angel. Not like you, no - but nonetheless, an angel.

But I am no painter of women, no painter of anything. Perhaps I could capture them in music? Ridiculous. The melodies which are still whispered to me by my only true and constant love could not possibly have anything to do with these creatures, these trivial, narcissistic mannequins, these brick walls, these perpetual sources of the profoundest disappointment - for which I have only myself to blame, since it has only ever been my absurd idealizations and expectations of them with which I've been in love - every flesh and blood encounter with their realities, their bodies, their absurd demands and inconsequential "personalities" - each necessitating my own unwilling encounter with my own - these have created only suffering - for them, and for me.

I can, and have, many times, grafted some title or other on a melody, sometimes a good one, which, on its own, means nothing - melodies do not mean anything, they please one, leave another cold, and may very well sicken a third, as if they were almonds or oysters. They can underline words, yes, but might have just as well underlined others - there is only ever the general sense of, say, something sorrowful. But sorrow is a thing of infinite varieties and colors. There is most certainly a sense of ominous tragedy in the Prelude to the third act of Tristan, but my tragedies have very little to do with yours, and, heaven help us, nothing at all to do with Tristan's bloodcurdling, erotic shrieking, which is so soon to come.

Music is a sacred place. A place for vestal virgins, not women in whose crotch one sticks this or that, and who inevitably shatter one's heart. One does not enter a sanctuary and shit upon its altar. I say that only in reference to this sanctuary - I would be more than happy to worm my way late some evening into any number of churches, synagogues, and mosques, to shit upon their altars - that is a very different matter.

Clearly, I am a monster. It is horrendous, I want only to be other, to no longer be myself - I am choking on this strangeness - all this talk of music, women, synagogues - none of it matters, it is all a dream, from which I only wake to another, equally insipid and monstrous - the dream of myself, from whom I cannot escape, yet wish so profoundly to escape. Perhaps if I were to follow a thought then, to its conclusion... But they never have conclusions! How then to rid myself of my self - there is nothing for it.

I touch the piano, suddenly it seems as if I've coughed up something of a tune, it is not quite awful, there seems to be something in it - and yet, there's nothing in it, there cannot possibly be anything in it, for I created it, and there is absolutely nothing in me - this talk, this nonsense, that a muse has somehow whispered to me - it's just some mutinous, aberrant cabal of neurons spitting up in some cleft within a brain which is rotting as I type - my fingers ten thousand miles away, the fingers of a monster - freckled, veined, hideous, skipping away like little chipmunks constantly running under houses, running from predators, looking for food - my fingers are running, running, running... Mindlessly! Oh no! From death, she is here, in my room, she is upon me.

Perhaps there is another fantasy I can now entertain that will kill some number of minutes, take me out of myself, at least for a few moments - some story, although the stories the others tell are always so dull, so imbecilic - but are mine any better? Of course not! But they are mine. But I am the problem in the first place! It is not my story I want, no, absolutely not - I want to become another, no, that won't do either - I want simply to no longer be myself. I am unbearably boring - to wake up as myself, again, like some vampire condemned to walk the earth for all eternity, flesh withered, insides gutted, yet still somehow here - how is such a thing possible? And yet it is, for such am I.

My young friend - does she experience any of this? This lacerating strangeness that she must needs be no less subject to than I? How is it then, that people are not running into the streets - screaming, trying to pull down the clouds, or find a way to be borne up by and within them. Ah, well - there are those fools who are waiting for precisely that, but they are blockheads, who expect to simply remain themselves - sitting upon clouds, yes, yet attending the very same church services, eating the same processed food and television. Perhaps their new pastor is to be a sort of ethereal, doubtless Caucasian Jesus instead of the ordinary dolt to whom they'd grown accustomed, but nonetheless - they are recognizably themselves, and, seemingly, not the least bit incredulous or curious - not bothered by any of it, in fact.

What I want is something quite other - to be, as I am borne up, to be ripped apart, cell by cell, molecule by molecule, and for all those infinite bits of misery which constituted this excruciating consciousness to be tossed so far asunder that there be no chance of any future communication between them. One wonders how much agony an electron is forced to bear.

My dear, beloved young friend. I pray you know none of this, that you shall never feel any of this. For you I can perhaps pull down some melody from the heavens, one worthy of you - be permitted to do so. But only for you. When you asked me, "Do you want me not to go?", meaning, "Do you need me to stay, because I will, because I love you?" at least that is what I understood you to mean - I had never heard, and will, doubtless, never hear again anything so beautiful - nothing has caused me such endless, joyful tears every time I think of it - no one has ever said anything to me even remotely like that, so artless, so kind, wanting nothing in return - you are a thing, a creature, nay, an angel that I thought could never grow, could never arise on this earth.

Of course I said no, for I had already received the gift - the gift was your offer, I needed nothing more, and shall never need anything more, from anyone. I am disarmed, paralyzed every time I recall it. I love you. It tears at me, it rips my flesh, this love - any love, it is an awful thing, and yet it is the only reason to live, that would cause anyone to want to live. And yet I want to do neither, neither to love nor to live, only to rid myself of my self.

And those are the only two means of which I'm aware. Oh yes, Ms. Music - there is she, now and then, she whom I praised to the skies above, and whom I now think a vulgar whore, prattling the most insipid drivel into the ears of self-important idiots who call themselves artists - who inflict upon the world chatter more insufferable than the babbling of toddlers, the taunts of adolescents on playgrounds, lunatics, politicians. And the fools want, nay, expect others to actually listen to it. And they do! Because one fool likes nothing more than another, who reassures him his ignorance is a wonderful thing, and encourages him to revel in it.

If I could but sterilize the planet, hire thousands of brutes to shove quinacrine up every awful crack of every awful woman, chemically castrate every male before they hit puberty - it's not eugenics I want, for there is not a one worth saving. Do I mean that? Of course I don't, yet of course I do! Everything is fragile, the world is collapsing, folding in upon itself - I am sinking, splitting, though there's nothing in me left to collapse - a pair of eyes watching fingers type, fingers which don't belong to me - certainly I am no longer human, they are all bound to see at least that - it matters not, in fact it shall be a sort of triumph, this becoming a beast, this sack filled with shards of glass which somehow propels itself through time and space.

Oh yes, there are my legs, I'd quite forgotten about them - rather, not mine - legs, there are legs, simply legs - legs, fingers, objects, the sounds of words being spoken, these words, by a voice half-familiar to me, and yet there is no me - that voice, is it out there? Well, once it's spoken, of course it's out there - where else might it be? Voice, words, fingers, legs - they've naught to do with one another, not really, they've minds of their own. I am not telling the fingers to type this twaddle, it's an agenda little or nothing to do with me - like some pack of voracious white blood cells attacking viruses, fungi, parasites - whatever it is such things attack.

It is a satanic circus, this universe, and its ringleader is Yaldabaoth - the mad, sadistic demiurge of the Gnostics. We're privy to just bits of it, we are just bits of it - each bit going its own way, foxtrotting in its own unique agony towards oblivion.

Of course these thoughts, this sorrow, these agonies, this dissociation - are they not all enabled by privilege? Would disembodied fingers be typing, legs which do not belong to me be twitching, were I being starved to death and dodging bullets? They would not. But I am no less a shoddily assembled machine here and now than I would be there and then.

Oh, that swooning idiot who sits just behind my eyes, a bit above them - he who watches and oversees fingers, legs, bladders which need to pee, who is nothing other than need, sickening, infinite need, blind animal need - it is all so disgusting, so appalling. I am disgusting, you are disgusting, the world and universe are disgusting, we and they are all abominable, gruesome mistakes, and to recognize that at least gives one a bit of tangible nobility one can roll between one's thumb and index finger for a few moments before it dissolves in the air and you want nothing more than to take those very same fingers and rip out your eyes, run to the kitchen to grab that one, particular knife - surely it is long enough but to do... What? Ah, but that is the question!

There is no "nobler", my friend - everything we see, feel, dream, eat, shit is imaginary - we are imaginary beings imagining -

hopelessly desperate and condemned to die, hopelessly hungry and condemned to starve - miserable beyond what words can tell - numbingly habituated, palsied, gangrenous - already dead. To die now would be to engage in the most unforgivable of redundancies - there's nothing for it other than to lean into the stupidity - embrace the prison walls of one's body, let the streets resound with their tone-deaf tunes and ignorant chatter, watch the jays pull the worms from the ground...

For there is one more senseless, imbecilic day to be gotten through - with the hope that in those few moments just before sleep, if sleep comes, which it often chooses not to, in those treasured, weightless moments of freedom, when even what I once recognized as great music sounds again as if it might be so - when the world is a bit less strange, menacing, and awful - one lives for those moments, though they be only seconds long. I live for those moments, that moment, especially because they come just before sleep, which is a little death, which is, when we are honest with ourselves, what we all really most want. To die in one's sleep, and to be assured there shall be no more of this horror - that it shall end. With the last B major chord of Tristan, the most perfectly orchestrated chord in the history of music. You hear it now, don't you? It is dying, disappearing, could anything be more beaut...

XIV.

"The woman in the theater, in my dream - was she not chasing me?"

The woman in the theater, in my dream - was she not chasing me? Was she not chasing me as one chases a fruit which is just turning rotten, which smells so momentarily sweet just before the stench of putrefaction and death sets in? Through the aisles, with the wide eyes, the silvery hair, the fingers pressed up against the lips in wonderment and expectation? Yes, it was she, I recognized her.

It was quiet, the sound only of a thousand faceless spectators breathing as they too drifted off into sleep, hats and programs falling to the floor, their looks of terror swallowed up in the fast-approaching stupor, in their numb anticipation of death. It was strange, as I was strange, as she was strange. Had I invited her? Was it she who had responded? Why yes, of course! We shall go together, or so I had thought, but then she had disappeared, without explanation - and yet now chased me through this bleached white dream which pressed me so close to its bosom, with its promises I only half-remembered, but by which I was soothed nonetheless.

I knew this place - I know this place, I know everything, I have been here countless times, I have never been here, I was born here, and I shall surely die here, perhaps even this night, perhaps this very moment. I hear the faces in my heart - they are buried deep within me, where other pairs of ears strain to see my own viscera wedded to those of the crowd, to those of she who still chases me, who has always chased me, whom I want to catch me, and who cannot, who gets so constantly lost, weighed down as she is with the grief of former lives stretching back into an infinite past, in which she and I were once one, intertwining lilies in a primeval forest, before the need arose for this beast to kill and eat that beast or plant, when all of creation still dozed in a blissful, sunlit stupidity, which we had all assumed would be forever, before...

That I do not know, that is to say, how we lost all that, how we were severed from one another, how we were taken up, as if we were nothing other than dust and dirt, into the violently swirling clouds of a tornado whose perimeter was so vast that it seemed poised to swallow up the earth itself. And then, for what seemed, or surely was, eons, we were jostled, throttled, strangled, cradled, choked, coddled, spun around with such force that we could only watch as our guts spewed out from our chests onto what seemed the solid walls of that violently swirling maelstrom, to dance in titanic, gelatinous, constantly fluctuating surreal murals of madness, horror, ecstasy, and oblivion.

I held your hand, nay, I clutched it, you were all I had left, you were all I had ever had - were I to have lost you then... We needn't think on such things - it was not to be. Sleep came - the balm of sleep, which grew boring - and so we began to dream, the two of us, and suddenly our bodies wanted nothing more from us - we saw them, far below us, discarded like soiled underwear at the end of a hard day of hunting and gathering - and now, left finally alone with one another in a bed stuffed with roses whose smell made us drunk with the lust we had felt for each other for so long but about which neither of us had ever uttered a word, now we were free - you, my sister, and I - to do as we wished on this bedspread of lavender velvet strewn with images of amethyst kingdoms, upon which we fused for an hour, nay, a day, nay, forever - for you live in me now, as do I in you.

And as the players tune their instruments, I hear the impatience which is writ on their brows, for this is a concert for which they've rehearsed since their parents first looked upon one another with the longing which one day would pull them down from the ether to shove them through crotches onto stages constructed of wood that's been carved from the maples in forests in which we first found ourselves, ages ago, when we hid in our rooms from the termagant mother who raged through the halls with our belts in her hands, poised to beat us for milk spilled when we were just toddlers - but that was a dream, was it not?

In the dream that we're now in, that is to bathe us in the narcotic, velvet music that's sure to begin in a moment, stands the conductor - she's ravishing, dressed in a gown which appears to have wings, and holding a baton out of which erupt legions of butterflies which somehow reflect all of the tints in the hundreds of chandeliers, and now begin their ascent to the eaves, in which they'll be cloistered and warm and delivered from all that is painful.

I am here, do not stop, you can, you must see me - no, look this way, not that way! In that way lies naught but a darkness in which there's a risk you'll be swallowed, and we'll lose one another forever - you must fasten your gaze on what's before you - not these women with their pearls, these men in their tuxedos, but rather me, only me - for whom you've been searching since we were entangled in ponds filled with longing, the pools of our eyes filled with tears of reunion, for we'd finally discovered that in one another we could be rid of these bodies, these selves which were choking our spirits, which longed to escape and embrace one another to the point at which our fusion would make of us not even a memory, just a sly wink out of existence, never to be found or seen again in this world.

I am tired, there is now the oddest sensation just behind my weary eyes, which are closed, for I am dreaming, am I not? Of a, how to describe it - a sopping wet sponge, which fills me, which is me, there is naught else, other than this odd feeling in my chest of a heart not quite sure it wishes to keep beating, and does so only grudgingly.

I am in here now, you must look with better eyes, with other eyes. Not for that body which I was, only a moment before, but for the spirit that lies cradled within it, or is it hiding - perhaps it has escaped entirely.

Yes, over here - no, no, not that way - over here, towards the end of the aisle, not far from that obese woman, who so greatly resembles a massive turtle which has been dragged unwillingly from a local lake - dressed, bejeweled, and made to sit next to a man who assures her, repeatedly, that he is her husband, there is to be no confusion on that account, they have been married for over fifty years!

And now that the music's begun, surely it will only be easier to find me. For heaven's sake, it is the prelude to the third act of Tristan - could anything be more appropriate? You are to find me then, surely - I shall likely engage in a few rounds of erotic shrieking and collapse in a heap, but nonetheless, you shall find me.

Is this not the music that was playing when first we met? In that house, that haunted house, patrolled by that sadistic fiend from whom I shielded you on countless occasions? Yes, we are alive, we live on, whether this be dream or no - we are here, there is this music. And we love one another. We have always loved one another. It's never been easy, or comfortable. That is not what love is, or life is. We are in constant danger. From the world, and from one another.

You must hurry - that idiotic shepherd's song may well begin soon - you must find me, sling me over your shoulders and carry me off, out of the theater and into the night, under a blood-red moon, which will surely be kinder, far kinder than this godforsaken music which has made of us drunkards, for decades, which robbed us blind as it fed us the most intoxicating delicacies, stuffed our mouths with sickeningly sweet confections, poured two-hundred year-old red wines down our throats, made of us fat, bloated decadent creatures who've grown wise enough now to run out the doors of this ambush to which we've been lured - you need only to awaken, and then to awaken me, you will see, we will live on forever - you and I, without her - she's been gone all these years, there is nothing to worry about any longer - it is simply that we must wake up and see and know one another as if for the first time, as we were, before we were drowned in those nets of imagination and longing which we threw upon one another.

We'll be free of them, you shall see, it shall all be burned off, all that madness - we will see one another for the first time, in the light of a day whose sun we'd been busy blotting out with our selfish machinations, the wish to make of one another things only -

things which soothed us, which bothered us when they dared to inhabit roles of their own choosing, which we had not previously allotted them, in which we had not cast them. None of that. That's all over. We are free now.

We can hold it in our hands. I have it in mine. You can see it, yes? Glowing? Warm and glowing? Here, it is not for me alone, drinking from it as I am - we haven't long, you must drink now, we must drink of it together - you first.

Yes, there is blood in it. It glows with blood, like the grail! It is our blood. I have pulled it up from deep within the bowels of the earth for us to drink with one another, as we gaze into each other's eyes. It will fill us, surely, for we are empty without it, without each other. Drink.

The world outside you, which you had considered real, will disappear - you will find it now within yourself, which is where it only ever has been. Drink. You shall no longer be you, nor I myself. That is what I'm offering you - it's what both of us have wanted since we first looked about, recognized ourselves, and understood that we had been trapped in these bodies, in these rooms, in this world.

I am offering you a way out, you must take it - you must come with me. You cannot retreat in terror now, it's far too late for that. Drink! Do you feel the screams we've been bottling up inside ourselves these many years? Drink of this blood! It will unleash them, you will be free - to hate, and then let go of hate. That is freedom, and that is what I'm offering you.

No, I no longer hear it either. No more f minor, now there are only the last few pages of Parsifal - flutes, Ab major, we have been taken up, we ascend with the dove to the dome of the temple. Drink! You must drink!

There is no why. Why is for fools - fools and young, ignorant persons. There is only how. I don't know what I'm promising - stop asking me. Rebirth, redemption - that's all nonsense. I know only that I am offering you freedom, and the possibility, nay, the certainty, that we shall never lose one another again, that we shall be safe, made whole, free.

Everything shall be as if for the first time - unsoiled, you, I, that which shall be after we are mingled and dispersed like rain over the earth, after we are together wholly, everywhere and nowhere. And in so being, nothing can return from what once so harmed us - it is like unto that last Ab major chord of Parsifal, trailing off into silence, into eternity...

There are no dangers, no villains to be found there, in eternity. What we both thought real, and because of its being real, feared could harm us - that was all nothing, only a fever dream. We shared it, yes, but that hardly makes it real.

The shared hallucination of siblings, of lovers, of friends, real friends - not the sham kind, the voyeurs, the vampires, the ones who want only that you help them to feel this or that, and who then discard you.

Perhaps there has only ever been you and I, and that room, in which I was so sure you had died, when I found you beside the bed - pale-blue, ice-cold - none of that was real either - we need only embrace now, close our eyes, and dream it away, as if it never happened, and was a bad dream only, a trivial nightmare, the result of an ill-prepared meal - surely, you are here now, you were chasing me, you have found me - you are to drink now, we are to drink now.

It is over, this nightmare. Dear God, God in heaven, if indeed you are God and if indeed that is your abode, bless this love! Do not again throw us into a pit of serpents, who rip us apart from one another, drag us deep beneath pitch-black, stormy seas to the ocean's floor, there to feast upon our bowels, to cackle and spit and fornicate all round us, to celebrate the separation you had incomprehensibly forced upon us.

Let our love part these black seas, and throw us upon the beach of a tropic isle upon which we shall live the rest of our days - happy, or as happy as mortals can be - safe, warm, bathed in light, eating the sweetest of tropical fruits.

Oh, and do not forget the library - we must have one! A monumental one! And, above and beyond any or all of that, you must allow us, nay, you must insure that we die at the very same moment - be it now, or decades hence.

So foolish, to address a being who neither exists nor has ears to hear. We shall die together, my love - of that we both can rest assured. No more screams, cups of blood, ill-tuned orchestras, fiends, harpies, deaths, or what we foolishly took to be deaths, no more. Only you. And I. And now. And what may or may not come. But let us not speak of any of that.

XV.

"And so the following morning I played
the C minor fugue..."

And so the following morning I played the C minor fugue from the second book with such sacred stillness, with such hyper-expressive, Wagnerian overlap and connections between every semiquaver that it was only with the greatest strain that I could follow the augmentations of the subject, when they came. Perhaps beings with far greater lifespans than I might comprehend them in the blink of an eye - perhaps an ancient redwood might sweep them up, in the momentary sway of one of its branches, examine them briefly, conclude that they're nothing but trivial artifacts of an ignoble and dismissible species, and let them float, deflated and soundless, along with several of its now dead leaves, to the forest floor.

I imagined that were I to continue to retard the tempo of this fugue, perhaps to the point of its taking many hours to perform, I would stumble upon some entry key, some mantra, some secret incantation that might facilitate my tunneling out from within this idiot world and prison in which I find myself - this body, this air, this tongue, these fingers, this cock which pees so frequently and through which, at this late date, I force my weary, indifferent, more or less non-existent libido to ejaculate a few bits of semen - this beard which so needs trimming, bits of which I can observe when I look down - all of it, no matter where I gaze - the hateful, idiot world.

And so, clearly, vision will not get me there. Perhaps then this fugue, played so slowly that I will chance upon that universe-in-a-grain-of-sand business about which psychotic poets and sham gurus are so fond of babbling on. And then what? What reason would there be to assume that this new universe, promised by all these either deranged, armpit-sniffing poets or, as is more usual, these megalomaniacal, pontificating hucksters, would not be every bit as awful as the one in which I presently find myself? Or worse, even far worse?

And yet, a man jailed in an underground dungeon he knows not where, when and if he chances upon some implement with which he can, over a period of weeks, or months, dig a trench which beckons to him with the promise of a freedom he so intensely imagines, will scoop handfuls of dirt, rock, filth, and worms with hands and arms growing progressively more bloody and disfigured until he catches sight of a ray of sunlight. His heart will then begin to beat madly, he'll pull apart great masses of vines, bristling with thorns - all the while knowing he is on the verge of, if not a better life, at the very least a very different life. And, lo and behold - what he instead finds is only that he stands in another, almost identical dungeon, that the light he took for that of the sun was only a spotlight roaming the premises of this panopticon from its highest barricade - that indeed, this universe, born of a grain of sand, into which he has entered, is every bit as horrendous as the one from which he has escaped, and that the oversized wooden spoon with which he has so arduously made his way through that hellish tunnel had been intentionally left in his cell, to procure this very result.

There is nowhere to go to. "Dr. Waldbauer, I am going CRAZY from all this!", she said, long ago. Was her name Barbara? Barbara Link? The missing link? Yes, yes, it was she - in that musicology class, which he taught. To which the good Doctor responded, in that Bela-Lugosi-as-Dracula voice of his, "But honey! There is nowhere to go!"

And so it is with me - in this room, at this piano, in the space between these notes, in the mad fantasy of happening upon some manner of burrowing out of this hell. Would death suffice? It's a clumsy experiment - it may very well be just another wooden spoon, another slug-filled tunnel to a worse hell. Then what? Ah, lose myself in art! Be creative! That's the ticket! Said the dung beetle to himself. The ten-fingered dung beetle who has spent his life practicing, studying, and attempting to compose music in a language no longer understood - the ten-fingered dung beetle who has devoted himself to the study of ancient Sumerian cuneiform in a decades-long, dogged attempt to soothe itself, trapped as it was in a venomous lair overseen by oversized scorpions, who, when the dung beetle was but a boy, used to disguise themselves as dung beetles in his presence, but who would, having shut the door to the dung beetle's bedroom, rip off their masks and costumes, to then begin a mad dance, in which the one would flail his bulbous venom gland and stinger every which way, finally inserting it into the other, as fierce shrieks of laughter shook their plated bodies, their eyes mad with lust, their brains bloated and throbbing with thoughts of the violence they were soon to inflict.

Silly to dwell upon such memories, to choke on these arsenic-laced Madeleines. There is a moistness within me, which begs for my attention. Which promises me, at the very least, a few safe moments - bathed in deepest sleep, or some generous, overwhelming daydream which ravishes me, that is until I become aware of it, aware of my being ravished - the moment the little homunculus behind my eyes puts on its spectacles to observe the spectacle taking place outside itself - at such moments it, that shelter, that refuge, vanishes in an instant, like a deliriously gorgeous whore giving one a heavenly blowjob on a dark pier on a moonlit night, who suddenly spots a constable turning the corner.

Homunculus, daydreamer, deep sleeper, dung beetle whose cock is being expertly sucked by a no longer young, red-headed vixen, whose face, thankfully, is not particularly well-lit - collector of wooden spoons, player of slow fugues, a stranger in long days' journeys into nights of melancholic pity parties, containing multitudes of pointless things which cannot and do not wish to communicate with one another, during which its bowels are so frequently in an uproar - there's nothing for it.

The hour of the wolves, the hours in which we scour what is ours and find it sour, and, overpowered, we dissolve into pools of mist, leaving the bedsheets damp - which will never be noticed, for no one ever has or ever does or ever will come into our room.

I am hungry, but for what? There is nothing that can fill the belly of the beast which lurks within me, which has gorged itself forever on these shards of glass to which it looks for love, to be accepted, to be known. And, when it learns that it's been cheated, and now stands betrayed, left to die in pools of its own blood, it looks then to a heaven it cannot see. Well of course it cannot see it! It's imprisoned in a belly, whose mucous walls are full of polyps which have faces bathed in hydrochloric acid - all it sees is a gullet, a disgusting sort of tunnel which it cannot ever hope to climb through - so it flops down in exhaustion on the floor, or is it the ceiling of the intestine? Through which it's fated soon to pass into a colon which will greet it with alarm or more likely giggles, snorts, and chuckles, which rise to horrid cackles as it chokes the beast in gases drenched in methane, where it will fester in an existential dread for weeks on end.

Such is the fate of bad metaphors. They ask for our acceptance - for our friendship, even for our love. We grant it to them for a moment, since we feel it reflects well on us somehow. For we are starving - not for food, but for some reason not to devolve into the madness which we bear within us, which we beg to keep its silence, whose outlines we become aware of so many times throughout the day.

And so, with heavy-lidded eyes, we sway our heads and hope for sleep to overtake us, and that this time it might be a kind sleep, bearing dreams which make us smile or, for a moment, believe in love - that there might be a sort of woman who is nameless, who is lovely and not awful, and who looks on us with tenderness, assuring us that this has all been somehow worth it, that she'll never, ever leave us, that she's sorry that it's taken her so long to finally find us, but that she has finally found us, and that we're now safe, and need only touch our lips and fuse our bodies and our souls in some exotic masque in which indeed the masks have been removed once and for all...

For it's my sister, from my childhood! Nay, my wife! My one and only wife! The one that mattered! Now arisen from the ashes to envelop me within her so that together we can fly from this veil of tears in a cloud of sweet forgetting and remembrance, in which we'll blend with one another into a thing that's made of light and which is perfect, which we'd deserved, and which was ripped from us so cruelly by this world through which I so much wish to tunnel to another which is better by the playing of slow fugues, by the mapping of the moon, by the letting go of every foolish hope I'd ever had, now that I have no more need of them. She's come and will not leave again, I'm in that timeless place, the one from which I cannot possibly be ripped. I've been here before, in fact many times before. "But this time's different!" So says a self that lives within me to another within earshot who may pass the news along then to a third.

Be still! I am inventing all of this, of course, in a corner of myself which is familiar to me and to which I latch on and about which I hallucinate, because I cannot fathom any other way to drag my weary body through another day of suffering without chasing after beauty which might soothe me if I'm lucky for a moment.

I want freedom. Yes, of course I do! But more than that, I want you only, to be drowned in you - and to forget all that which presently defiles me, and to remember you so clearly that your every pore and hair and mucous membrane is a painting by some great master of the Renaissance into which I can now enter and be lost, that is to say, I shall finally be at peace, and rid of everything - of all my past, but above all, all my selves, including this one - who is writing, writing, writing, always writing - but who now gives himself permission to leave off and beg for visits from a daydream, from a melody - or, most of all, a word or glance from you.

XVI.

"Dear God, it hurts, and yet..."

Dear God, it hurts, and yet...

Wire me up like Malcolm McDowell at the end of Clockwork Orange! Glue my eyelids tightly shut so that I cannot close them! And play the film for me! Not of my crimes, or not of mine only, but of theirs, play it over and over, not because I wish to be subjected to any sort of "exposure therapy," in which I am to be made somehow desensitized to it, rather in the hope that I should be made to bleed from every pore, that my heart should run up my esophagus and dive outwards into the room, to then run madly about like a mouse stalked by a rabid cat, like a fawn hounded by a pride of lions - like me, haunted, as I am, by myself.

Look at it, that blood-red, pulsating fist, wearing a top hat, seeming to dance, as if in a vaudeville routine, or perhaps a cable television commercial for a box of chocolates. No close-ups, pray tell! For a close-up would reveal the expression, which would immediately turn to ash anyone who saw it clearly - well then, that is the point, is it not?

I feel for my pulse - there is none, or, rather, there most certainly is one, but presently its bearer is to be seen scurrying about on the ceiling, ping-ponging from wall to wall, madly trying to put an end to itself and failing, failing, failing.

I ask the lab technician if she is entertained - she seemed kind enough earlier, perhaps good for a chat. But she is no longer there - in her place is what looks like a Komodo dragon in that very same nurse's outfit, large-bosomed, and, hey, not at all bad-looking, actually - scribbling away on a clipboard, paying me little or no attention.

I ask her if my heart, which had just hopped on her lap, only to rapidly scurry off a moment later, was disturbing her concentration. She scribbled for several minutes, looked up at me, smiled, and returned to her scribbling.

My heart had meanwhile dropped down from the ceiling, climbed up onto my chest and was staring intently into my eyes, sobbing, trying desperately to speak, which proved quite impossible. All that emerged from it were guttural grunts and squawks, for, as now became unpleasantly apparent, where there ought have been a tongue, there was but a bloody stump.

Had it swallowed its tongue? Had this nurse...? Had this been its condition since its birth? Since my birth?

We looked at one another in mutual incomprehension, its face etched with the deepest melancholy - mine, I would imagine, displaying whatever signs of curiosity of which I was then capable, in the face of the fairly severe optical discomfort I was presently experiencing.

It adopted the most heartrending, beseeching, desperately imploring expression, frequently nodding its topmost part, which I supposed was serving as the metaphorical equivalent of its head - less than metaphorical, actually, since its face, and the expressions on that face, could not have been any clearer.

I opened my mouth. The thing could not possibly fit, could not possibly make its way down my esophagus to burrow its way into whichever appropriate spot within me that was likely eagerly awaiting its return.

And yet, as much as I had wished for exactly this, to be heartless, and this was now quite literal, there was some other self, or perhaps a half-dozen of them, maybe more, that wished no such thing - all of whom caused me to open my mouth, lick my lips, and adopt, as best I could, the seductive expression of that quite appealing college-age gal, that stripper, in that vile midtown club, who had, once upon a time, attempted to entice me into a lap dance, and, doubtless, into giving her large sums of cash.

I recalled that look - my eyes, tongue, mouth dutifully reproduced it - I opened my mouth, and quite immediately my heart catapulted itself into and through it.

I had the overwhelming sensation of choking, of being unable to breathe, of beginning to assume that, indeed, this was to be my time - that this was to be my more than a little strange death - in this very room, with my eyes glued open - with this nurse, on this table.

Everything went dark.

I awoke, blood gushing from my mouth, eyes still forcefully glued to the endless loop of childhood horrors which had been playing on endless repeat those many hours, and felt for my pulse. There it was, at somewhat less than fifty beats a minute.

I would have dismissed it all as nothing other than a more than a little peculiar nightmare, if everything else had not remained in its place.

The nurse spoke - her words were garbled, yes - she was, as I have said, a Komodo dragon, or something very much like one. I, being less than expert in such matters, assumed that it was not every day that Komodo dragons walked upright, dressed in nurses' garb, scribbled on clipboards, and, not least, had what seemed endlessly enticing, utterly delicious-looking, humongous tits.

"Your wife is in the adjacent room," she croaked. "But I've already mentioned that."

Had she? What on earth was she talking about? I was only this moment learning that she could speak!

And so she continued - "...and that we had attempted, the doctors and we emergency room nurses, to implant a pacemaker to get her heart started once again, but that, after a bit, we had informed you that she had passed away. And you must also recall that it was at that moment that we had the security guards fasten you to the table upon which you now find yourself, glue your eyes open, and begin the film, the film that you so specifically requested."

This was insane! Cathy was not dead! She was sleeping at home! I had merely gone into the living room to listen to Act 3 of Parsifal, that particularly stupendous Knappertsbusch live recording with Thomas and Dalis.

"What I did not tell you at that time was that, although she was indeed dead, in this world, in the world of the film you are presently watching, or, rather, being forced to watch, the one in which your heart was romping about not all that long ago, she is in another, fully awake - confused, frightened, and, above all, desperately longing for you.

Are you willing, and do you think yourself able to go to her? This would not be a simple matter. And not some Eurydice scenario, in which you would have some chance of bringing her from where she presently is to this world. This would involve you leaving everything you have ever known, other than her, behind - with no goodbyes, no chance of returning - it would be quite irrevocable. Do you understand?"

I told her I absolutely did not understand - that I hadn't the slightest idea where this world in which she now found herself was - what it was like, and what our life together might consist of, were I to go to her.

"You don't get to have a single one of those questions answered. That's not the way this works, and, honestly, I find it more than a little amusing that you, of all people, would ask such a moronic question, given that you know full well what the answer is, that answer being: if you indeed desire the truth, the truth of her, of your life, and of the love you shared, you will accept the consequences, whatever they might be. Our time is running out - I have another patient, and I must engage the technician who will be involved in your case, obtain the appropriate film, and on and on. I need your answer. Now!"

I answered yes, of course. "Yes!"

The ninth circle of hell! To be submerged there in boiling oil as a limbless torso would be preferable to anything that this world, this shithole, could ever offer me, given that it was now devoid of her.

My chest thumped wildly. I thought I heard words - no, not words - proto-words - tongueless, barely formed, gibberish words, gurgling up from within me. Words whose tone of voice was still sufficient to convey their assent, and their longing, which were my own.

The bottom of the room suddenly opened.

Blackness within, without - everywhere.

Had it been a lie, a ruse, another betrayal? The final betrayal? A surreal treachery perpetrated by I had no idea how many onlookers and conspirators, who surrounded this former annihilation chamber, now-become abyss?

I only know that I heard laughter, the laughter of what sounded like overfed aristocrats at a ball, toasting one another - perhaps it was some sort of ancient Roman gathering - perhaps it contained a horde of Caligulas and Neros, fucking their siblings while dousing themselves with wine - my dissolution and devastation being merely one of the many merriments with which they were all pleasantly entertaining themselves.

It came from far above me, this laughter - from ever further above me, growing ever fainter, echoing at greater and greater intervals.

The thumping within me? Which I felt was about to cause me to burst apart like a cheap firecracker? That had ceased.

There was only darkness, my breathing, and my heart, beating ever more slowly and feebly - so resigned were the two of us, that is to say, my heart and my self, that we both laughed.

At least I did.

And the gurgle and sputtering I heard from deep within me gave me the sense that he, too, that is to say, my heart - I shall call him "he" now - that he too found, in at least being granted a death not, at least yet, excessively painful, a source of amusement, an amusement half-familiar, yet new - still funny, more than a little clever, and not a bad way to go after all.

Or so I thought to myself, and assumed that he did, as well.

As for the others I carried within me? For them I could not and cannot speak. If this goes on for any time at all, they will, doubtless, speak for themselves.

The nurse had not dropped her clipboard and pen, not to mention that it was pitch black - and so I had neither the means nor the perceptual ability to precisely record their reactions, were they to have had any which I might have otherwise have seen, as written words, at any rate - and yet I vowed to I have no idea whom that I should take great care to commit their reactions to my memory, if, indeed, I were able to finally hear any of them.

I am nothing if not responsible - capable of the most atrocious verbal ugliness and abuse, yet nevertheless, fundamentally a good egg.

XVII.

"They are not real, all these others."

They are not real, all these others. They had never been real - I had simply not looked at them carefully enough, with sufficient intensity. They are like words one fastens upon and repeats endlessly, which degenerate into meaningless sounds which fall to the ground like leaves in autumn - colorful and momentarily entrancing, but which one then simply walks past, steps over, because they are boring, and I am on the way to - where? Where was it exactly I was on the way to? Surely nowhere any less absurd, no less a lie, no less a dream - a dream which, like those leaves, distracts me for its duration, sometimes not even that long.

I finally wake, fed up with myself - is this the best I can do? Cough up this nonsense? In deepest night, in silence? And that's it? I so often told myself that I was something of a genius in my dreams - and yet?

The majority of the dreams I produce are those of an idiot, those of a teenaged boy - of engines overheating, of exams not studied for or missed, of courses I had been thought to have attended and in which there was some final examination, and all of it quite unknown to me, that sort of thing - the dreams of a perfect moron, one without the slightest right to draw breath, to walk the planet - to speak, to shit, or to be given the opportunity to dream again, if that is, indeed, the majority of what I can manage.

The dreams of a dung beetle - dearie me! Where on earth is my ball of poop? Mother shall be ever so angry with me! And she may very well stab me with her pincers, sever this or that leg! Yes,

I've six, but no matter, one wants to keep all six, this does not become acceptable simply because I have six, no matter Mother's anger!

And so the dung beetle rolls over and finds that it is possibly human - there's no assurance of that, of course - and yet there seem now to be two legs - a warm, milky feeling pervades me and enervates my limbs! It is sweet - it is blueberry sweet. It is more than sweet - it is a pleasure mixed with just enough apprehension to make it more or less exactly as uncomfortable as it is sweet.

I am on a tightrope, and do not wish to fall - it is an acceptable mix, far better than that of waking life, no question of that, for that is awful, the world is awful, walking through it is a perpetual nightmare - the trees are eating one another, constantly lashing out at and brutalizing one another - as both I, and the birds, flit from one to the next, carrying their messages of promised vengeance out to the hundredth generation.

And yes, they do indeed have ways, these trees, of following every last acorn, seedling, it matters not, to the hundredth generation! The birds' concerns are much more to do with me. It's me they're gunning for, these, these mostly crows - the Canadian geese are too stupid to constitute a tenth the threat posed by these crows - they're talking now - in the trees, the ones I see, and the ones I don't.

They are everywhere - they are inside me, they will gnaw their way out of me through every last pore - flee the forest, hop a train, a spaceship, for that matter. I can't escape, even in dream, especially in dream! That's where they nest, inside my mind, inside my soul.

I shall devour myself, it's been decreed. And so I begin with my left hand - is it not delicious? Is that a feather I'm now grasping? A black feather? How did it get there, I wonder? It was not there a moment ago, when I rolled over, onto the side on which I hardly ever sleep, but upon which I'm now aware that there is someone in the room. Or some thing - I am not certain, it's very dark. I'd rather focus on my milky limbs, which are floating - I am floating - why not lean in? There's no harm in it, certainly.

Yet it's quite clear I'm being watched, and the agenda of this watcher is not something to which I am privy - there's been no sound, there's been no movement which might give away the ghost who sits beside me.

But no! Behind me! At the foot of this great bed, which is too big for me alone - that's why I have my dog beside me, whose feet I've wiped, as if that made this whole scenario any less repellent, less ridiculous. But I, too, am ridiculous! Perhaps that's what this being has come to tell me - the one at the foot of this king-sized bed in which there writhes a pauper and his mutt who's somewhat sweet but less than special, not like the one I had before, or the wife I had before, who has been gone for seeming eons through vast spaces - perhaps it is she, who is now sitting at the foot of this huge bed?

No, not tonight. I know quite well that this is not the sort of evening on which she'd come to pay a visit - with her whispers, never clear enough to make out just what she's saying, only that she's so terribly lonely.

The melody of her words is always unmistakably sad - as if it were played on a cello, though she was an alto, or is an alto - for she's eternal!

Like the being who now appears as if he's fidgeting, perhaps rustling something - are they papers? Is it indeed a he? How can I know? I cannot see him, I only hear him - but not even that, I simply feel him.

I cannot open my eyes, I am bound in sleep, tangled up in milky limbs - or are they branches of the trees in which the crows sit? Who are now discussing the many ways in which they will get even for all the crimes for which they blame me, and yet who take great care not to inform me of their nature - only that they'll never cease to torment me until their wrath is satisfied.

I don't begrudge them - they've got a point! I feel the same - for all these creatures I'd mistakenly thought were real, only to discover I'd wasted all, or almost all, of the years and days and hours that had been given me, on a loan, which now it seems they all are claiming is in default - and that the agreement is now over, that the collector's on his way, and that I'm to count my blessings, which they say belong to them - I suppose that's possible, even though they are not real.

I'll play along - I know enough now, having lived this long, that it's a farce - we're all just lizards, shedding skins, lost in thoughts about ourselves which count for nothing, amount to nothing, are composed of nothing but soothing fables that we repeat on autopilot to ourselves, because we're zombies.

Yes, we too are zombies! We've always known that they were, that's long been obvious - but that we are, as well? It's only lately that we've come to that conclusion.

And now we seem to be required, to have the duty, the obligation to slog through all that's left of life until the end, which is not much, at least in my case, that much is true - without relying on another or believing in another, for there are not others on whom we can rely or in whom one can believe!

There is only us, you and I, who've been forced to live as zombies. We - who are every bit as unreal as these delightful, viscous feelings in my legs - are they in your legs as well? Are they not delightful? Will you keep sleeping, as I intend to? Am I insane? Most people say so, but that's no matter, they're not real either.

And if they were, I'd just dismiss them with a wave of my left hand in which this feather now is sitting. How it got there I don't know! Perhaps the window was left open - perhaps a raven sat upon this regal bed of mine. I have no bust beside me of the goddess Athena, and yet he must have certainly been here! For there's this feather, and the window is quite open, and it has rained - no, it has poured! And it was violent, that's for sure - there had been lightning, utter chaos... But now there's only grief, and nothing else. There are no creatures by my bedside, there are no bedclothes - there is nothing.

This thing that's thinking? That's proof of nothing Descartes was wrong. I don't exist. I've never lived, and yet can die. There's only death, naught else is real.

Please take me now, in deepest sleep - while my limbs feel somewhat warm, before the frost and then the ice and then the glacier, my final tomb...

Will that be it? But that's so silly! There are no glaciers where I'll be going - I'll just be dying, and that's forever. It will not stop, shall never cease - it needs no cause, it is the nature of the world - this constant danger, the sound of prehistoric jaws masticating, of desperation and exhaustion, of the endless, poisonous habit of being me and not some other, on the lookout for an exit, maybe this way, maybe that, perhaps a swig of Southern Comfort, or a bit of masturbation - like this writing now, which scans the whole horizon, on the lookout for an exit where despair is on vacation, and the passions are not ugly, at least not mostly, and the birds are not these nasty, beastly black things, but are rather sweet, and colorful, and kind - though they may be harboring dark schemes, for there's not a one that wasn't predator or prey during the Triassic? - or Cretaceous? - or that other, which I've forgotten, it doesn't matter - I will pretend the ones who look to me as if they might be kind because they're lovely, that that's enough - it's always enough! To generate a somewhat pleasant dream in which the woman is no monster - rather an angel, poised to give me what I'd always thought not possible, non-existent - the reassurance that I was not a piece of garbage to be thrown upon a bed under a roof in which a harpy roamed the halls -an ugly woman, more man than woman, more beast than man - a thing I knew spelled only danger, and yet I listened to her lies and let her infamies wind round my neck and pull me deep beneath a cesspool onto the bed on which I find myself right now, on which I'll die - that much is certain - I'm only spinning now - it's rather pointless, of which I'm more than well aware. It's entertaining, on a good day, on a good night, though those are few - but these dreams! I can't control them, they're in the basement of the house, they're in the basement of my self - they arise without being bidden, they are climbing up the stairs - they are here, am I to greet them? That seems so silly - they're paid assassins! They want no greeting - they assure me they'd still do this out of love, were they not paid - that they'd just as gladly slit my throat and throw my entrails down to hell. Hey, it's a living! Nothing to scoff at - I'd do it too! Had life been different, had I not been raised by vampires, had I the willpower, had I the mettle and the spine that other children seemed to possess. I had desires, I have them still, and yet volition? Of that I've none. It is still sitting in the bowels of my first crib, biting its nails, crouching in terror - in that crib, which has long been torn to shreds of wood in mouths of maggots who pay no mind to frightened children, to their long-forgotten stories - I've not forgotten, they're in my belly now.

And speaking of bellies! There is a dog now right beside me, whose belly craves attention, so there is something I can do, some small excuse to go on living - and as I listen to her breathing, her gentle snoring brings my attention to the window, and the wind, and to the thought of moonlight, which is so stupid - with naught to say, paler than death, and such a constant disappointment. She has been shining, no, reflecting, upon eons of earth's suffering, without a hint of her awareness, much less compassion - only boredom, only cemeteries.

I could scream, it might well soothe me, but she'd not hear it. Tears count for nothing, thoughts for less, prayers for nothing at all. There are, after all, no ears to hear, no words to be heard, no others, no you, no selves of any kind.

There is death, and there is silence, and all that noise, all those flurries of activity, all those wails of agony, everything I ever thought important, felt as painful, every notion I had ever had of a "being" that could possibly think these thoughts, and feel these pains?

Merely the rising and falling of black waves in an infinite ocean of silence, and of death, which look, for a moment, at themselves, at one another, call and think themselves "waves", and then are nothing again.

Well then, not quite nothing, given that they are now free, at last.

I have been to no mountains, much less mountaintops - and there's no God to thank or curse for it, but nonetheless, perhaps I ought consider doing so.

XVIII.

"Is there anything in me which is real?"

Is there anything in me which is real? Was there ever? I
don't recognize the self I was an hour ago - in the park, on that trail,
alternately entranced and impatient, looking forwards with
anticipation and dread, looking backwards with regret and sadness.
There is none of that at this moment, or very little at any rate.
What is there, then, that remains?

I recall being that fellow as I recall a character in a novel, for
whom I felt not much empathy, who merely served, or so it seemed
to me, to carry the not particularly compelling plot along, who had
been pasted into the narrative only as an afterthought - a cardboard
cutout, a more or less philosophical zombie, mouthing words I
knew full well had just randomly dribbled onto the page - perhaps
their author had just had a meal, was racing against a deadline, was
considering how in God's name he might push the action of this
deeply inconsequential story along... Oh, I know! I'll invent X!
There you go! He'll serve me for eight or ten pages, at which point
I'll discard him - from my memory, from the memory of any reader
foolish and small-minded enough to have paid him any mind up
until that point, and from the memories of the other characters - a
being so inconsequential his behavior should rightly have been
written with invisible ink.

I am that vague - even now, at this very moment, I'm
nothing more than an odd desire - a whim, a flurry of anger, of
longing - the sense that there is something of a speck in my eye, and
the worry that it might need tending - my annoyance at the dog,

who is now barking at a closed door, wishing to be let in, because she prefers the bed upstairs to the downstairs couch - all of this, not a one of which has the least bit to do with the other - a flurry of thoughts and sensations and feelings of the most trivial miscellany, a hodgepodge of nonsense - one of the universe's most inconsequential drawers of junk, nearly all of it unspoken and beneath my consciousness - a seashell to which I sometimes bend my ear, expecting omniscient reports of the sort Aithra was privy to in that silly opera of Strauss, but invariably containing nothing - not a footnote, not a number preceding a footnote.

There is pain, surely. Experienced by whom? I can't recall the self that experienced yesterday's pain. Any griefs I feel now are the flutterings of a bird who exists only in this moment, who will not fly off, intact, to somewhere else, or accompany me through the rest of this day, simply because he cannot. Palpitations and tremblings, vague pains in extremities, the sound of my stomach gurgling and a train's horn in the distance - one no more real than the other.

"I am." What a silly thing for a God to say, for a God who wishes us to take Him seriously to say. You are WHAT, pray tell? I take you as seriously as I take myself, that is to say, not at all. There is just the scattering of fragments, nay, not fragments, for that presupposes a prior unity - there is just scattering. And I would just as well dispense with the verb "to be". There - scattering. Here - violence. Within - violence. Now - violence. Always - violence, silence, terror - terror in silence, the wish to cast off the body.

Oh, how I grow weary of this constant looking within, knowing full well I shall never find a thing. One finds nothing in a vacuum other than the sense that there is someone peering into it. One is thrown back on something, but surely it is not a self, for I have no "self", am not a "self" - it is a seeing, a hearing, of nothing done by no one.

OK then, I have left the body on the floor - it lies in a heap, underneath this cheap computer on which someone's fingers type away, but they cannot be mine, for mine are there, on the floor. My hands are clutching one another, the last sputtering of an entirely forgettable hot spring at which no visitor would spend a moment gazing.

Suffering deepens us, so they say, the ones who suffer and so desperately need to soothe themselves. It teaches us to live - they say that also. What a horrid student I must be! I am a landfill of suffering, yet haven't a clue how to live, have never lived, don't even know what it would mean to live, even for an instant.

I am waiting, I have been waiting, it seems forever. For life to begin. Even now, as it inches its way towards its close, I am waiting still. Surely it will begin? Is this wishing itself a sort of life? Surely not.

There was that fly on the kitchen counter earlier this morning, seemingly stuck there - it would not fly, though I encouraged it to - I felt as if the future of the universe itself depended on the ability of that little housefly to right itself, to be off, up, up, and away - alive, hungry - for food, for mates, for more of life. No. I was watching it die. It was unbearable. It was myself, it was my first wife, it was everything good in this world, which is not much, admittedly, but for all of it to die? At this very moment, with this fly? I could stand it no longer.

I thought that perhaps I might gently scoop it up on something - a matchbook, a paper plate - but feared I would end its life finally, instead of this gradual extinction I was witnessing. I walked away; it was intolerable. They feel, these things feel, perhaps as deeply as we.

There is a holocaust taking place on every windshield. There are planets, solar systems, being vaporized out of existence on our porch steps, in our gardens. There is agony, screaming at pitches we can't hear, but surely they can. They know full well that into which they have been born and by what they have been made to suffer.

That creature on the counter, he carried the weight of infinite generations of his kind - their pain, their longings, their occasional ecstasies, and it was all to be snuffed out in a moment. It was intolerable. No one could stay in that room, given the monumental nature of what was occurring - least of all I.

I needed to do something, anything - play the piano, scream, walk the dog, perhaps stab myself, not fatally, just enough to make this go away, this horror. I climbed the stairs and pissed in the upstairs bathroom. I vowed to not return to the kitchen anytime soon, and returned to it quite immediately.

The fly was gone. Where? I did not know. There was no buzzing to be heard - it had not righted itself and taken to flight. It had simply vanished. Perhaps it had never been there in the first place. Perhaps I had just been witnessing myself, glued fast and slowly dying. Perhaps it was a vision given to me by that idiot God, who says, "I am", yet is not.

I was tempted to walk through the park again, but was sure that this time there would be other creatures, far larger creatures, mammals, if I drove to the larger park - fawns, adult deer, beavers - and that they would all be frozen, glued to the spot, and slowly dying. And that, coming upon them, I would suddenly be rooted to the spot and begin to myself melt - burning with the desire to resurrect them, and if that proved impossible, to at least give them a proper burial - something, anything to symbolize their agonies, their lives which ended this way and not another, something which no one would or will do for me, and which, were I to somehow be able to look upon the world after my death, I would, ironically and sadly enough, be relieved that they hadn't, think it just, think it appropriate.

I want there to be only disappearance - my barely noticed footprints in a fast-melting snow. How silly! There is, of course, no danger of any such thing, any such memorial taking place, and no reason for me to obsessively wish such a thing in so unseemly a manner. It would be equally likely that a horde of flies playing brass instruments of every variety might march across my counter, conducting a jazz funeral, after which they would gather up their fallen comrade and fly off to some winged burial for him at sea, or perhaps alight upon a log being ingested by termites and beetles, who would welcome them with termite applause, all of them eager to ingest and digest the corpse, with the help of both their little mouths and of all the famished microbes busy roaming their guts.

I would wish that for my vanished friend. I would attend, and with great reverence. There are no words to be said at such events. A dirge, perhaps, a curtsy towards the moon, who appears to oversee such things, at least at times.

I would curl up horizontally with the others on the forest floor, taking sufficient soporifics to carry me through until the onset of winter, at which time I would either wake, or not. That's the gamble, to which we all happily sign on. We need not be taught what to do; we will all know what to do - we are all born with these instincts - to feed when hungry, to fart when bloated, to wake when freezing.

Unless, unless... Unless there is a being of greater strength within us, and of far greater wisdom, who decides otherwise. Who hungers for shadows, for pitch-black night, for death.

XIX.

"And then - pop! At a stroke, and in a jiffy..."

And then - pop! At a stroke, and in a jiffy, and almost wholly by surprise, I find myself inside a dream, fully awake, in a sort of cavern, pitch-black and, hence, quite colorless, or, more likely, a place where color has no meaning - a womb, without a view, which nonetheless looks out upon each and every possibility of the multiverse, if that's a thing, which it's likely not, but no matter - it's a vast, uncharted space, and I am in it.

But am "I" one? Two? Or even a vast multiplicity of selves? Can I find this dreaming self? Perhaps shake his hand, embrace him? Slit his throat? Get on my knees to thank him, list my grievances, my demands? All I know is that I now am somehow writing from within this place, this place of deepest sleep, and of dream.

I'd always thought it lay within me, or perhaps beneath me, inviolable and inaccessible, its entry gates patrolled and protected by demons, flaming swords, perhaps even serpents, that sort of business - certainly not that it would open quite this freely, invite me in, and pose no threat. At least this seems to be the case as I now wander, but is it wandering? How can one wander in such a space? A space which has no features, much less rooms, or tended gardens, or wild forests, or dense jungles - it's just a space, yet not a space. It's got no length, no width, no dimensions, and yet I'm here, and most definitely within it, looking about, though I've no eyes, and keenly listening, though I've no ears - and yet I do, and they are far sharper and more able to attend than when I am awake.

Perhaps I'm God now! I've always said that, that when one dreams, that one is God, that when I dream, that I am God. But then WE are Gods, my dreaming self and I, if indeed he's someone different than myself - that is not clear. Perhaps he'll speak, or show himself, and make this somehow plain to me. In any case, we are together - I've the sense I'm not alone and that I'm safe, and if he's watching, or he's waiting now to see what I'll do next? I've not decided!

I could go this way, or go that way, which is odd, because I'm floating in a womb that has no mass nor has it features, and is clearly just my mind, perhaps the mind of something greater and far larger than my mind - or even of the mind I share with him, who is my dreaming self, who is now me!

What is that noise? Ah, it is familiar, it must be just before the morning, when he wakes, that other self - you know the one, that cortisol-awakened self, the one who vibrates, full of thoughts which gallop by at breakneck speeds, so full of worries, of apprehension. And now he's entered, the call's been sounded, we're all awake!

Perhaps we'll pee now, all the members of this ghostly trio, though not quite ghostly, at least not entirely, for one is clearly wide awake - the one who swings his legs up and then off the bed. So now we're all dragged off to the bathroom, to find ourselves behind our everyday companion, this pair of eyes, which now looks down to watch a stream of piss that plummets like a waterfall to splash into the toilet, for the most part in the toilet, and with the customary, long-familiar music of this minor waterfall, heard then by ears which have returned, it now appears, and which seem to function in their ordinary fashion.

It's a music which goes far deeper than the musics made by men, which only sound like mindless chatter, rarely anything more than that. Oh, we are done now! The dick's been shaken! It's been returned to where it was, and now the three of us shall wander back to bed. That should be nice. Perhaps we'll sleep!

We need not waken for some hours, all of us. Perhaps the dog is turned aright now! As in not a-wrong now, that is to say, when her ass has claimed a spot which is all too near my face. But no matter! I can still stretch out my arm to rub her belly. Oh, this is nice - the agitation is subsiding, perhaps the three of us can join now, become a solitary creature on a raft which now sets off upon a river - you know the one, it was a Greek one, was it not? Perhaps Lethe? It hardly matters.

So he was willing, after all, that half-crazed beast, so full of angst, addled with cortisol, or with varieties of whatnot - the stuff of life, the horrid stuff, which is the source of what one suffers when awake, the endless creatures in the woods and under cars that he is worried will be dead soon, the ones that rip his heart out as he contemplates the cruelty of the universe in which he finds himself. But now we've managed, the three of us, to surmount this, and to find ourselves in deepest sleep, where we can stumble towards the morning and its horrors, in a fashion which, as a rule, more or less delights us.

It seems I'm still bound up in words, and yet I know, inside this space, which is so vast, there are no words, just getting lost in one's own warm and milky limbs which extend into a void.

No! Not those words! For this delicious, creamy feeling? This tasting? Is it tasting? Of a body which I no longer seem to be in? There is just space, prior to dream, a sleep so deep perhaps I now am just some tiny blood cell, perchance a red one, or a white one in a battle with intruders of whom I'll never be aware, because I'm floating in this milky, viscous space, as if I'm stumbling towards oblivion, which now calls, and I pick up, for that's a call I wish to take, I need respond to - I want directions! And assurances that this will be that bliss of which I've heard so many tell, most of whom are shameless frauds and shameful grifters, but that's no matter - I still believe I'll make it there! For now I'm here, and this ain't bad, that's for damned sure.

The self that wanders through each day in abject pain is now adrift on purple waters of the most delightful river, and it seems as if I now possess a will, which I most surely don't possess in waking life, for in that life I simply shudder, as I wait for what is surely now to come - abominations and distress, which it's decreed I must submit to, but in this dream world, it is different, I can act, and I can do! I can make the boat go this way, or stay still, or make it rise into the sky, which seems to offer me some peace, which is enchanting in in a strange and very different sort of way than anything I've ever known.

I'm rather happy - well there's a concept! No, not just happy - I am ecstatic! Although I know I'm in a dream, that dreams must end, and I'm just stalling, for the morning's not far off, and when it comes, this all will end, and to awaken is the worst thing that can happen to a man, just as the drifting off to sleep is quite the best.

Well that's to come, but this is now, and may it linger for as long as it is possible for such serenity as I feel now to tarry, to hover and to dawdle deep within me, in that soul of mine in which I don't believe.

Am I dreaming this dream alone? How many dreamers might there be? As many as there are turtles holding up the world? Which one is "I"? Is this a foretaste of my death? Perhaps I am dead. Well then, it's not all that bad! What's all the fuss then? It's quite comfortable!

I need for nothing! I've got it all! I've got my will! And because of that, there is a way, indeed there must be! So it's been said. But then I pause - a way to what? I want for nothing, only to stay here, and that forever, not to waken to a world in which I find that there bunnies are under cars, which makes me dread that they might die there, and if that happens, it's quite certain that the sun will just shut down, or will explode, but either way, the world will shudder for an instant, burst into flame or turn to ice.

That is not something to stick around for, how much better to remain in this cocoon, which is delicious, in which saliva tastes like nectar, in which my blood has turned to wine, made out of grapes all grown in Eden, which were stomped upon by dancing, smiling children, who are eternal, as I'm eternal.

I want to follow. I want to find them! I ask my comrades, "Can we turn in that direction? Try to find those joyous children, stomping grapes with such abandon? I want to see them, I want to join them, my blood is wine that's of their making - I need to tell them, I need to thank them, I won't use language, they'll simply know when I approach them what it is I wish to tell them without words - it's not a thing that can be told, just understood - they'll understand, they are my children, as I am theirs."

Dear God, don't let the morning rip me from this womb which I have yearned for since before there was a world, which I preceded, as did you both - it was the three of us, remember? Before this spinning globe appeared? We were in space - it was tremendous, it was ecstatic!

There was that woman - no, not just one! There were a thousand, they all bore us on their shoulders, do you remember? To that place? Yes, we had anguish, not all that much though. For the most part, there was love - they saw quite through us and were delighted, you must remember! I see you do. Thank God you do.

We're going there now! I've turned the boat in that direction! It shan't be long. The anguish simply means what follows will be exquisite. Don't be discouraged! I understand, I get that way, but just recall what I've recalled - it's in your minds just as in mine.

We shall soon get there, you must believe me! The river's silent, nay, it is breathless, it is eager that we trace it to its source. It was born once, as were we, it's being born while I am speaking, but I shall stop it, as I stop myself, and we shall row, and we will get there before the morning sucks the air and dries the river. We've not long, but long enough.

This is ridiculous, of course, I know that well and know it truly. But I am sick of being modest! It has eaten up my life, it has shredded all my soul to blasted bits, it has crushed me to a bloody, mangled pulp! And so I've tossed it from this boat, this "modesty", as you can see, into this river, where it's been swallowed by - were they sharks? Perhaps piranhas? It doesn't matter, because it's gone now, and there was nothing as ridiculous as what I have just mentioned and which has now been cast aside.

And there is nothing we can do, nor that we need to! That's why we're headed now for Eden, where we'll be greeted by those hordes of Amazons for whom we've yearned so, who'll simply greet us and invite us to the most ambrosial orgies of both the body and the mind.

It's not just hours till the morn, we've all eternity! You will see. We can stay here, or rather there, where we'll dissolve into the mouths and breasts and cunts and hearts of women who'll adore us, who will arouse and then delight us with such pleasures as we've never known before, which shall make up for the horrors that we've...

Well now, that's strange! I can't recall them - how about yourselves, the two of you? Have you forgotten them as well? I understand them as a concept, they were the mainstay of my life - the main event, but for the life of me, the life to come, I can't recall a single one. For now there only seem to be these mouths and breasts and cunts and hearts and soothing, loving words.

These are embraces of a sort one can't imagine, though I am trying. Not doing badly, truth to tell! There are these fireworks in my brain, and in my milky, viscous limbs and in my cock, which is on fire in a way I thought not possible anymore. Am I now twenty? It would seem so.

And am I human? Hand me a mirror! But dreams contain no mirrors, at least I thought not. I am alive, that much is clear. I am this vast, uncharted space. Well, they'll explain it. There is no question that they will, as they rub their milk-white breasts over my face, and laugh like angels, who will never let me go into the morning, that hateful morning, with its blood-red sun and thoughts and fears and pains felt in a body I never wanted in the first place, but which now here just gives me pleasure. How am I to understand such a thing?

I am happy now. Were I to suffer here, with them, it would not matter, it would be a different thing entirely, a thing to learn from and to cherish, and not a thing which lays me low. Life is deadly, but dreams are lively, and for now, I am alive.

Please do not wake me, at least as long as you can manage. Yes, I hear it! It is dreadful! I can feel it without seeing it! It's dawn! It's coming soon! Why am I weeping? Of course I'm weeping. It's like always - these foul Gods, who dangle joys and offer promises that desires can be fulfilled, only to yank them from our hands and to throw us once again upon a pyre which consumes us, like the one that's on the doorstep of this space that I've been privileged to inhabit these few hours but am now forced to abdicate.

I will awaken, and I will tell myself, or selves, that I must do this thing or that, not for a reason, only to help me slog through all these hours, all these endless, brutal hours of which my paltry life consists. Until the door which guards this space, this sacred space, opens once again, and I rush in to taste of happiness, for a time.

That is all that I can hope for, and is enough, other than death, which won't be long, and, it is hoped, not be that bad.

XX.

"That is indeed the hope, that it not be bad..."

That is indeed the hope, that it not be bad, that it give more than it takes. Unlike this monster which is sitting to my left, which pretends to be inert, which I discovered centuries ago, or perhaps it found me? That's something I could never quite determine. But that it's conscious? That I know, for even now, this very moment, as it sits there, it is grinning - perhaps with delight? In its anticipation of vengeance?

It often sits in living rooms, which really is amusing, because, as a living thing, it seems, indeed, to have these miscellaneous, almost human requirements. It can be generous, that is true, and so it was towards me, amongst a multitude of other qualities, including jealous, shrewd, and desperately, diabolically cunning. The latter's the most dangerous, for it's attached to its intuitions which fasten so invariably on the innocent, particularly on those who've been exploited, victimized, and violated, who are looking for a friend or a protector whom they can trust, for, as a rule, they're far too young to realize they ought be very cautious, since nothing comes without a price, be it distraction, be it protection, or be it hunger, masquerading as devotion or as kindness.

"You need only touch me, need only stroke me," so it would whisper, "and I will take you to my bosom, where I'll cradle you in safety, forever. You'll be encircled in a halo, and there'll be music - you like music, yes? Well then, it is settled! It's a deal! You'll not desert me, and I, in turn, will see to it you're safe, that you'll always have this place, this refuge, and in return, ah, that's not something we need discuss now. It's but a trifle I'll be asking, you will see. You'll have the better of the bargain by a long chalk, for I ask only for company, for curiosity. Well, to be completely honest, it will all be a bit more complicated than that, but that needn't be discussed presently. Now that we've met, perhaps you ought make note of precisely when it was?"

And so I did, dutiful little boy that I was. I recall awaking in the wee hours of some morning or other - was I four years old? Perhaps I was. I recall only that I sat bolt upright in a sweat, because I knew I had to note the exact time at which we'd made this bargain - I, and this "thing". But how was I to do it? I was four, maybe five. I had no pen, I had no paper, so I slithered to the bathroom, and wrote the date of our first meeting in the sink with gobs of toothpaste, which I somehow thought would last, perhaps forever.

Yes, I recall it! My pea-brained hope was that it might last forever, for surely something this monumental, something as grand and memorable as this clearly was, need be inscribed upon the heavens themselves, for I'd somehow awoken to a new and kinder world which now offered me an exit, an asylum, an escape valve which was to be constantly available, and to which I could turn whenever I wished. It only asked that I caress it, in order that it might answer me with music, which would save me, that much was clear, for it had promised, though I knew of other promises made by those who had assured me I could trust them, with their words or with a glance I should have seen through had I been older and more worldly.

Yet the promise of this thing seemed rather different, for, first and foremost, the others in the house would have no way to know we'd made this bargain. They just assumed it was a dead thing, they barely saw it - it was just furniture for them. It never beckoned or intrigued them, they passed right by it on their way to make a meatloaf, or grab a belt with which to beat me. They didn't see it, didn't know of its existence, though it was said, was often said, in fact there was a legend in the house that, at one time, the hobbling crone had known full well of its existence, nay, was even forced to marry it for a time, and to spend countless hours in attempts to please both it and her own mother, who had made that marriage mandatory.

And for years! At least that's what the myth had been both in that house, and in the house in which I'd grown up - that is until the crone grasped that she'd be able to bamboozle some young man and to impale him on a meathook, and then drag him to this house, our house, the house in which I lived, which now contained both him and her, as well as me, along with this monstrous, toothy, black behemoth former husband of hers, which held no further interest for her, and which she took great care to never, ever touch, for that was how she thought it fit to recompense the mother who'd engineered all that so many years ago - all that enforced unpleasantness and drudgery, that slavery to a chore which she so resented - that mother who'd made her sit obediently for hours and for years, caressing furniture she loathed so deeply, and which she could not wait to cast aside at the very first opportunity.

Well then! Now she'd done so, she had two victims, who were made of flesh and blood, not wood and steel and melodies for which she'd seemed to have some aptitude, but never, ever the slightest feeling, and which now she'd never have to play again. And yet she'd dragged this former husband, this black behemoth, and had placed it in our living room, a seeming place of honor, which was odd, for she despised it!

This is a story far too deep, or far too simple, either way, it can't be known, or finessed to mean something. And furthermore, there's not one reason it should be of any interest, for fairy tales of witches in bad marriages are legion, and the point is that the monster beckoned me now, as if it were a woman, who'd be my savior. There's a bit of fire and brimstone of which this business smelled and smells. I can't deny that was the case, although there wasn't any poodle, no dramatic trails of fire, just this behemoth, this great black box, sitting there and salivating, seemingly benign, and even cheerful.

I began at once to play. This wasn't bad! Not as great as it had promised, as she had promised, but even so, if I could soothe myself, if I could cast myself in some fable in which I'm something, something worthy, who, in between the many beatings, might be praised? Well that was better, was it not?

I had no reason to refuse, and signed the contract. It was hardly an ecstatic thing, but when you're on fire, and see you're bleeding, and that you're being flayed alive, a distraction of the simplest kind is welcome, though this distraction wasn't simple, it required commitment - endless hours of study and practice, but that was fine - I was a curious boy and have remained so. This was as interesting as anything else of which I was aware, so I could hardly turn it down.

No one had previously made me any sort of promise without shortly after having done so plunging one or more sharp objects in my bowels, and that hardly seemed what was being offered here. There was a contract, a mental promise, but no compact to be signed in blood, or so, at least, I thought at that time. Rather I was being offered shelter, an identity, a way to navigate the filth, to survive the violence, the unpredictability, the hatred, the constant wishing that I'd die, not just by my hands, but by hers - above all from her, loud and clear and almost daily proclamations. She made it clear that's what she wanted!

Well then! Now I had a way I could fight back. Why I wished to I don't know. There was this thing in me, it's in me still - this idiot who just wants life, to keep on breathing, and not to die. Why that should be so I did not know, I don't know now. I only know that I embraced that marriage, and said I do - to that identity, to that commitment, this was me now, I had a path, was on that path. Yes, it cut through dangerous forests filled with phantoms and with harpies who desired that I suffer, that I come within a hair's breadth of extinction, like a comic on a vaudeville stage who's yanked offstage by shepherd's crooks attached to canes and poles, wielded by her, at first, but then by me, yet always thrown back with great force upon that stage a moment later, naked, terrified, and forced to perform.

In point of fact, I remember quite clearly, when playing upon my new mistress, without the slightest clue what I was doing, in the presence of the hag, she seemed delighted! And, when delighted, was not dangerous. It was seductive, it was revolting, because she might as well have been fingering her twat with great abandon, as her little boy pressed buttons on this curious piece of furniture, which had promised his survival, and which had filled him with the notion that he might well have a future, that he not be forced to die at any moment, at every moment, after having been through tortures of the most abominable sort, with which he was more than a little familiar, which, in fact, were his near-daily bread.

And now the point of this sad tale, the question which has no answer - it's the only one that matters, so why not ask it? But of course there'll be no answer! Not a simple one, at least. But nonetheless.

Who was that boy before that fateful bargain? Am I still him? That terrified boy, consigned to a solitary hell, who possessed no weapons, who clutched a piece of furniture to his breast, in hopes it might protect him, give him a self to which he might then cling - that boy who hung now like a madman on to bits of floating debris on a black sea poised to swallow him, and which did, indeed, swallow him, and on very many occasions, only to cough him up a moment later, panting, and spitting up seaweed - looking for her, she who would save him.

She surely must come soon! Ah, there she is! Floating there still! My lover, my protectress, a mighty fortress she to me! Who am I, Tristan? In the third act of that shriekfest? What is going on??? No matter. He'd be safe now, that little boy. I'd be safe now - for an hour, for a month, a year or two - who knows, perhaps be safe for even longer.

It was a lie, needless to say, like all marriages are lies - a lie, but perhaps a slightly less noxious one than most. A white lie, perhaps.

But enough now with these two-bit parables, these metaphors, this horseshit! I gave her, this hellish thing, this duplicitous, famished piece of furniture, I gave her my fucking life! I entrusted it to her, and what did I get in return? Yes, I got something. I did. Sixty more years of life, for had I not met her, I would have been gone at five or six years old, perhaps even earlier.

Would that not have been better? And how much better still to have never existed in the first place! But who is that lucky?

I had very little talent, I'm fairly certain. Anyone who spends forty thousand hours masturbating over a piece of furniture will become somewhat adept at negotiating its needs, something of a carpenter, as it were, learning to encourage it to do this or that, even wheedling out of it, out of her, a bit of something that he'd liked to think he'd created, which was somehow novel, but of course that was always and ever bullshit, these things were no more novel than the shits I might have just taken on the way to sitting another six hours in front of that greedy, insatiable, satanic contraption.

I gave it, I gave HER my life, and she gave to me a way in which to continue living that life - a perfectly stupid arrangement, benefitting no one, at the very most a venal and cowardly arrangement, at least on my part.

That's not a grin I see when I look to my left - it's a grimace, or, more likely, a scowl of contempt, a licking of lips, the smirk of victory.

"I have swallowed your life, you fool! I blinded you, made you my hostage, you've been walking down a lethally lonely path - down, down, down, with, at each and every moment, the noose you never noticed I had cast about your neck, and which I tightened ceaselessly, the function of which was to insure you not look this way or look that way, that you only go on doggedly and blindly, drowned in this fictional character we'd colluded in creating.

Now that this tale is drawing to its close, there's no need to continue the charade. You've lived a reasonably long life, and it's been, no news to you, utterly empty and utterly meaningless. Are you surprised by that? Then you are still the fool I took you for six and a half decades ago! Music is utterly empty and utterly meaningless. As you are!

What did I get from all this, you ask? That I shall not tell you, it's unlikely you'd understand, in any case. Goodbye. I leave you so you can be again that four year old in the basement - alone, terrified, minutes away from being eviscerated for the umpteenth time - no longer by her, that is true, but by the world, which is only her, after all, writ large.

Yet she is everywhere! Beneath you, in the skies, in your dreams, and in your bowels! In the food you eat and upon which you choke, in the life you lead upon which you choke no less. In the face of which you are equally helpless, equally naked, as you were when she would so viciously attack you - with her fists, with your belts, with those bedroom dresser drawers, and, worst of all, with her foul tongue. Which is now your tongue! For she lives in you. You use it now - on those by whom you're threatened, on those you love, and whom you wish to love you. She flays you alive from the inside out, you have become her. Her fondest wish, your worst nightmare: your life."

But of course it was not just she, the ghoulish, fiendish, piano-harpy that spoke to me thus. It was the crone herself - it was all women. It was my wife, it was my sister, my first girlfriends, my first wife, the horrid second one, and life itself - my every doomed-to-fail attempt to rip through this cage of flesh, of pain, to find something, to find someone, that would hear me, who would see me, who would know me, and not simply, reliably, inevitably, and so incessantly betray me.

The world is on fire - with laughter, with the most hideous laughter, at me, and me only. This is the last act, that's clear enough! And, apparently, the most hilarious! I am a contemptible, desperately gullible, and apparently still incomprehensibly hopeful thing. Hence, the most contemptible sort of idiot, a squashed and macerated thing, who can no longer hear, speak, eat, piss, shit, breathe, swallow, blink, move. And who is to write the music for this scene? Not I! Not anyone, for there can be no music sufficiently awful, horrifying, eviscerating enough to paint this moment, this tightrope on which a marionette stumbles above a planet engulfed in flames. There can be none, for there are no players left, they've all been incinerated, the lucky bastards. There is only me, dangling, drunk with grief, clutching my torso, through which a harpoon has been passed, and with this maddening, incessant tingling in my extremities.

And dancing. I! Who cannot dance! Shrieking to no one - no one above me, no one below me, no one beside me, and if there were, it would make no difference. The world is this Ouroboros, devouring its own poisonous tail, and I am that terrified child

again, eating another stumbling, shrieking marionette, and another
- becoming again the child who eats...

What is that sound? Dear God! Is it the slow movement of
the Schubert cello quintet? Of course it is!!! Who's playing it? For
there is no one left to play it! This is not possible. Perhaps it's the
voice of a God I wish existed, I cannot say. But why now? This last
gasp of that wondrous, pockmarked, syphilitic sorcerer, a couple of
stumbling steps from death?

Another lie, of course, but such a beautiful one. Such a
beautiful, magnificent lie! The one I was promised. It's still playing,
yes, very faintly, but nonetheless. But this time it promises nothing.
And nothing is precisely what I must come to desire, for it is upon
me.

XXI.

"This godforsaken habit, what has it made of me..."

This godforsaken habit, what has it made of me, this habit of having thought myself a "musician"? Now that I look upon this dreadful, cruel black comedy, or, rather, pitch-black commode, now that I see it, what in God's name is it? What has it always been, ever been, since its very beginning?

I will forget it, of course. We jettison even the most long-lived of habits and, after a time, forget we ever had them. They appear to us ludicrous, incomprehensible. We cast through the catacombs of our memory trying to locate that self who had once cared a fig for such things, such avocations, vocations, and, let us not forget, persons, lovers, wives, who are also things of habit, and, when gone, eventually become the mysterious accompanists we'd long ago engaged to accompany us in duets which now sound, at times cacophonous, the sorts of things from which one flees, but more often, far more often, things for which we have only the most profound apathy, which no longer touch us in the least.

If I still grieve after all these years for my first wife, could it possibly be about or for her that I grieve? Of course not! That would be an utterly preposterous assertion. She is no more, and the self who told himself he loved her is long gone, as well. Of what, then, could such a thing possibly be constituted? Shock that lives in the body - it is quite unlikely that it is anything more than or different from that, and that alone.

But what of the habit of being one's "self"? That's a tougher one, an enigma on the order of Schopenhauer's world-knot. I have discarded and buried the tens of thousands of selves who've combed the earth bearing my name and social security number without batting an eye, but what of this one, the one to which I am so seemingly firmly attached, the one right now? What of him? Can I attain to that state in which I see only the pockmarked actor with the paunch and balding hair and never again Hamlet? Why certainly I can, and do, and have! Why then, not with my self? This one! The one within which I am presently incarcerated, at this very moment. Can I not look upon this steaming bag of viscera, shit, and foolishness, and reach a similar conclusion? As if I were some word endlessly repeated, which has been reduced to nothing but a perfectly idiotic and profoundly annoying noise? Gibberish?

My mind says of "me" very much the same: I am nothing more than an idiotic and profoundly annoying sound, sight, and stench, among other things - all of them annoying, nay, infuriating, and that's on a good day. And yet this hunger, this moronic will-to-live, how do I rid myself of it? Philosophy can't manage it. The Stoics were such fools, such endlessly prattling blockheads and poseurs. The passions are all! And the passion which is concerned with continuing even the most horrid of existences is the profoundest of all of them.

Yes, there are exceptions - in extraordinary circumstances, or perhaps, at times, even in banal ones. One hopes for the latter, for there is no one more banal than I. I want to feel towards my "self" what I so sadly experience now in and with music - it has become chatter - mindless, narcissistic, chatter - narcissistic masturbation to no purpose, an admittedly redundant turn of phrase, although there can be pleasure in the latter. And yet, alas! I no longer take any pleasure in music, nor do I in my grubby, putrid, and all-too-familiar "self". Therein I perceive only a leering, contemptible inanity. And yet, were I to attempt to wrestle against the instinctual revolt of the body envelope in which I find myself, I would lose. I know that! I've tried it. Several times.

All this very like what has become of music, which has become, for me, little more than a den of narcissistic monsters, coughing up and out the purest nonsense, Roman fountains full of trombone spittle and bow hairs, rooms full of perversely shaped diaphragms belching rank, fetid air out of rancid gullets, through instruments, and into auditoriums - very much as former lovers have become beings about whom I never give a thought. They have all of them devolved into a worthless collection of vibrating larynxes, distorted nipples, blemished faces, and idiotic verbiage - their every former "beauty mark" now the obvious, actual deformity which I had previously not seen or wished away, renamed, or, at least, reframed, in order that it not disgust me, as it does now.

And so too have "I" become to my "self" - a thing, an automaton, a mechanicus - a machine any sane person simply drags to the junkyard and never thinks of again.

I have, at times, remarked to myself that I have fallen out of love with this "self", and yet there has never been anything out of which to fall, certainly not love. There has only ever been loathing and disgust. And yet I hang on, like a rat on board the sinking Titanic.

I want nothing more than to sleep, the sleep of death, that's true enough - and yet it's always the sleep of not QUITE death, the hedging-of-one's-bets sleep of death. For tomorrow I may... I may what, pray tell? Drink of the nectar pouring out of some woman's pussy whom I have attempted to convince myself I love? That seems less than likely. Cough up another page of crap no one will ever read? Some trivial, pleasant-enough-sounding tune to which no one will ever listen? To slog on a bit more through the perfumed, poisonous, cork-lined rooms within the mind of Marcel Proust, that sick fuck? These are the reasons my idiot body supplies to my obedient mind, which is almost, but never quite stupid enough to believe them. I go on, because I must. Because the painless suicide clinics on every other corner, which one would find in any even remotely civilized society, do not exist. I possess no lust, no passion, and no enthusiasm for anything anymore. I see right through to its transparently hypocritical, here-we-go-again heart, though they so rarely have hearts, at a first glance or hearing. There's nothing new under the sun, which is like most other suns, all of whom, I assume, must be as bored shitless as I. The sleeping earth must necessarily pray for the kindness of a collision with a planet greater than itself.

I cannot even flatter myself that it is sorrow I feel - it is far too inconsequential, far too generic and stupid. And if it is a sort of sorrow, it is precisely the same sorrow that every other fool feels, when he wakes up in the foul pool of each new morning to find that he is again drowning, and that there's nothing for it. I've hardly got a patent on it.

In the beams of your home there are countless tribes of beings, some of them insects, others slimy invertebrates of this sort or that, all of them engaged in ritual slaughter, and all of them shrieking in desperation, in agony. Put your ear to the wall, you hear it, yes?

The very same rituals are taking place this very instant in your guts, and in your bloodstream, full as they both are of weeping microbes, begging, praying for death, imploring their neighbors to end their shabby, imbecilic lives, for they are too weak or have not the proper means to do it. Just like me! And like you.

Of course it's best to not think upon any of this - you just end up spinning, screaming, and clutching your bloated guts. You want to tell someone, anyone, what it is you've seen, what you've become, what you're experiencing, but they cannot hear you and won't listen, because it is precisely the same for them, the difference being that they've erected ramparts against the enemy, and, my friend, if you are anything like me, and see what I see - rest assured, for them you are the enemy.

You walk through the park, dropping selves like flies with each step you take. Don't look back! They are slipping beneath the gravel, trying to claw their way upright before they disappear, wailing, praying that you'll offer them your hand, and not simply cast them off like dead skin, without a thought. And in the course of your short walk, you have murdered ten thousand selves merely to be the one who the very next moment is to be murdered, suffocated, buried, and forgotten.

Ah, but the smell of lilacs! So lovely, innit? How even more delicious it would be were you a bee, a butterfly, a hummingbird, or a caterpillar. And yet you are! You silly person - you are all those things. When they shed those selves, more quickly than hummingbirds flap their wings, those dying selves are not the least bit different from you - it's the same toilet in which I, you, we all end up. Listen! You can hear it flushing, no?

Whom am I addressing, again?

Yes, you are violently alive in this moment, as alive as an endless line of veal calves stretched across the dung-filled walls of a factory farm, all hung on meathooks with the speed of those hummingbirds' wings flapping - each thinking, nay, knowing, "I'm the REAL veal calf, no question of that! I feel as if I am, and hence there's no denying that..."

Whoops! Next veal calf! Same ideation, same comical, fantastical notions of continuity.

The savage intensity, the wild aliveness of the dying moment, which you call "yourself", and I "myself", for we love stories, don't we? They seem to be what you are, what I am, what we all are, so we continue to pretend, hope, and sometimes even believe that these things are the case. We must tell ourselves these stories. Otherwise? Otherwise, the spinning begins, the vertigo, the sickness unto death, towards death, and of death.

I look about - there must be someone to whom I can communicate these horrors! They look somewhat like me, perhaps they see it as well, and feel somewhat similarly! Perhaps we can hold hands for a moment, the moment just before we're thrown on a meathook.

But this line of veal calves? Wait - that's not quite right.

The veal calf thrown on the meathook is the one just cast off, sloughed off. Yes, of course! The meathook is behind us! The abyss is tracking us, from just behind, swallowing our cast-off selves, the idiot selves that keep walking through the park thinking themselves somehow continuous - all the while they are simply mutating, becoming other, unrecognizable, new selves, all of which sounds as if it should be delightful, no? How delightful! Not knowing what one's next thought shall be? What pain shall arise? Which hunger, regret, longing, speck in one's eye, lump in one's throat, tumor in one's abdomen, sensation of a bursting bladder, or of an explosive, wildly constipated colon? What are to be the future remarks by our idiot neighbor, or when shall be our next unpleasant sighting of that noxious moron? What shall it consist of, this next moment? No matter, it won't be "I", in any event - that "I" is already behind me, half-swallowed by the gravel path - screaming, reaching for my hand, and begging for - what?

Another moronic nanosecond of stability - begging "me", this "me", which is already gone as well - swallowed, begging, screaming, reaching - gone.

Delightful movie, no? Would you like some popcorn?

Popcorn, yes. Indeed!

One wants to feel it slithering down one's gullet, plopping down into an inferno of hydrochloric acid - it's a scenario very much like our own, like the fate of each self we each shit out hundreds of times a minute, nay, an infinite number of times - they, like our popcorn, which we imagine might shriek and beg for mercy somewhat less, though there's no assurance of that, are cast into a vat of acid, there to be torn asunder, dissolved in a ravenous, satanic stew, in which they splinter into barbecued bits of lonely grief, crushed hopes, and existential terrors.

It's all been futile, this death march - you see it, no? You know you're on it, of course you must know at least that. It cannot be only I that see it, that is not possible.

Let your spirit fly upwards for a moment! Towards the vault of, well, surely not heaven - towards the stratosphere! Breathe deeply of the nitrogen and whatever the other godforsaken poisons are that float about up there, but look down, that's the main thing, that's the point - look down!

And do tell us, what is it you see?

You see it, surely you see it? The death marches at every scale of existence? The countless souls being cast off, billions of times a second, into that blood-red ocean of flames?

I see it. I see nothing else these days, only that.

And not just the infinite holocaust of beings gorging on one another, that's the least of it - I recall how I busied myself for so long thinking that was the worst of it! No, the other holocausts, those of nature herself, and of time - chasing us all through scorched and desolate deserts, all the while stabbing us gleefully in the ass.

We are all Muammar Gaddafi in his final moments, are we not? That "thing" called Muammar Gaddafi? Which was, and had been, an infinite number of beings, each disappearing the moment it was observed by the others, and by itself.

Pretty picture, innit?

You can weep about these things - I do, I am, as a matter of fact, weeping right now. It's a bottom-end form of being alive, and, hey - it's a living. I know a few others as well, all of them hopelessly undependable and unsatisfying, some sick jokes not worth repeating, a few tunes, and not a whole lot else.

The world is an ill-composed tune - do you hear it? Those she-devils scratching away at their mutilated cellos with those two strings made of cats' guts? Some of whose bloodied, eviscerated corpses lie at their feet? Their audience composed quite entirely of other, garroted cats? For they're all about, a few of them still sufficiently alive to wildly howl, as cats do, particularly those who have been recently so viciously eviscerated. They are a less than ideal audience, and yet, still, one weeps. Ah, there is no explaining these things. Still one weeps. I weep. You weep.

I wrote that little ditty, by the way, that trivial little cello tune. Ya, it's quite awful! I know! And I was quite certain I had trashed it! I haven't the slightest notion how anyone could possibly have chanced upon it, much less arranged it for six mutilated cellos, nor where they might have found she-devils willing to work for such low wages. Is there not a union of some kind? A she-devil union? Of course there is! I married into one. I've been paying its dues ever since. But that's another story.

Don't listen too closely, for reasons explained above. You'll hear only cat guts, and see only the carcasses of dead trees, cats, and the grimaces of she-devils. No matter - it will all reliably implode, momentarily. And yes, that is what is really going on.

And this is all very far from a deep insight, my friend.

Is this reality the one you wish to experience? What all of this, in fact, actually is? This random assemblage of endless bits of debris, each of which has not the slightest real relationship with the scrap of litter against which it has been momentarily thrown? The idiotic static and black noise which is the world? Do you not prefer your little stories, the ones you tell yourself you see and hear, the ones you tell yourself you are, the ones about your "life", and its "meaning"? Of course you do!

Pass the popcorn, if you've not yet finished it, and would be so kind. And do your best not to notice how each word that comes out of my mouth, or of yours, or of any mouth, none of which any of us can remotely predict, drops down to and disappears within the famished ground beneath it, which we believe serves to hold us up, and upon which we tell ourselves we walk, but which, rather...

No! Do not look down or behind! Look only ahead, replay that soothing, innocuous story in your mind's ear.

And do have a bit of popcorn, before it, and I, and you, and we, the we of this particular nanosecond, who are already gone - before we disappear, die, are swallowed, incinerated, buried, and forgotten - all of us lightning flashes in a pan who shan't be ever heard from again, known, or experienced - all those "I"s of but a moment ago.

Before we, um..., well, you know...

XXII.

"And so there appeared before me now a parade of discarded selves..."

And so there appeared before me now a parade of discarded selves, as if in some sort of celestially generated magic lantern display - not on some wall, but as if before me, or, rather more accurately, from within me. Is it not wise, is it not brave, and even noble to honestly reflect upon how ridiculous this all is? That one reads a book and emerges a changed person? That one bumps one's head, not at all badly, and transforms into what seems another person?

Well then! At the point of death, we shall all indeed become another, whether it be a collection of distant, lonely molecules, maggot food, incorporeal beings of this or that sort, fretting about what's next for them, whatever or whomever they might end up becoming. All these things are equally ridiculous, no? A pointless charade in a hall of cold, cruel mirrors? And, hence, not to be taken remotely seriously - a parade of momentary delusions then, each replaced by another equally foolish, and not a bit less awful or violent.

That foolish boy caged in a basement in which he assumed he would soon die by his or others' hands? He had no notion of what death was, and did not fear it. He dreaded only the getting there - the brutal death march, overseen by mangled mothers bearing whips and scowls and shouting at - was it indeed at him? For he had done nothing wrong, nothing at all! Why at him?

I hold him close now that I am walking by this river, and with each step I take I slough off cells. A very simple matter, when I compare it to the sloughing off of selves, which fall behind me and are immediately dragged beneath the water's surface. I try to catch them as they fall. I catch the boy who I once was, if indeed I really was that boy.

But no - I see him veiled now, beneath a curtain, upon a stage five miles away, beneath the waters of this river. I can't save him, and I don't want to. There had never been anyone who cared to save him. Let him drown! I've other matters to attend to. I'm being chased by Nazis, and Rwandan Hutus with machetes! From whom I'd fled, and thought myself safe. But they were me then, and they are me now. They are inside me, I can't escape them. They are hacking me to ribbons from within, while casting numberless of my former selves into this river.

And can't you hear them, those former selves? They are all screaming! They are begging me to save them. Of course I can't. I've got this new grief, it is immense. It is my life now, that thing I loathe, that thing I've always loathed, that I'd give back, were it allowed, but it is not, so I keep walking by this river, which is choking with the selves that I've sloughed off and that I barely recognize, when I look, which isn't often, other than as pictures in some gallery within me that I hardly ever visit, because when I do I feel empty, and the emptiness coagulates and grows into a grief which is immense and is inside me and which makes it hard to walk along this river which is choking with all these selves.

The little boy I was - was it in first grade? My sad encounter with the little blonde girl whom he so loved? Who slammed the car door as he stood there with his soul smothered in longing, with his heart grown dry as bones and cast in vats of bitter acid, of bitter tears, seeping down some tube behind his mouth and nostrils, seeking refuge?

I remember! I began to gag and wheeze and lose my balance, and the world began to spin. "Why did she do that? She must hate me! It is all over! I must die!"

I'm in the basement now again. But no - I'm simply walking by this river, suffocated, as it is, with the bodies of the selves I have discarded, nay, which have been ripped from me. And yet I never signed a contract stipulating I'd be ripped apart this way!

Is that an infant I hear sobbing? In the river? I can't place it, though I hear it clearly, and the gases in my guts gurgling away seem its tender, attentive, somehow magically appropriate accompaniment.

I hear a frog who sings a song I might just yesterday have thought was simply croaking, but which now I sadly realize is a desperate plea to she who has just spurned him. He is sobbing on what seemed to be the banks of this same river. And yet I cannot quite make it out. Is he out there, by the infant who was sobbing?

No!

The gases that were gurgling as that boy fell to his knees upon the slamming of that car door by the little porcelain angel whom he'd never see again? Whom he had dreamt might come to save him in the basement? Down in the bowels of his unbearable aloneness and despair? They're in the storeroom of MY guts now - in an uproar, belching complaints I can't find words for.

And all those limbs I see beside me? Beneath the waters of this river by which I'm walking, reaching out as if to grab me? I've not sufficient hands to pull them out, nor do I wish to. They are not me, not any longer.

The little blonde girl? She was no different from the next one, the one after, and the one... They served their purpose - an evil purpose! Which hardly matters, for my heart is throbbing still. It is pounding in my ears, part of a symphony of belches, croaks, and screams - of prayers and drowning selves who beg to breathe and walk and drink and eat and piss and shit and maybe fuck and tell themselves they're loved just for a moment! Then they'll repair back to the river, disappear, without objection. That will suffice. They all were so terrified of girls and so in love they couldn't speak. They thought they'd die, and now they have, at least been cast into this river, here to drown and be no more than stamps on letters opened now and then inside a dream. There's no returning, though they try. They try to speak - I never catch just what they're saying, like the night in which my wife died, when she came into the room and mumbled something which I didn't understand, then stumbled through the hall and back to bed. It was the one and only night I fell asleep upon the couch, only to find her in the bedroom on the floor, ice-cold and blue, many hours later, in the cruel and pale light of dawn.

Was that horror, that nightmare - was it not happening at this very moment? For this moment too is ice-cold, blue, and terrifying. I am coming undone before my very eyes, which are bleeding - I am shivering and imploding now as then.

Yes, the world turned upside down and there were screams - which came from me! They came from me! Which I did not realize at first, but I hear them now quite precisely as I did then. Indeed - Dear God, I hear them now! They live in me. But are they different? The ones in me now? From those that poured out of me then? Are they different? And am I?

Well then! It was, it must have been me who screamed those bloodcurdling screams, who ran lunatic into the street at dawn. But am I not now again in that street? Is this path by the river not that very lane? Surely that self is in the river? The one who screamed half a century ago? Who should have died? Who wanted so desperately to die? To be with her?

But no, he's here, he's still inside me. I still am he, I've never ever shook him, he cannot be cast away like all the others. He's like some nameless beast who lives within me and who feeds upon my entrails, who's turned all that remained for me, the long, black as pitch, solitary path of my life, into a posthumous existence in a gray and cheerless world, an upside-down world which I'd never dreamed existed, in which I live and breathe not deeply anymore, for there's no point in breathing deeply anymore.

This world is airless and contains nothing of interest, although there's still the quite occasional, I guess it's hard to think of what - perhaps the sweetly fragrant smell of purple lilacs? Perhaps a mother doe and her fawn? Perhaps some tune a bit less insipid than most of the others I've coughed up over the years? Although they are so rare, the very good ones - so very rare, so sadly rare. Perhaps a thought, a book, a smile? But no, it's over. It was over on the morning when I found her, and the world in its entirety became that ice-cold, pale-blue body, and has been that, and only that, ever since.

Then there is me, this or that momentary self, this shuffled deck of cards which I try to put in order, or pretend exhibit some sort of order, but which perforce spill out of my hands, for I am nothing but a zombie whose appendages are frostbitten, who drags his frozen limbs beside this river which is always to his right. I make a point of making sure that this is so, I'm not sure why, perhaps because if I'm to be grabbed by some strong arm which is protruding from the river, an arm that's mine, or once was mine... Well, in that case I know my right arm's somewhat stronger! There'd be some chance I could escape the grip of memories hellbent on pulling themselves out of the oblivion in which they find themselves.

But this is all so very silly. It is not real! He's like the moon, that little boy. As am I, as well. Like the moon, which has no fire of its own, emits no light, for its light is borrowed from the sun, which is soon to swallow up the earth and which shall eventually die. The moon's a dead thing, as am I, and as are they, all of those selves in shattered mirrors, stumbling blindly by this river where the countless me's are pulled beneath its surface by those creatures in the folktales who appear sometimes as sirens, but who are in fact demonic, and whose business is to drown you.

But there is one whom I wish they'd belch up from their depths. Not hard to guess who that might be! So I'd suppose, at any rate, if you've been reading, which you haven't.

It is my mother, that filthy bitch. Please spit her out upon the banks of this black river.

For there are other things which seem to live eternally, to persist forever. There is grief and there is hate - otherwise just this shuffled deck of selves who are submerged beneath these waters, beneath the ground, in vaults of memory.

But if you'd be so kind as to cough up for a moment that vile hag? So I could slit her throat and spit into her face, then wrench her head off from off its body? Medusa she was not! (Though she'd ambitions.) I'll kick it quite as far as I can manage, past the croaking frogs in search of mates, to the depths of the inferno, to that frozen lake where sinners are encased in sheets of ice and pissed upon by little boys who've now grown strong and who seek vengeance. At least this one, who is walking by the river in this upside-down, disgusting world of madness, and of filth, and of all those little blonde girls upon whose altars I have ripped my very heart out from my chest, and gently offered it as sacrifice - as a prayer, and as a gift, to be taken freely, or in barter, or however they might accept it.

But they never did. Not a one did. Although lies of every sort were told, and promises were given of both rescue and protection. And the worst lies? Those of love. That two-bit whore whose filthy mouth spills vile poison and whose cunt is overrun with fetid sores and foul pollutions which they'd taken care to hide. But what of them? They didn't matter then or now - their throats need not be slit. There need be no reprisals, for the truth is they're as dead as all the selves that once were me, for the dead are no more dead than are the women who still live, but who are not who they once were, and, hence, need trouble me no more.

It's just a slideshow, or a sideshow - nothing more, a parlor game. I'll laugh it off, I'm sure of that, at least eventually. It has finally ceased to rain, the sun is shining. I no longer hear their shrieks, if I heard them in the first place. That's a question I can't answer, and with which I need not bother.

I am hungry! That is all those growls and gurgles signified.

It's all so silly, so embarrassingly insipid, all this pointless ruminating. It's not worth a second thought. For I have learned, perhaps the only thing I've learned, is that the horrors of one moment are as nothing in the next, as are its sights and sounds and thoughts and melodies. One's heart can't catch them, nor one's ears or eyes retrieve them. They have bubbled up from deep within us to reveal themselves as what? A belch, at which we chuckle. Let them sing their wretched one last song now they're about to drown.

XXIII.

"And in this desperate circle in which I find myself..."

And in this desperate circle in which I find myself, alone, it's not myself I find at all. It's just a cubicle that's silent, that is true. And yet these voices in my head make of this place a pinball game that's full of echoes - I am a God here! And that is true as well. But I'm a Gnostic sort of god, a demiurge that seeks destruction. I am a bad god who rejoices in my evil, and yet I take it out on no one - just myself, and in my mind, and in my sleep, and in my fantasies of vengeance, which are cruel beyond imagining, and when examined, on reflection, cause a violent wish to puke, which has happened on occasion, when I've swallowed my own vomit in disgust at my own wishes.

But what is more, it's all the others - it is they that are so frightfully atrocious that the thought of being near them, much less being forced to listen to the drivel which they foist upon their company of listeners who can find no place to which they can retreat except for vats all full of arsenic and hydrochloric acid which then boil in their entrails, ending up as thoughts of murder of which they ought to disabuse themselves, not relish - yet they do! There's very little that can give them near the pleasure that the fantasy of ripping all those cretins quite apart does, if not with words then with utensils they have sharpened in their kitchens, while they cooked up lethal dinners to be served to all the morons whom they're forced to tolerate - but not for long!

For they retreat into their cubicles of silence and are deafened by their longing and their lifelong disappointments and betrayals which have made of them these mangled and exhausted things who find their only solace in their cubicles of silence. I'm in mine now, where are you?! I'm only asking to be polite, for the truth is I don't give a tinker's damn about you, and wouldn't care if you were crushed upon some train track and were left a paraplegic, just so long as there remained no chance I'd end up in some room in which you happened to be staying, holding forth, as is your custom, on a multitude of subjects, concerning which you've not a shred of information, you pompous blowhard - can you please just have a stroke? We'd all be much obliged! We would applaud! And then we'd stuff you in the fireplace and turn your bloated corpse to ash, while we roasted sweet potatoes and discussed the final volume of Remembrance of Things Past, which was authored by a man whose mind was quite as diseased as yours, but that's a very different story, and he isn't here at present, being dead these many years, and, heaven help us, we are not the sorts of folks who roam about in deepest night, and who rob graves outside of Paris, not to mention all his bones have not a shred of flesh upon them - hardly suitable for roasting sweet potatoes, which, as you know, is our intention.

Have you died yet? That's the main thing! Please don't tarry, we've got lots and lots to do. And, by the way, and speaking only for myself: I'm not the least bit fond of yams.

The main thing that's worth noting is that my life's completely miserable. There are several rooms inside my head worth visiting, sometimes for hours, sometimes for days, but nonetheless, there's this appalling isolation which I cannot drive away, for to do so would require me to not become impatient with how purely idiotic I find all I see and hear and, God forbid, all to whom I'm forced to listen - there's nothing for it but to run back to my cubicle, a sort of Führerbunker, which, luckily for me, contains no Joe or Magda Goebbels, or their snot-nosed little brats - no Eva either, though a dumb, adoring blonde might be rather helpful in my case. But, good heavens! Not one who's dumber than a Bratwurst!

Thank goodness cubicles akin to the one in which I find myself now come equipped with links to porn sites, so I used to think at one time, but these days I find them all so very boring, so pathetic, that I can't be even bothered, it's just my godforsaken cock, for goodness sake, and what of that? Or, rather, what to make of him? Don't I have better things to do than look at pigs with tits of silicone and brains made out of jello, high on coke, and, as a rule, all headed straight for early death?

How much better to play music for the virginal upon the piano, though it's entirely inappropriate. Honestly? It's awful! Completely wrong, but I don't care. What I really care about is coughing up some new idea, but it's been ages since I've done so - I'm all spent, there's nothing left, there's nothing for it, the situation of my spirit quite resembles the condition of my cock. I am that tattered coat which sits upon a frame which sports a tattered stick which has no function anymore, is just a nuisance, more or less like I am - this self that watches from behind my eyes, the one those greasy swamis with their orange duds assert is what I am - that self, that watcher, who's revolted by that other self as much as by my cock, which are both impotent appendages, needless to say.

But what about my bladder and my prostate? Though the latter's good for nothing as of late. In fact they're both just weird accretions to a house of bones that's crumbling - the prostate an appendage that's quite certain that its singing and its clapping days are over. The best it does these days is grimace, and to wish it could at last escape the body, leave all the bones on which it hangs in a heap upon some sidewalk where some poorly paid custodian might come and sweep them up, if he's not crumbled into dust before he does so, which is a reasonable hypothesis, though quite beside the point, at least for now.

For if the prayer this stinking soul now utters finds its way up to some heaven, which is foolish, there's no heaven, to some bastard of a god who's feeling generous, that's more plausible, methinks - perhaps he'll yank me through some tunnel for a pleasant game of blackjack with some geriatric players like myself. I just hope he's taken care to make quite sure they're not as stupid as the average set of kvetchy, grizzled, half-demented geezers one encounters as a rule.

No, this won't do! The thing is - I must disappear as if I'd never been, that's what I've always begged for, and it's what I yearn for now. I only need to happen on some calling card of this or that exhausted demiurge who at the moment hasn't anything to do, and would be willing then to grant me the oblivion I seek, the one I've sought since long ago. That thing! That monster! Who has me popped out of nothing into a world I never thought could be this awful. But - alas! Such is my fate, and the only things that seem to still remain to me consist of all these prayers to minor gods I am quite sure do not exist, so barring that, I may break down on sleepless nights and turn to Pornhub or to Gibbons or to Byrd - perhaps I'll hear tell of some book of which it's been said might offer me some pleasant sort of explosion in my brain, which is so famished, which is dying of starvation, truth to tell.

Unlike my cock, which is purely atavistic at this late date, purely vestigial, more or less a thing of horror which reminds me that now and then I need pay it attention, or I'll die of my insomnia in my cubicle where at least I am assured that I'll be safe, but safe for what? For more of this? This is godawful!

Perhaps I ought now take a walk, but that won't do! For when I walk there may be people. Oh, the horror! What is worse than other people! Which serves then to remind me how depressed I'd always be just after fucking, how I'd want to die, or, barring that, to murder the repulsive piece of meat which was then lying by my side, spouting lies, gushing promises, professing bullshit, full of sweat, and foully reeking - and that voice! Dear God, that voice! Hell is the cackle of the woman you've just fucked, the only honesty's in solitude, nothing else is bearable, for the moment there's someone else, some other person, one then falls right through the earth into a pit of fire and brimstone and of monumental boredom and the threat that all this filth might be eternal, that there neither will nor can be any exit. And that any sweetness in one's nerves or in one's joints needs must be followed by a pain so huge and vast that it's as if one is a cavern, nay, a canyon! Full of hydrothermal poisons on which one's gagging, in which I'm gagging! There are no windows in this room! This cubicle which I have fashioned out of hatred, lust, and sadness has no windows, and it's shrinking now, how could I not have noticed - it is shrinking! I've not long, what can I do?

They say a man's last thoughts are great, that they're profound, but that's absurd, all I'm aware of is the violent need to shit and how I wish that I had said more vicious words to that fishwife with whom I spent the latter half of my existence. It should be she who's being squashed, like the dogshit that I stepped in on the way to this apartment. It's too late, she's probably busy reading chick-lit, watching rom-coms, while eating chocolate.

Had I simply thought to tell her what she was? What she had done? Or, better still, to slit her throat? Then I would welcome, I'd congratulate these walls about to squash me, I would fall upon my knees and genuflect in acts of homage, I'd express my gratitude in countless sonnets, well, perhaps there'd be no time for countless sonnets, but a few! There is no question I could generate a few, it's not hard to write a bad one, surely walls are not good critics, they'd be grateful for the effort, it's the thought that really counts, that is a given.

It's somewhat hard to breathe at present, hence might be a challenge to recite them - nonetheless this is a good thing! I've always wanted nothing more from life than being able to create a fresh, newfangled thing of one sort or another. These are strange thoughts to be having in my last "most cherished moments", which have never, ever been the least bit treasured, not a one - so why start now?

Oh dear, this hurts! Will I be nothing but a postage-stamp-sized bit of former flesh? The molecules of which will now be smashed together, be made nothing, with no space for their reflection in some mirror which I'm glad I do not have, for it would show me as I am?

Is that a cricket? I think it is! And it seems to me a healthy little bugger, and quite friendly! Well, so much then for all the fools who say we're doomed to die alone.

XXIV.

"The thing that's really me, that is within me..."

To be rapidly and rhythmically read aloud - "swung", if you will, in the manner of an accomplished jazz musician

The thing that's really me, that is within me, that which came before I was this pitiful and broken human being is more important than the nonsense that's accrued to me like barnacles, like names and traits and habits which I carry like an albatross which feeds upon my viscera, which steers me this way that way through this life I never wanted, and which hides from me what's far more fundamental, indescribable, microbial, molecular - all of which has naught to do with what I see before me and which I've been taught I am - this freckled thing with dandruff and a bladder full of piss, who had been told there was a place for him at table, where the fare the mother served had been extracted from his bowels, and where the milk, when it was spilled, caused violent scenes involving carving knifes and words which were far sharper than those knives and which eviscerated hearts and lungs and hopes and dreams through countless plates and services, and courses not in miracles, but curses quite empirically demonstrable, observable, and of which hell is full - which roll through vague casinos where the yes men tell their women, who know precisely what is kneaded in their undistinguished pantries (not to mention all their lacerated panties) and who also wear these ripped black nylon stockings full of candies which before they are excreted will be greeted by the microbes which will grope them in a wild, demented frenzy.

Yet there's this sense he hadn't wanted this to happen - it was a happen-circumstance then taken for the truth was he'd been shaken and not stirred to gird his loins in quite the way they probably ought have been, for this was not to be an ordinary circumcision! for the decision then was made for the incision to include a full castration to be followed by a well-thought-out and quite prolonged damnation which contained the names and traits and habits nailed to a cross fit for a drawn-out crucifixion on that table on which soured milk was curdling as the throats of all the guests who had been stapled to their armchairs were now gurgling snowy alpine cataracts which made the eyes of all those persons who were seated quite opaque - which is something one can't fake out of their minds or of the asses of the lasses which were all now being buggered by their lovers whom they hated and degraded with their words and lips and eyes which still could see in spite of clouds and feathered canyons everywhere, which were a hair's breadth from their dreams and schemes and bones, which had been broken by the host who, though unleavened, was now living in a consecrated crack house which his family found degrading on a curved ball made of wax which always dripped so from his ears - so full of braggadocio and all so terribly crapacious yet quite spacious but not quite large enough for families such as this one which had made of all its children serving spoons made out of lead by ears attuned to what was then in fashion and was rationed by the culture into probiotic yogurt which was somewhat tasty, that was true, but since it had ingredients that harkened back to ancient

Greece, when little boys were forced to eat it they would look about with vigilance and fear of being buggered by philosophers who belched then spoke of love at some symposium where they supposed, quite rightly, that their rosy pinkish buttocks were quite soon to be impaled by the cocks of windbag geezers whom we find ourselves still reading for some reason, weeding through another dialogue or garden where the grass is being choked by kids engaged in what they call the blackout challenge - either stroking cocks or sneaking out of doors which were all left wide open and through which their evil mothers cart their bags of groceries to a table where the children sit in silence stunned by guns which are embedded in the food which they are fed and in the words which are then said and through which they all lightly tread, taking care lest carelessness could make for more than should be uttered, which might result in an assault or battery being inserted up their anus by their crazed sadistic mother who's besotted and beside herself - there's no one else but her! Only she can give direction to this nightmare! hire the actors, tell the cameraman to roll his belly fat into a lump of ashen charcoal which will fire up the barbecue upon which all her children will be roasted to a crisp, perhaps laconic bits of bacon, who's to say?

France is sure to send its troops - one might very well assume they'll then erect a sea of scaffolds, upon which they'll then throw the children who'll be hanged if they've been nice, yet if were naughty be beheaded towards a future in which children are not seated at such tables but are able to escape and to reshape the broken promises and limbs into a plausible facsimile of families not composed of scowling demons wielding pitchforks knives and spoons made out of wood with which they're beaten boiled fried and often poached upon some porch on which their genitals are scorched as they are hoisted on a pole and lit as torches to illuminate the concert of some emperor laying eggs in the antarctic, a gigantic pear-shaped oval which she then rolls to her mate who sits upon them while she takes off on vacation, galavanting on some beach with other penguins who are every bit as whorish and depraved, and all the while those hapless husbands who are freezing to their deaths in their attempts to nurture children they don't want, and who cease to eat and wish for nothing other than a quick and speedy death.

The kind of plot which only can be hatched in all the deepest darkest recesses of women's minds when left to their devices and to their nature not their nurture. Oh, there are some that return but even those lock up their chicks inside of rooms where they demand they spend the night in utter darkness with no toilet, left with toys with which they sometimes try to while away the time when they're not peeing in some corner of the room in which they're locked for sometimes days and sometimes weeks and often lives in which they never have the chance to realize what's fundamental, indescribable, microbial, molecular - that thing, that thing they are, that thing they always were before they ever winked into existence, that they'll be again though they can't see it hear it feel it as their asses have been glued upon some egg they do not want and cannot love and which is starving them of nutrients, as all the while they watch in abject helplessness as waves of blood are poring from their entrails - for who on earth could have a sense of who they might have been when this is all they've known since they were little children?

It's impossible to miss what one has never known or could have possibly imagined - they can hope for death, that's true, that it might free them to stop thinking, to roll their eyes quite backwards and to look within in an attempt to suffocate themselves in search of some transcendent thought or vision that's entirely within them which they'd never known was there - to finally recognize the only way to live and to have pleasure is to feast upon their entrails, to dream and not to waken, and to find within themselves the raw materials on which they might now nourish all the microbes fungi plankton dying stars they'd always been but had forgotten all about, of which they'd always been deprived for they had thought by living less perhaps they'd not offend the gods or not be noticed quite so much, escape a beating or some dressing down to hell in which surrender was required when the workers were about, although they'd sometimes pick a fight with one another, even slink out of the pit in which they'd long been held as hostage to some circle further down the road where punishments were somewhat less is more than they or anyone could bear.

You just want anonymity! To be nothing they can find at any rate at which one taxes one's ability to find some opportunity to fade and to dissolve into obscurity and shade from scorching suns and words and daughters led to slaughter in arenas lit by torches which themselves are flaming corpses stuffed with waxen figures skating triple and quadruple jumps and axels on the chassis of some stripper who is dancing on the laps of Wall Street guys hyped-up on coke, whose diet now consists of booze and seamen

and of sailors bearing razors poised to slit the throats of managers
in mangers, now the food for famished cattle-calling distances, all
of which have been so very shortened for so long.

Thanks for the fish that smells like pussy, or does pussy
smell like fish? and why do pussies so like fish? they're always
coming into kitchens when you've opened up some can of perhaps
salmon with those hot tin grooves, those grooves deep in the
pockets of the Wall Street guys whose cocks are being sucked in
VIP rooms of the strip clubs on ninth avenue where parvenus who
now are hedge fund managers in mangers where the Christ child is
still squawking like a pig who has been flayed alive and strung up
on a cross like some poor veal calf on a meathook, just like we were
long ago when we were children at that table by that mother with
the serpents in her hair and in the air and spewing out from every
orifice, her nose her mouth her eyes her twat her ass - you must
remember! there were vipers everywhere! how we'd be bound and
then be bitten how the things would sidle up to us and stare into
our eyes from eyes which looked like blazing coals and which had
long been dead, but in which we could still sense the hunger the
agenda of this mother - all the while the bleeding bread upon the
table was dissolving as was she for we were melting all of us
engulfed in flames encased in ice and being strangled by the
serpents who were egged on by the mother who was shoving gobs
of meatloaf down our throats that's what she told us, you
remember! it was only bits of bread which she would roll into these
balls! dear God! what was that meant to be, and what exactly was it
we were meant to feel?

I am sleepy and my fingers which are freckled just remind me that I'm still this sort of person or at least that's what they say, but it's not true, I'm something other - something heavenly, primordial, eternal! which survived that fetid feast! it always was it always will be naught to do with what I see extending outwards from this torso inside of which there's something other which no mother can destroy - it always was and always will be, quite unlike that vile bitch who's been dead these twenty years and upon whose grave I'd spit and piss if I'd the means to find it, but I don't - but that's no matter.

What's to come I do not know, only that there is a thing that is within me and that's precious and will slog and sputter on for maybe days or perhaps weeks or even years without regrets or guilt or meaning what I've just been busy saying which is nothing as it should be as it is and as I've finally come to know it and accept it and embrace it and go gentle into what's to come, which doubtless shall be very bad, of that both I and you can be quite sure, there is no question that what's coming will be awful, it's bad now, and shall only get far worse, but what the hell - when one is thrown into a world which is this stupid, this ridiculous, there's nothing for it other than to shrug one's shoulders, laugh it off, and then go on.

XXV.

Beyond the cork-lined room,
and the Proustian illusion of timelessness

As I once again extended my hands through that room, through clouds, vapors, steam, fog, and threads of sweaters I wore as a boy, as I felt again the warm nubby texture of my flannel shirt, the particularly lovely one that I so treasured, the deep-blue, plaid one, suddenly there was, again, vividly before me, my social studies teacher at the blackboard, Mister Shelland, the one of whom it was said that he had suffered, and continued to suffer, from the symptoms of shell shock - that Mister Shelland in whose class, I, being the obnoxious little prick I was, had dropped a large textbook on to the floor from a height sufficient to enable both me and my classmates to learn if indeed the rumor were true. The poor man's legs rose before me once again, seemingly carried, by an unseen force, quite off the ground. They shook, violently. He then began to stare at me with a gaze I had not seen since I had held that little turtle in my hands as a boy, and, with a great deal of curiosity and not a little touch of sadism, poked its head, not meaning to seriously harm him, and most certainly not meaning to kill him, but very definitely to annoy him, to learn about his inner life and responses with sadly little regard for his feelings. And now here was that gaze again, fastened upon me with that very same rage, and, being whatever age I was, perhaps fourteen years old, I was still very much that obnoxious, little, turtle-torturing boy, now become his hopelessly obnoxious, adolescent descendant.

I recall a bit of shame and regret, though not all that much. Had I carried out that little experiment this morning, at this point in my life, I imagine I might very well intentionally drive my car into a concrete trestle later this afternoon. Who was that little boy? Where did he go? I don't miss him in the least. He was a monstrous little shit. I should feel pity for him, for he was constantly beaten, wished dead, and suffered a thousand other existential insults, and all those on a very regular basis. But I do not. I haven't the slightest bit of empathy for him. If he is my "inner child", I want him once again promptly and savagely whipped and beaten, with belts, drawers, fists - all the more and all the harder. The little fuck. It was almost certainly a very good thing that my child was not born a boy. I remember worrying myself sick that the future little crotch turd my abominable second wife was ferrying about within her would be a boy, and that I'd involuntarily become his abuser. This terror came upon me one afternoon midway through her pregnancy, after observing my reaction to some little piece-of-shit kid on a park playground, some snot-nosed brat, scurrying about, pretending a tree branch was a sort of gun, or, more likely, that it was his dimly-hoped-for, gigantic future penis. I wanted to swat that kid so very badly, and hence assumed and feared I would do precisely that, were my child to be a boy. As had been done countless times to me, when I was a boy.

Thankfully the crotch turd emerged female, which made it ever so much easier, even intermittently delightful for a good number of years. Until, say, twelve? Fourteen? At which time, sadly, from that lovely little feminine chrysalis there emerged no butterfly, but rather a vile, winged harpy with razor-sharp fangs, a dreadful, loathsome creature, whom I, to this day, have a terrible time acknowledging had sprung, at least in part, from my loins. But that is another story, for another time, or, better, for a time which shall never occur, at least not as a result of my once again telling the squalid tale. I leave that for another, better writer of horror. It, and she, are far too inconsequential. And who was that man on the playground? The one that so wished to smack that little brat? Or who took such delight in so many of his daughter's achievements? Her birthday parties, the "family's" trips here, there, to parks, malls, the houses of relatives, friends, and lakeside cottages? Not me, surely. I cannot touch him, find him, be him. Nor do I wish to. I can still see him, through countless mists, and buried deep in smoke, ash, cinders, and, above all, stupefied bewilderment. But that he is I? That there is a sort of Platonic realm, some timeless realm, in which he and I are one? Some block universe whose praises I ought sing now? A ridiculous assertion. And if it isn't quite as preposterous as it seems to me, it might as well be, for it is a "truth" to which I have now, and will never in future have, the slightest meaningful access.

I have had my Proustian Madeleine moments, indeed I have. Were I to walk into a room at this moment, and were it to smell of stale cigarettes and mothballs, it would be more than likely that the image of my kind, at times cranky, yet always utterly adorable Nana would rise before me like a goddess, and fill my heart with joy and love. And perhaps, for that moment, but it would indeed only be a moment, I would be that boy in her kitchen in Providence, much loved by her, or so it felt to me at the time, and so I would like now to believe.

But to claim that in such moments I had ascended to some enduring boundless world in which time has no meaning, nay, death has no meaning? That is an assertion weak-minded people make in an attempt to soothe themselves. That, and nothing more. There is not a shred of evidence for it, nor, granted, is there any evidence against it. But it is only a fable.

Yet would that I could embrace it! It would make navigating through what shall surely be the shitshow of my remaining years somewhat more tolerable. I could look upon old age, illness, and death with the grace of God knows whom. In point of fact, I've never met such an evolved person, such a God-knows-whom, and doubt very much that I ever shall. I hardly consider Marcel Proust to be one of these mythical beings, even after reading all his gorgeous, flowery, self-soothing assertions to the contrary. Every person I've ever known who has found themselves a few paces from the grave has been more than a little miserable, terrified, disappointed, disillusioned, and, needlessly to say, stupendously depressed - just as I will most surely be! Of that there seems little question.

When I've my wits about me, which is most of the time, I find all this a laughably kitschy little fairy tale, worthy only of contempt, as is anyone who professes it. Those who do are inevitably the sorts of fools who wish to convince you that we are "spiritual beings", "spiritual beings" on a "journey", that we've chosen this particular incarnation because we saw quite clearly that it was the one in which we could most "learn" and "grow". As if the universe were a kind of poorly-funded Buttfuck, Arkansas public school, writ large. These are the sorts of persons I would love to slap silly every bit as much as I did that little fuck running about the playground with his imaginary machine gun and much-hoped-for, future, gargantuan cock, which he had sculpted and idealized from a bit of tree branch.

And then there is the claim, of Proust and others, that through "art" we can reach this timeless realm. Not only that we can, but that it is, obviously, the only way in which we can do so. Let's pause for a moment. Who is it that is most likely to make this claim? Well, that's more than a little easy to answer, is it not? The self-described "artist"! Big surprise there! He who is not a whit more or less grandiose and narcissistic than the self-described landscaper or plumber whose "timeless realms", one imagines, consist of eternal dreamscapes containing numberless, transparently ethereal bags of organic fertilizer, heavens full to bursting with toilet plungers, water heaters, and drainpipes. In either case, a world of angels in which no one pisses or shits. Am I any less guilty than any of these imbeciles?

Am I any less the star of my own idiotic soap opera? Surely not. I'm probably the worst of the lot at the end of the day.

I occasionally feel these Proust-like ripples. I am something of a two bit poet, I have something of a soul. I hear the music in the claim. I do. And I am touched by it at times. At other times, I am revolted by the painfully obvious ways in which those that embrace and prattle on about it reveal themselves as cowards simply attempting to comfort themselves, to prop themselves up in the most unseemly and craven of fashions. If indeed there is this "transcendent realm", about which all these fucktards so constantly crow, one assumes that every last shit I've taken, every idiotic thing that has ever come spewing out of my mouth, in other words, the substance of very close to the entire, disgustingly mundane and awful timbre of my life would analogously occupy very near to the entirety of this hypothetical, abstract, timeless "film", as it were, of my life. And that it all sits in some tin can, in the projection room of whichever demonic Gnostic god it is that manages the theater, that theater being the whole of time and space, the entirety of the universe. Thus, it's not just my beloved Nana sitting at her kitchen table in some high-end, believable virtual reality that would caressingly envelop me, whom I would find upon entering this supposedly enchanting, timeless realm, it would be, rather, the entire nauseating fabric of my life, a life which should never have been, a life which I have wished, from its very beginning, to have never occurred. That the tin can would never so much as have arrived in the projection room.

And so, what is the ACTUAL takeaway from all these ravings, these absurdly infantile folk tales that these nincompoops so constantly tell themselves? Simply this: that there is a timeless world of very close to comprehensive and total banality, venality, vanity, moral rot, evil, physical decay, betrayal, pain, and boredom - that the vast majority of one's life, if not all of it, has been and will for all eternity be nothing other than galaxy upon galaxy of unspeakable frozen horror. Granted, perhaps containing the very occasional, good-natured comet or meteorite, bearing some small whiff of inspiration, some legitimate pleasure. Surely I can concede that, and still be legitimately appalled. I simply ask of anyone who professes to be the least bit honest with themselves to place the positive and negative contents of that tin can, of the totality of their life, its joys and sufferings both, on opposing sides of a cosmic balance scale, and to then observe the behavior of its pans, beams, and pointers. And that they take care to do it quickly! Prior to the side which bears all the physical, spiritual, and moral refuse and filth which constituted the vast majority of their life collapsing into and upon itself, and becoming that primordial black hole in which is contained the shit-engulfed world in which we all unwillingly trudge onwards, whipped mercilessly from behind through our weary lives and to our doom. In which those extraordinarily rare, momentarily revelatory comets rifle, for a few moments, through a wildly accelerating cloud of gas, and are then stretched, ripped apart, and swallowed. They are nothing, not even a speck in the eye of Polyphemus. Nothing.

There are to be no luminous, numinous reconciliations or reunions, no coming together of the tens of thousands of selves we have all cast off, unaware that we have done so. And of which we continue to be unaware.

So - recite this fairy tale to yourself if it helps you drift into a temporarily soothing slumber! I don't in the least begrudge you that. It's the fable Marcel Proust told himself. He was a genius, and I am anything but. And yet, being perhaps two percent more clever than the average slob, I can recognize that even this stupendous genius was nourishing himself, in the face of death, on fairy dust. So - do not dare to profess such things to me, unless you can dress them up in prose as ravishing as Proust's! Do not assert them in my presence, nor have the wish that I take them seriously, as revealing anything at all about this nightmare into which we've all been thrown, without our ever having or having been asked. That is to say, as revealing anything other than your own, soul-crushing, existential terror. You are nothing but a two-bit charwoman, indulging in a vain attempt to sanitize the bottomless cesspit which is your existence. And, as you scrub, scrub, scrub, you play to yourself, through your dearly purchased, noise-cancelling headphones, the most vapid and jejune of musics. Spare me its impoverished harmonies.

I, too, when I am able, attempt to siphon the endless bags of manure hanging from my shoulders like so many voracious birds of prey, as I slog through my days. I, too, attempt to draw them through some fine straw of my own invention, or so I like to tell myself, into the temporary shape of perhaps a lily, a precious jewel, a beautiful woman's smile or teardrop. The difference being this: I know I'm lying. I accept that I'm lying.

Lies have their place! They MORE than have their place. They are the most wondrous of things. Without them we would drop to the ground like flies after a single breath, a single step. I eagerly and happily embrace lies and lying. I embrace anything which hides from me, if only for a few moments, the abhorrent nature of the world. And there is nothing better than a good lie to achieve that result!

But I have spent far too much time on this, on you, and on your weak-minded drivel. You are all too much the low-hanging fruit, and, I might add, a very far from pleasant tasting one. Rather, you resemble far more a sort of brown banana or bitter melon, a foul thing from which one ought rather simply turn away and flee.

Do I look in the mirror, smile a deceitful, hideous Dorian Gray smile, and tell myself I have in some sense "transfigured" all these countless bags of shit through my lies and diversions? I do not! Not for a moment! I am hopelessly vain, and horridly narcissistic, but I do stop short of making any claim quite as ludicrous as that one. I do, nonetheless, give myself a pass for momentarily indulging in them. No one can survive ten minutes without an infinity of falsehoods and self-delusions. The world is a pig sty, and I am in pain. They soothe me. Case closed. That hardly makes me a monster. Nor do they make you one. In your case, however, it makes you, in addition, into an idiot.

And yet, we are all idiots and monsters, I as much as you, as much as anyone.

If a bunch of wandering carbon atoms are forced to become a diamond, is the universe thus enriched? For me it is, but only for that moment. To create some tiny bit of beauty, to devise a confession of some sort - to tidy it up, to make it sing, glow, stare up at the sky from the gutter - to make of one's rage, grief, or humiliation an idea - that is no small thing! For the maker, that is. It enables him, that him being me in this case, to keep moving, breathing, shoving this or that bit of food down his gullet. What does it do for others? Very little. More likely? Not a thing. If it does do something for them, it is only their affair, and has naught to do with me. They could have done the very same with a bit of drivel in a magazine, with this or that weed in their garden which they'd inspected particularly closely, with a mango, or with a remark from a stranger which touches or enrages them. It's their world, and theirs only, as utterly inaccessible to me as is mine to them.

These things arise only out of pain, boredom, envy, curiosity, and wounded pride. One seeks to impress, to enchant, to wound. That's the first impulse, a very natural one. And it is as far as most folks get, can get. To make something else out of all that though, that's the trick! To turn it into an idea! Don't misunderstand! The goal I just described remains every bit as much the perfect fool's errand, the purest bullshit. Yet one can soothe oneself in so doing in a way that, it appears to me at any rate, is quite a bit less unseemly than the ignorant assertions and fables of "timeless realms" and "spiritual beings on journeys" described above. Yes, I am quite as full of shit as those who profess such things! Full of vanity and snobbery and jealousy and grandiosity, there's no denying it - nor do I wish to! And yet, I think, at the same time, that I am somehow marginally less laughable than them. Less loathsome, less ridiculous than them. Why? Because I've seen through the joke, I've heard and understood its punchline.

But then again, you think the very same. Which leads us where, precisely? To what conclusion? That we're both simply trying to survive. I tell myself that I'm wearing somewhat better duds than you while doing it, that I'm sporting some dapper, stylish tuxedo while you're staggering around in a white-trash flannel shirt and work boots, but that's just another lie. Nothing can or does absolve either one of us for being the despicably vain morons the two of us are, or, more accurately, the nine billion of us are.

What we do is absolutely necessary if we wish to survive. Necessary, yet nonetheless, awful. Were I a sculptor, I would not, for a moment, tell myself that my trivial, pint-sized David was not born of mud, and is not sitting in it right now, not actively engulfed in it.

When I am lazy of mind, self-serving, and vain, I tell myself I've found a sort of sacred frequency in my disgust, in this life of mine. That I've made something lovely, or turned a bit of malice into an artistically rendered "idea", but that's all self-serving nonsense. And while I know that perfectly well, I still find that I continue to soothe myself with the notion - I cannot help myself! To put one foot in front of another, even for a fraction of a second, requires lie after lie after lie, endless suspensions of disbelief. One becomes a veritable walking suspension of disbelief. We all ought wear the t-shirt or hat making it plain to everyone we meet!

I'm redeemed by this sort of bullshit for, on a good day, ten minutes. Redeemed, as in "saved". "Saved" as in, perhaps, not blowing my fucking brains out for the next half-hour. My pain has been forced to do tricks! To dance, to walk through hot coals, and not to simply live rent-free in my head. Those things are true, for the moment. And that is an achievement some grandiose blockhead might refer to as "redemption". Especially if that blockhead is the worst and most loathsome sort of pretentious twat.

You can't go on, yet you go on. Not a new thought, of that I am well aware. Looking at the sky for a moment hardly removes one from the gutter, for the clouds above are streaked too with its filth. But you are able to catch a glimpse of that cloud for a few moments, shit-stained though it is. You briefly smell a lilac in the midst of the overpowering stench of dung in which it grows, which is everywhere, and not least within you. You have by no means "transcended" your miserable, hopelessly corporeal state, but, for a moment, you are lighter. You have taken the most delightful of craps. There is a momentary bounce in your step. It is quite marvelous, until it is not, which will be all too soon.

To expel, to evacuate, is to grab hold of a bit of relief, if only for a moment. And it shall only ever be for not more than a moment, perhaps an hour, even a day. And that's as good as it shall ever get. An acceptable day, one somewhat less engulfed with the usual suffering, good enough to consent to continue one's part in the obscenely perverse comedy which is the world. An absurd moment of grace. Not one I would care to call "amazing", but grace, nonetheless. The burden is temporarily less. The constant stench, for a moment, a bit less appalling. Your hands are a bit less full of mud, of shit. There's a bit less toilet paper hanging out of your ass, that sort of thing, the sort of thing which most often passes for "happiness". With no self-pity, or, at the very least, a minimum.

You take the horror, the loss, the malice, the waste, and the absurdity, and, although you know that a moment later it will all return with redoubled force to convince you the world is the shitshow you've always known it to be, and that the arbiters of eternal punishment are still busy sharpening their knives, as proofs of the futility of absolutely everything - for that moment, that one divine moment, perhaps two, even three divine moments, you will have spun something delicate, graceful, and momentarily beautiful into the web of awfulness, and it will take its place there, if only for an instant.

And that is something! No forgiveness, absolution, or cleansing. Just seeing, making, and creating form, a thing that does not and cannot hurt you, and that does not wish to hurt you. A fleck of light in an underground cavern, the one you're still in, that you've always been in, and in which you will die. From which you've emerged and to which you shall return, yet, in which, for a few moments, you have managed to feel alive, and be glad of it.

This is not some "eternity in a grain of sand" bit of horseshit. No! Unless that eternity is the cosmic weave, which is composed almost entirely of spun threads of fecal matter, that "dark matter" all too rarely remarked upon. The gift the universe occasionally provides is this: for a moment, for an hour, you are not neck deep in garbage trying to not simply choke to death.

You can do it with a tune, a poem, a joke, a tender word. Do it whenever and however you are allowed.

And, by the way, you cannot "choose" to do it. It will simply come upon you, arrive now and then. Don't snuff it out, that's all. Don't turn away. Allow it to pass through you and out of you into the larger world.

For a moment then, you, and if you have an auditor or reader who pretends to themselves or to you that they understand you, which is, needless to say, utterly absurd, but no matter, you will both be momentarily alive, that is to say, not swallowed, macerated, or flayed alive. In that moment, and in that moment only. You haven't connected in the way either of you might like, or imagine is possible, that's a given. But even this, just this, is quite a bit better than nothing. It is a distraction, and only a distraction, as is absolutely everything which isn't entirely godawful, but it is a distraction of a somewhat more noble kind.

You are alive, if only for an eye blink. Oh, you were alive the moment before, when you were gagging on arsenic-laced croissants and knee-deep in shit, yes, you were alive then as well. But you are now somehow lighter. For a moment.

Someone might feel a vibration from all this narcissistic archaeology you've busied yourself with, but it will be their vibration, and theirs only, having naught or very little to do with the one which has passed through you. You will, ultimately, have shared not a damned thing of any significance with them, not really - there can never be any actual connection or fusion between you both. The gulf is vast, bottomless, and unbridgeable.

You don't do any of this for them! Oh no! Most certainly not! For their needs and desires shall be served, if not by your dogshit, then by the dogshit of another, or by a bit of moonlight, a tunafish sandwich, whatever it might be. You have no obligations, and you are to have absolutely no expectations or wishes either involving them or in that regard. You have, perhaps, provided some tremor, some resonance with which they feel momentarily in sympathy, but the only cavern in which that echo matters or has meaning is your own, the hall of endless mirrors which is your life.

Look out your window at the shit-stained clouds. It's a sunny day! Do you not see a fleck of light there, drenched in shit as well, that is true, but nonetheless, a fleck of light? That fleck of light is within you, presently dissolving in the pools of hydrochloric acid in your guts, that is true, but still lighting up your stomach walls, if only for an instant. For the instant you manage to tell yourself this self-soothing little bit of smug, rehearsed, self-satisfying nonsense, at any rate.

XXVI.

"I thought I'd retained the ability to have a thought, or perhaps at least some feeling"

I thought I'd retained the ability to have a thought, or perhaps at least some feeling, but instead there's just this numbness. It comes upon me, it lives within me, and is, perhaps, the most authentic part of me - this deadness, this unwillingness to feel. Why is it here now? What does it want? It is clearly frightened. It is intent on feeling nothing and giving nothing, on being dead. Yes, literally, dead.

There was that teacher, that meditation teacher, all those years ago, whose fondest wish for sentient beings was that they "be dead while alive". I still recall him, decades later - his poisonous advice, the flatness of his affect, and that unnerving deadness in his eyes. At the time, I thought it wisdom, for I was falling very fast into a nightmare from which I have never emerged.

I'd hoped, up until today's bombardment, that it might now be different, that I'd manage not to suffer all that much anymore, that the beast who lives inside, within me, which stays silent for a time - for a week, sometimes a month, sometimes even years - that I'd somehow finally escaped him. But here he is, in all his beastly ghastliness. What does he want? I am terrified - suddenly the plans, the equilibrium I thought would linger for a moment are gone, and I'm behind this wall.

I'm frozen, no longer in my body, and lacking access to a single tool that might help return me to my self - the noise of the heater no longer a simple noise, but now only this menacing omen, this infernal whistling, hissing - of what is now to come, to befall me. Have I not been through enough Hells? Is there to be no grace, no peace that is ongoing? Can the old age which is upon me, which was coming but is now here - can it offer me no solace, no release from these numberless Hells?

Suddenly my limbs no longer are mine - there is no "me" to whom they might be said to belong. And this has all happened so very suddenly! The world in which I existed but an hour ago is now gone! Where am I? Who am I? It's half-familiar, like some half-forgotten nightmare. It lives within me, deep in my viscera. I have been here, or somewhere and someone very similar, before. I cannot tell either you or myself when that was, but I know it, for a fact.

Dear God, please let this pass! It was just a day or two ago when I said to myself, "Well then, at least you're not getting dissociated these days, that's a plus!" Perhaps, at this moment, I see myself as others might or even likely see me when I am as I am at this moment - as an ugly, dismissible, unpredictable, mentally diseased monster. Perhaps that is the core of what I am, and of what I've always been, my "better selves" only momentary anomalies. Surely such a thing as I would do the world and himself a favor by ending his life? By putting himself and those around him out of their misery? I simply need think of the countless times I spent innumerable hours researching the tragically few ways in which I could end my life with minimal pain, the two times I so very seriously attempted to do so, and the aftermaths of those attempts.

Dear God, they were all so awful! Nightmares beyond what I could have ever imagined! Weeks and months of involuntary incarceration and humiliation, the ever-present sensation of falling, falling, falling... Dear God, is there no bottom to the world, to my despair, to this Hell? Can one, can I sink any lower? Are there countless chambers, infinite pits of Hell, and have they all been reserved for me, and me alone?

There is not a one whom I see, to whom I speak, or who speaks to me that understands. They think and act as if I am in their world, the one in which they're speaking, the one in which they live and work, from which they even, at times, extend their hand to me, but it is not so. I have left their world, if I were ever a part of it. I have been dragged very much elsewhere, how and why I do not know, nor by whom - perhaps by myself, perhaps by some ferocious, insatiable, sadistic beast which lives within me, has always lived within me.

Surely that last is the explanation! There can be no other! But what does it want, this thing? What does it want from me, need from me, demand that I do? Is it somehow perversely trying to save me from a worse fate, or does it simply wish to torture me? Why the latter, if that is indeed the case? For what offense, pray tell? I am awful, a loathsome thing.

It's been a great deal less than an hour since this horror arose within me. Can it, could it leave, exit, evaporate just as quickly? If it were to leave, where would it go? Where has it come from? Can I address it? Plead with it? Learn what it wants? I do not believe such a thing is possible - a great deal of my sad experience attests to that.

It is not a thing to whom or with whom one can speak - it is an ugly, primal, bestial thing which wants exclusively ugly, primal, bestial things. It simply WANTS, or so it seems, so it feels to me. Yet it's foolish to attempt to imagine what it wants - it is not a thing that wants, it is a dead thing, a frozen thing - it is a set of frozen limbs emerging from a sea of ice, pulling me down, down, down, unattached to any sort of consciousness - there is only this mindless pulling, pulling, pulling...

And yet, dear God, it is me.

Am I to die today? At my age, my father had been dead almost for four years - it would hardly be a tragedy. The tragedy would only be were this horror to continue. And yet perhaps it may abate, as quickly as it appeared? That is not impossible. Exactly that has happened many, many times before.

And so I should, undoubtedly, hope for exactly that, but I am not a thing which possesses either the talent or the inclination for "hope", even in the best of circumstances. And, on top of all that, at this moment, I am nowhere, I am bleeding at the bottom of a black sea, and being gnawed upon by savage, primeval beasts.

This is all so very ironic. I had thought that I could, perhaps, write, even write something warm, alive, with a bit of depth, perhaps even full of the deepest feeling. It has happened before - why not now? But I am a dead thing now, and the fingers of this dead thing are typing from a dead, rotting, festering place - not one of "composition", rather of its opposite.

That place is not "somewhere", not some cemetery, crypt, or whatnot. That would be ever so much better! They could locate me, come to save me! "He's been buried alive! We must unearth him, resuscitate him! Surely there's someone who loves him, who wants and can manage to breathe life into him again! Who will revive him, love him! Surely someone loves him! Look in his notes, there must be some address, some phone number, a way of contacting SOMEONE who loves him, who cares for him. It is simply not possible that no one does, for there is no one whom SOMEBODY does not love!"

And yet there is. That "somebody" is me. And I am frozen, and don't even care to save myself. I suppose I might, if it were easy, and I had some idea of my location, but I have none. For I am an already dead thing. As I said. Forgive my repeating myself, I don't wish to trouble you.

I just walked through the living room. But it was not, by any means, MY living room, not the one I ordinarily walk through. It was a bizarrely different space, an eerie, menacing, cold "thing". THING. Everything has now the quality of thing-ness, or, perhaps, "thingy-ness". Take your fucking pick, you academic psychiatrists who help no one, whose insights are reliably dogshit. People are, for me now, either zombies, or these entirely unknowable, beastly creatures. I am terrified. Of this, of them, of the next moment - which might be even worse! But would that even be possible?

I am paying for a crime I must surely have committed in a former life that I don't recall. It must have been an absolutely appalling crime, an unspeakable abomination. There can be no other explanation for a punishment of this kind, one of this severity and strangeness.

There is no point in asking or expecting of myself to write each day, for I have become a chest full of pale-blue ice, that grizzled geezer who gazes back in horror from the mirror, a few unbalanced, staggering steps from his death, that THING they must all think me when they look upon me - a freak! A monster! Whose every additional day on earth is a curse, an abomination - whose death would be a blessing both for it and for the world.

I was able to give the dog her medicines, but surely it was not "I" who did so, not the "I" in whom I normally find myself, or consider myself to be - the relatively untroubled one who peers out from just above my eyes. That "I" has disappeared.

There is just this thing now, which has returned here, to the desktop computer, for some reason, and is typing again. Whose fingers now smell of the butter and cheese with which it tempted the dog into swallowing her medicines moments ago. But smelling involves a one who smells! And the drinking of coffee a drinker! But now there is only a disembodied warmth, felt by no one, an unrecognized, and perversely strange gullet through which "things", "breath", and "saliva" pass, and these "eyes" which somehow manage to look out from nowhere, upon nothing - none of which are in any communication with one another.

There is just this idiot buzzing, this thing which breathes, which has no past, is not really here, and which surely has no future, could not possibly have a future. For could it not be more obvious that a thing which is not alive can have no future?

The second hand on my watch seems still to be moving, although it is no longer "my" watch in any meaningful sense, any more than the wrist on which it sits is "my" wrist. The face of the watch is black, I'd never noticed that before. Hmm...

And now what seems the sound of a plane... Surely that is not simply the sound of a plane, there must BE a plane? Does either inhabit the same world as I? The smell, the coffee, the gullet, the disembodied fingers typing, the sound of the plane, the plane itself, presumably, all unattached to any sort of self which oversees or directs them? Where are "they", and where am "I"?

There is just this moronic typing - I see the fingers there, I see quite clearly that they're still at it. "My" fingers? No! Not "mine"! Surely they are not "mine". "Mine" has become meaningless, absurd. What could "mine" possibly mean at this moment?

They are all just things in a world of things, which I only call things and observe as things out of habit. Not "creatures" of habit, for they, and I, and anyone unfortunate enough to encounter me in this condition are, to me, only "things" of habit as well. Aha! In my agony I have invented a new term! Which will surely become utterly meaningless and evaporate if and when I return, even minimally, to my former "self".

Surely that cup full of pens would resist being moved? It's been there for it seems forever. I won't disturb it, it's likely as capable of getting angry, of feeling disturbed, ruffled, and annoyed as I am. But there is no "I"! Just these monstrous, severed Peter Lorre fingers, typing!

This is ridiculous, but not in an entertaining, or even entertainingly absurd way, rather in a desperately empty and contemptible way. I am terrified, and yet I am nowhere to be found. It is a most curious thing.

Things, yes, it's a thing, they are things, I am a thing. Were I to meet you, you would also be a thing. That's the operant word - THING. Everything has become, well - I've heard people say "thingy", it's become a sort of slang word for inarticulate folks attempting to be adorable, but it is for me now an adjective, and a quite horrifying one, for it includes absolutely EVERYTHING - the fingers typing every bit as much as the cup of pens before me, as the deadness I see in my own eyes when they stare back at me in the mirror, and in the eyes of "others".

I am no adorable hand emerging from a black box to pick up the receiver of a telephone and hand it off to Morticia Addams. No, I am now only a poisonous, radioactive, black hole of blankness and pain.

It is as if a sort of serpent has taken hold of - no, no - those are not the words, that's not what's happening - it's just that the air is made of ice, there is this coldness, this deadness everywhere - out there, within me, although there is no "me"! This "deadness", but that won't do either - it's a place where words are only sounds, as "thingy" as cups of pens and fingers.

Everything is ridiculous, perverse, and nightmarishly absurd in an ice-cold way, in the most brutal and terrifying way. Can I punch my way out? I wonder if I'm trying to do precisely that, right now, by attempting to write. "I" wonder - but that's wrong too, necessarily wrong.

And yet I see them - there are these "fingers", typing - typing nonsense, needless to say, worthless nonsense, 'tis only the vomit of a drowning man clinging to a fast-sinking raft. And yet - what was it I was thinking just before this came upon me? Oh yes, I was reading all sorts of crap I'd written about the implosion of my "family", a word which now makes more or less as much sense as "I" or "my" or "fingers".

How can inert things such as "they", the so-called "persons" in my "family", have so crushing an effect upon me? Perhaps that's the point? But now I cannot follow the thread of my thoughts. What am I trying to uncover? What thread am I trying to follow?

I am trying to unravel something which I must believe can free me from this frozen hole, this dungeon of ice beneath the earth into which I've fallen, but I cannot see it, or, if I did, I've now lost it. There is no thread, perhaps there never was, perhaps I'd only imagined it. In any event, the thought is gone, the hope is gone, and time itself has now become "thingy". I am presently in quite the jumble, nay, a jungle, it is a jungle, and an absolutely terrifying one! Of absolutely everything, rather, of every "thing".

Have I been here before? I think so, though not exactly, as I said. Or did I say? "I" cannot recall. Perhaps. Equally awful places, of that there is no doubt. But not precisely this one.

Perhaps I can still escape! No, that's not how this works. Perhaps the prison bars will dissolve! That is my only hope - the escape is never something I effect, something I generate, something "I" "do", or even can "do". That I recall and am sure of.

But perhaps it was precisely those thoughts, those awful thoughts about my family, rather "my" "family", which triggered the onset of this horror. But maybe there was some other trigger, or worse, no trigger - perhaps this is all just some great white shark randomly emerging from the deep, which has no overriding interest in "me", yet which now munches away contentedly at my bowels. A deadly bolt of lightning, if you will.

Oh, how I despise that word "triggered" - it's a buzzword thrown around by morons. What's a better one, "stimulus"? "Springboard"? Oh, fuck me in the ass, it doesn't matter what word I use - there's no one listening, not even "I" am listening. Or speaking. Or writing. Or existing.

The point is: there might, conceivably, be some spur or spark or whatever the fuck that could conceivably spring me out of this hell as quickly and reliably as I've sunk into it. What could that possibly be??? Time? Sleep? Death? Walking the dog? I just did that though, for over an hour, in the freezing cold, just before this began. Nope. Didn't help.

Why was that Indian man in the park wearing that bizarre turban, and chanting like that? And those deer whom I confronted on the path, when I decided to turn back - who were they? What did they want? Were they what I should have understood as unmistakably clear omens? But of what? Nothing good, that much is clear. Were they famished? Were there mouths full of massive incisors poised to macerate and devour me? Did all those things mean something? Did they have to do with, create, point towards me, towards this, towards what has just happened?

None of those hypotheses make any sense. They're all ridiculous! I cannot think. Why? Because I've lost my "self". "He", that "self", is, for "me", now a sort of Eurydice, that is to say, perhaps the more "I" look up, down, back, or despair the present catastrophe, the worse off "I" shall be.

I shall stop now. Perhaps lie down. Which will solve precisely nothing. Time will pass rapidly, through a sort of strange funnel which no longer has the slightest concern for me, and with which I cannot interact. I am no longer in time, nor in space.

The point is this, only this: I see the thing I presently am as a thing of horror, a reptilian thing, a vile thing, a thing which engineered my marrying, or acquiesced to my marrying a woman I never loved, and having a child I never wanted in order to - WHAT? To fulfill my destiny? To have the opportunity to feel the rage I was never allowed to feel when it was literally life-threatening to feel it? To acquiesce to a situation which was sufficiently similar to that of my early life to provide me the opportunity to once again be the boy who wanted to fight back, but could not? To enable me to now feel a rage, which was appropriate then, but likely out of proportion now, within my adult self? At the present-tense disgusting, appalling situation in which I find myself? Fueled by the Chernobyl-sized rage stuffed onto the head of a hatpin that I had never been fucking able to unleash, and which now, finally, has exploded?

How can I not accept that it was myself who engineered all this?

Perhaps some Schopenhauer-ish magnets beneath the world dragged my wife and me together in order that I might acquiesce to this nightmare. I don't fucking know about any of that crap, nor does it matter. Nor did he know, he admits it's all pure speculation at the very start of his cockamamie essay.

Yet there she was! At precisely the necessary time and place for this cruise ship disaster to be set in motion! And now I am able to read this dreadful novel in its entirety, of a life lived forwards but able to be understood only backwards. And it is a vile, awful, far less than human novel - disgusting, loathsome.

The protagonist is like some creature from the black lagoon who momentarily donned a suit of pale white skin, red hair, and freckles, to then stalk the earth - waiting, waiting, waiting for the perfect opportunity in which the original awfulness reappeared in a guise upon which he could then light the fuse of his wrath.

Let it all fucking fly off to hell in a handbasket! For had there ever really been anything else within him, within that creature, within me? Perhaps those dopey little tunes I'd so often busy myself writing? Yes, some of them were pretty, even lovely, perhaps even "pretty lovely". A few of them were, at any rate.

Ach! Another fable the sniveling coward who is "I" tell my "self". But none of them emerged from the real "me". All those things were coughed up by the terrified "me", the one uttering faint whispers of gratitude for a hobby which had saved his fucking life, in order that "he" might manage to survive long enough to let this fucking gamma-ray burst violently explode within him, this ravenous supernova rip the world apart, this cataclysmic volcano he'd been carrying within him for six and a half decades to finally, at last, detonate.

And so it has, and there is nothing for it. This is far worse than any post-coital "tristesse" I've ever experienced, during which some malevolent demon or other would laugh his horns and tails off at the foot of my bed, after I had finished fucking some ill-chosen creature. No, no, no! These are all the hosts of hell in one go! Whom I've carried within me since I was four years old, finally erupting! Leaving me, leaving me - WHAT? As WHAT? Leaving me the empty, nondescript nothing I had been before I was violated - a vulnerable, worthless piece of tender, unremarkable, forgettable, thoroughly disposable meat.

I would love to claim "I coulda been a contender", even to simply laugh at the prospect of saying it, but for it to be even remotely true would require the totality of my life to have taken place in a very different universe. In this one, I was simply one of the bad, dark jokes of which I have become so fond.

I am a Vesuvius which explodes only into nasty, snarky remarks, and vicious poetry and prose. I didn't get to bury a town, murder anyone - it is all so very disappointing! Given the life into which I was thrown, that is the only possible sort of contender I could ever have wished or dreamed of being.

But sarcasm doesn't quite cut it when one's real wish is to have been an assassin. And so I am strung on this slenderest of threads beneath heaven and hell, though far closer to hell, in a cyclone of impotence, in a tornado which is spinning at the speed of light but which picks up only the occasional weed or discarded coffee cup - a laughable, discardable idiot, whirling violently about, dizzy with rage, and signifying nothing.

And, when I find myself finally thrown to the ground, exhausted, I am left with nothing, because this rage is all my life ever was, all it ever could or can now possibly still be. A hideous fate, but it is mine. I survived it all.

But why the fuck did I survive it? For what?

Love and rage are completely indistinguishable for me - they are the same. They are the same?

I've been inhabiting a lie for nine-tenths of my life. I am only myself when I am exploding with wrath, with my wish to rampage over the earth like some gigantic, monstrous, serpentine fiend, ripping flesh, faces, limbs to bits, grabbing babies out of strollers and throwing them in the air, skewering them on pitchforks, slicing their mothers' bellies open, disemboweling them, eviscerating their wombs, castrating all their despicable fathers who prance about so, with those shit-eating smiles of self-satisfaction pasted on their faces.

That is what I want! For the devastation and annihilation I have carried within me for close to seventy years to be OUT THERE! In the world! From whence it came! From whence it entered into me! I want it OUT THERE! I want the most appalling suffering, and I want it everywhere!

But hold on - not in the animal world. No, no, no, not there. I do not want it there! Not in the least! I want that all made right. For they have done nothing, they are without sin. I want it only and ever in the human world. I want the heads of every last person on the planet to burst into fucking flames. I want shrieks and car wrecks and famines and beheadings, all lit by shrieking human torches, of the sort Nero favored.

And were I to actually see this? Or were I able to bring it about myself? There would be no satisfaction - only a different, far worse Hell. The one I'm in. Impotent, exhausted, dissociated - a walking sob.

I walk the earth with this blast furnace inside of me. It is a constant, it is always there. When I'm feeling what seems to me fine, it is there as well, roiling and boiling away within my bowels, waiting eagerly and cagily for it to be called to the main stage.

I am a fiendish thing, an alien thing, a thing of horror. But walk I shall. For, in spite of the galaxy-sized rage ripping my flesh to ribbons and crushing my soul, I've never lifted a finger to any sentient being, other than myself, and I've no intention of doing the latter now, for whatever reason.

I ferry crickets, spiders, and flies from the house - while weeping, for fuck's sake. I am a laughable thing - a mouse who occasionally spits hints of flame and thinks them bonfires, wishes them supernovae. Nothing more, nothing else.

Dear God, would that I could have a laugh over all this?

Ok then - walk...

I shall walk again...

If only for the dog's sake...

<Subject uses highly elaborate, often poetic language to contain overwhelming affect. Writing functions as a self-regulating mechanism, preventing enactment. Presents strong moral awareness despite violent imagery. Insight preserved; judgment intact.>

XXVII.

In which the narrator of In Search of Lost Time finds that he is, suddenly and without warning, able to very faithfully and vividly recall taking his beloved dog for walks, long ago, through a certain, much-beloved park...

And at the moment in which I realized I had, in fact, slipped on a vile, slick wad of dark maroon skunk cabbage in my grandmother's deeply beloved garden, the one she had tended with so much care and devotion since her earliest youth, so mottled as it was with delicious yellow-green streaks from which there always so reliably emerged that particularly sharp and acrid scent so long familiar to and much cherished by me, the memory of all those afternoons and evenings in the park with Lulu rushed headlong upon me, as if I had been, in that instant, entirely transported through all of time and space to a quite particular path frequently trodden by, and, hence, quite well-known to me, a path which traversed a great deal of the terrain of that very same park, and upon which she and I had spent countless pleasurable hours walking. It was as if my adult eyes were now the very eyes of the boy I had then been, and would never be again, but who, at least for those few moments, I somehow was, in fact, again.

And for that boy, who I now felt I was, it had always appeared to be the case that all the bicyclists in that local park who so often violently pulled their front wheels up from the ground as they rode, in an attempt to impress those unfortunate pedestrians whom they whizzed past with their charisma, strength, and, by virtue of the inferences they assumed would necessarily be drawn by those astonished onlookers, the presumed sizes of their penises, had been designated, by certain other bicyclists, although it is perhaps worth noting that some of them were, in fact, unicyclists and skateboarders, all of them of at least somewhat, and often decidedly less strength and bravado than the macho cyclists of whom I have just made mention, though it must be said, possessing infinitely more cunning and sadism than they, to be, upon their passing a certain boulder adjacent to one of the park's main paths (a boulder whose position was considered most fortuitous in its location by these other cyclists, those of the lesser strength, though it must also be said, of equal vanity), viable targets for massive volleys of large rocks flung, with the greatest force and enthusiasm, by those very same boys, whose intention it was to strike down the aforementioned aggressively macho cyclists, if possible to incapacitate them entirely, and ultimately to put an end to their displays in the most definitive manner imaginable.

When the latter did not occur, and by that I mean to say when those initial volleys failed in achieving their intended goal, by virtue of either less than expert aim or force applied, or by some combination of the aforementioned, it ought also to be noted that those boys who had thrown the rocks and failed, and who tended more often than not to be extremely ashamed of this failure, would, as a result, be subjected to enormous verbal ridicule and, on occasion, to forms of physical correction by the others, an activity in which those others appeared to take the greatest pleasure. They would then, all of them - the ones who had succeeded, as well as those who had not thrown so much as a pebble - immediately rush upon the unfortunate, once preening but now grievously compromised fellows, if indeed they were still capable of movement, and bring matters to a conclusion of a sort that ensured no further exhibitions of their athletic bravado would be forthcoming.

Their bodies were then invariably disposed of in the river that ran, and continues to this day to run, through the park, and for which the park itself was named, at the turn of the century, by a noted naturalist, to whom we will refer in later volumes, as his part in our tale is a not insignificant one - this disposal serving, at least in part, as sustenance for the very great numbers of trout whose home was, and is, in point of fact, that very river.

It ought be noted that the town had frequently informed, and, so it was reported, continued to inform, its inhabitants that there was not, under any circumstances, to be any fishing in this river, nor were these trout ever to be eaten. This prohibition was due to the various environmental toxins which these very same trout had ingested over the years - toxins which the town's mayor and his colleagues had been intentionally and systematically permitting to enter the water, the precise composition of which had been the subject of many local, state, and federal investigations, as well as academic studies, some of which had appeared in the most prestigious of scientific journals.

The reason for the poisoning of the river's fish population was simple: the park's officials had been, all this time, receiving enormous bribes from local chemical firms, all of which had moved intentionally to the town in order to reduce their tax burdens, in exchange for permission to introduce their by-products into the river in precisely this manner. In addition to these financial incentives, that is to say these bribes, these firms had also made any number of threats to local officials, promising consequences of a most unpleasant and far-reaching nature, extending, according to rumor, beyond the officials themselves and into the private lives of their families, were such arrangements to be refused.

The young boys who so eagerly and cheerfully took part in those activities, and whose adolescent vigor and abandon in doing so was the stuff of legend, took great care to place the bodies of those unlucky, once vain and charismatic bicyclists, as well as the bodies of those boys whose volleys had been unsuccessful, beneath a certain waterfall, which had been named for an early seventeenth-century explorer of the area, a figure often mentioned in contemporaneous journals read by many of those early settlers who were sufficiently blessed to have had the good fortune of being educated. These early colonizers were, as a result of said tutelage, literate, a condition far from universal at that place and time, as public education had only just begun to take a tentative foothold in the region, though such schooling did, on occasion, occur, a fact well documented in more than one surviving chronicle of the time.

Beneath the above-mentioned waterfall, the bodies were extremely unlikely to be observed by the general public, many of whom were often visiting from adjacent counties, several of which possessed similar, though somewhat less rich and variegated parks, in that the vegetation in those places was rather less impressive and colorful than that of this far more popular and well-attended one. In the ordinary course of a day, those persons walking dogs, jogging, and riding bicycles just above the bodies, on that particular patch of the path from which such things were entirely out of view, a result of the somewhat unusual angle at which the bridge had been constructed, given the curious whims of the architect, who suffered from an uncommon form of ocular disease, which physicians had done their best to correct through numerous surgeries at the time, but which nonetheless continued to affect his plans, at times rendering them more than a little unfeasible, and at other times producing what was, admittedly, a thoroughly inadvertent yet nonetheless striking architectural interest, were never privy to matters which were easily known by and visible to the small group of boys who possessed prior and intimate knowledge of the terrain.

It was only when they, the boys in question, descended upon the rocks beneath the waterfall itself, where the bodies lay, that these matters became fully apparent. This they did, and often for rather extended periods of time, during which they would cheerfully wave to passersby above, laughing all the while in voices of various pitches - some prepubescent, others beginning to crack and squeak, still others sounding more than a little adult, that is to say, full and stentorian.

There was in this group a pair of twins who seemed to exercise a commanding, iron grip on the others. Indeed, the other boys appeared more than a little terrified of them. And it was precisely these others whom the twins would consistently compel to take part in certain acts involving the remains of those formerly laughably vain and athletic bicyclists. The pair took very great care to ensure that such participation was both unavoidable, as well as rendered with extraordinarily meticulous care, as per their instructions, in that the threats they issued to these other boys included the promise to put an end to the lives of every member of their families in the most appalling of manners, according to rites of their own invention, and in in the most bizarre and disturbing of ceremonies, were such participation to be refused.

These were ceremonies which those boys had, in fact, witnessed on many occasions, and in which several of them had even been forced to take part when earlier refusals of the twins' demands, always so loudly and vigorously intoned, had resulted in swift and memorable consequences.

The motivations of those twins? That had never been entirely clear to either the others or to me.

It was said, and there were reasons to believe this, that following these ceremonies the twins would enter into a state of extraordinary agitation and excitement, one which manifested itself in a sudden and intense interest in the more secluded stretches of the park. There followed, according to rumor and fragmentary testimony, a series of encounters with young female passersby who had been unfortunate enough to be alone, encounters which involved varying degrees of force suited to the strength and capacity for resistance of those affected, and which resulted in injuries of such number and severity that the bodies of the young women involved, though still largely intact, were nonetheless said to have been permanently altered in ways best left to the reader's imagination. These alterations were attributed, by those who told the tale, to the use of implements of unusual size and sharpness, and applied with a level of enthusiasm and exertion that those who claimed to have heard the events described afterward could recount only obliquely, noting chiefly the sounds - laughter, shrieks, and other expressions of misplaced delight - which issued from the surrounding foliage during these episodes.

There were also reasons to believe that local law enforcement was perfectly aware of all this, and that they chose, for reasons best known to themselves, to ignore it. And why was this? The rumor circulating as to the potential reason the provincial police might have brushed aside not only the arrest of these perpetrators, but even what would ordinarily have been regarded as the most elementary forms of inquiry or prosecution - nay, even the utterance of stern and cautionary words - was one the veracity of which I was, and remain, not entirely equipped to assess, much less to verify. It was said, however, that for reasons most likely involving the substantial quantities of organic matter introduced into the river as a result of these faux-ceremonial activities, the fertility of the trout population had been, and continued to be, very much increased. And so, less than surprisingly, as a result, there was now less of a financial burden on the town to restock or otherwise encourage the growth of these numbers, which had, owing to the circumstances just described, reached the most extraordinary proportions, so much so that one often saw hundreds of fish in the space of only a few yards of river, their glistening, silvery bodies catching the light in a manner that reminded me, at any rate, of the most exquisite impressionist masterpieces of that painter who, had he been afforded the opportunity, would surely have devoted countless inspired canvases to these gleaming, lustrous creatures. They appeared, at times, to be flying high above the water in their efforts to either dislodge parasites, capture insects, or to signal their biological worthiness as prospective partners to members of the opposite sex, this latter reliably heralding the most furiously urgent and visually astonishing episodes of mating.

Yet, most often, and above all else, these trout, in their desperate attempts simply to survive, seemed chiefly concerned with avoiding being crushed to death by the innumerable others of their species now occupying the river, all of whom barreled so wildly, brutally, and incessantly through its waters. It was, needless to say, a curious rumor, given that, as noted above, the town's inhabitants had all been repeatedly, and quite sternly, warned neither to fish in these waters nor to consume these trout.

All of this was, and remains, for me, even at this late date and remove, deeply confusing, ironic, and, at the end of a long inner journey in which I have repeatedly tried to make some sense of all these facts, persons, and behaviors, ultimately incomprehensible.

So you may make of all this what you wish. I myself, for the most part, believed every last bit of it, and was, like the police, more than happy to ignore everything I have described above as well, though for very different reasons than they, reasons which are, I imagine, unique to me. First and foremost, I was overjoyed to encounter far fewer of those moronic, preening bicyclists on my afternoon walks with Lulu. There was also another reason, perhaps less crucial but still consequential, which was simply that both Lulu and I greatly enjoyed the very frequent, jaw-dropping, and maniacally entertaining dances of the fish.

Their wild frolics and gambols were, and remain to this day, a thoroughly delightful and utterly breathtaking sight, one not to be missed, the memory of which, along with so many others, so inevitably overwhelms me on those occasions when I chance, through this or that seemingly random accident, to find myself suddenly inadvertently inhaling that long-familiar and much-cherished scent of skunk cabbage in which my grandmother's deeply beloved garden was, and is, always so reliably enveloped, a fragrance which provides me with a sort of window, that is to say a metaphorical entry key, into a celestial, eternal world in which neither time nor space exist, a world which I greet and embrace with the most ecstatic eagerness and gratitude, and into which, when I am lucky and privileged enough to be granted access, I invariably, ardently, and blissfully dissolve.

And, as if this were all not enough, later that afternoon, in my grandmother's old, abandoned, and far from pristine outhouse, immediately upon being overcome by its familiar stench of mothballs, urine, and the whiff of things so prodigiously, egregiously, and unmistakably human in their presence as to resist any honest attempt at description, the very same miracle washed over me once again. But more of that anon.

XXVIII.

The disillusionment of Swann. And of "Swan".

The disillusionment of Swann. And of "Swan". This ornithological disillusionment with women and love appears, in fact, to be quite widespread. The only thing capable of causing Charles Swann to feel anything at all was the fact that the object of his initial affections resembled a figure in a painting of Botticelli. She was, for him, at that time, an image only, a false goddess from the start, this "Odette". Not his "type", said he, but no matter - once she began to betray him with other men, he was nevertheless consumed with jealousy, that is, until the absurd caricature he'd made of her finally revealed itself - when her mask, for this and whatever other reasons, dropped to the floor. Seeing her clearly ended his torment, but not his folly. He married her anyway, for the sake of his respectability, and because he so loved his daughter. It might all have been quaint, even comical, as if a certain, rather famous Thurber illustration had somehow been made flesh, if her desperate superficiality, continuous betrayals, and venality had not finally killed him. This once suave, socially brilliant man was gradually replaced by a pathetic, tormented shadow of himself. If you wish to be generous, you might choose to consider Odette's crushing of Swann's soul as inadvertent. If you wish to be accurate, you'd describe her behavior as monstrous.

We can assume that his cousin, Wagner's "Swan", from the composer's desperately and comically ridiculous opera, Lohengrin, this other "Swan", about whom we have far less psychological information, and obviously not even the remotest hint of Proust's rapturously glorious, poetic, and psychologically insightful prose, became equally disillusioned, and for somewhat similar reasons. This creature, so feebly and lazily drawn by its composer with those oscillating f# minor and A major harmonies, is forced to return to Brabant by Lohengrin's bride, the utterly gullible and revoltingly needy Elsa. It is a doomed love, from the start, no less doomed than Swann's, although this time for psychological reasons minimally and poorly rendered. But nonetheless, whether you are a Swann or his avian fellow-at-arms, a "Swan", it would seem to be the case that you will necessarily have all manner of hell to pay. The former dies of a terminal, unnamed illness, although, let's not be silly - the name of the illness which kills Charles Swann is Odette de Crécy. Just as the name of the woman who brings about the unhappy fate of Lohengrin's boatswain, or shall we perhaps say, rather, "boatswan", if you'll be kind enough to forgive the term, is Elsa. One imagines him drooped over a barstool in some dingy Montsalvat saloon, drinking himself to death, as one of Kundry's aunts offers him a lap dance, or perhaps some overpriced Hebraic fling at the nearby Jewish bordello at which she is employed. Both Wolfram and Wagner remain unclear as regards the matter, obstinately and devotedly vulgar rakes though they were.

And so the question remains: are all women as shallow, venal, and selfish as Odette? Or as hopelessly foolish, gullible, and terribly annoying, all of which lead to devastating consequences, as Elsa? Must all those who find themselves subject to the whims of women's momentary passions die of thoroughgoing despair, or end up slumped over in an alcoholic stupor in some dingy Monsalvat tavern?

One might choose, instead, to become a "Don Juan Swann" or "Don Juan Swan", to wit, to indulge in all manner of sensual dances with all manner of females, either simultaneously or in succession, that is to say, to resolve to invest as little emotion in such matters as one can manage. To worship one's penis, if a man, or the "cloacal kiss", if a swan - to make of it, and of them, nothing. That, plus a healthy dose of cynicism, nay, of refined nihilism, of cruelty, and of superficiality, can go a very long way in these matters. It was Odette's way - one need only consider the means by which she flourished, and in which she advanced her social and financial position. To seek to be Aristotle's happy idiot - a person possessing a minimum of intellect and self-awareness, and flourishing constantly engorged genitalia, to which he or she pays the most devoted and constant obeisance. The secret of, if not happiness, then, at the very least, of a sort of contentment which prioritizes one's pleasure.

And what of the larger avian world? To what extent do sensual and emotionally intense relationships inevitably and necessarily become cruise ship disasters when one is a bird, more specifically, a male bird? To properly answer this question would require a dull and somewhat academic slog through the worlds of bowerbirds, peafowls, and other feathered exhibitionists, who endure all manner of grueling physical tasks, deformities, and enforced displays, and who sacrifice both their health and social standing in order to win five or ten seconds worshipping at the fetid altar of this or that hen's cloaca. Ironically, swans have been perennially famous figures in myth and legend all over the world, embodying themes of transformation, beauty, music, and the divine for millennia, and wild swans seem to do all the better, what with their elegant courtship rituals, long-lasting monogamous bonds, and shared parental duties. And yet here we have a Swann, and a "Swan", who have voluntarily allowed themselves to be disemboweled in a sort of spiritual seppuku, as sacrifices to cruel, calculating, two-bit sorceresses. Only in a world turned quite upside-down could such things be, could this fall from grace be so complete.

And yet here we are. And not only "we", in the sense of simply observing all this, or of observing and remarking upon it. The truth is that I am Swann, and you are Swann, and that all men are Swanns, or "Swans" - either way, the analogy holds. Yes, you, the reader, are Swann as well. Not to mention Lohengrin himself, that laughable buffoon, who was, at least, able to cruise back to his buddies, and return to his familiar, daily life as a gay monastic. Swann, on the other hand, was to die of an Amfortas-like wound - there was to be, for him, no healing. And worse, his wound came not from some ditzy, adorably mad and psychologically tortured gal in a laughably absurd opera, which has, at least, a few stupendously gorgeous passages, but from a venal, manipulative whore in a pink dress.

I too eviscerated myself for the sake of a daughter - in my case, a daughter I never wanted, after having been dragged into a marriage I never wanted, to a woman who advertised herself as an Elsa, but who gradually revealed herself as quite entirely an Ortrud. To survive, the swan, THIS swan, that is to say, "I", became an ostrich, and it is an ostrich I remain to this very day, hiding my head in the hole I've been forced to dig in order to avoid danger. I am, then, a former swan, possessed now of no lake, of not even a puddle, of not much more than the occasional teardrop. Ponds such as I have are to be found in my mind only, the place in which I've been forced to nest, and in which I shall draw my final breaths. And there is a name for the illness which has crushed my soul, and which will ultimately kill me, a name far more straightforward than that of Odette de Crécy. And although I might very easily state it here, I will refrain.

One is forced to conclude, as I have, that it is only one's imagination in which one ought spend one's time. Would it not, then, have been far better for Swann to have only loved the Zipporah in Botticelli's fresco? The one in his imagination? The one with whom he dallied and took such pleasure in his inner world? In safety and contentment? Rather than the greedy, grasping, two-bit whore in the pink dress with whom he ultimately set up shop? For in that inner world, we too, all of us, can find ourselves performing the most elegant of courtship rituals with the most demure and deserving of mistresses, with whom we can have invariably and reliably spiritually nourishing, monogamous relationships of the sort wild swans have. In this manner and this manner only, we can most enjoy and cherish her - she is there a source of infinite, reliable comfort, delight, and solace. And in utter safety and comfort.

When, on the other hand, we encounter and experience this creature in the flesh, she, who was for us only moments ago the most delicious of angelic white swans, very quickly metamorphoses into a hideous, flightless monstrosity with an enormous hooked beak - a terror bird, ready and eager to rip the flesh, tear the genitals, and fleece the pockets of any gentleman foolish enough to become involved with her. We, who have grown so soft in civilization, who have become such ineffectual weaklings, were once hunters, who, it is said, drove these selfsame terror birds to extinction. And yet here they are! They walk freely amongst us, wearing disgusting, vulgar, whorish pink dresses!

And we find them everywhere! In drug stores, markets, on the covers of the magazines in those markets, in taverns, workplaces, and in homes, masquerading as lovers, wives, and mothers. We poor, myopic swans saw only what we wished to see, until it was too late, until we found ourselves, courtesy of them, in states of terminal spiritual and even literal sepsis. If only we can manage to hold on to our initial, fantastical impressions of these creatures, the ones which existed in our minds and dreams, and take care to not make ourselves vulnerable to their fleshly reality in the waking world, if we are able to carry our impressions of them within us as ideals only, we will remain happy, content, and productive.

In so doing, we shall find that they speak to us only in hushed, kind, mellifluous tones, every syllable a note in one of Fauré's loveliest songs, every one of their steps that of a Balanchine girl, not a real Balanchine girl, heaven forbid, rather the Balanchine girls who dance, smile, and with whom we make love in our mind's eye and in our dreams, all of it taking place as if on a distant stage, observed behind endless, seductive scrims. More often, we learn, when it is too late, that to engage with these diabolical organisms, these she-devils, in the corporeal world at large, is self-destructive, masochistic madness.

Run while you can, Charles. Run! You cannot save your daughter. She is destined to become the creature her mother is, no matter what you do, as was mine. Look only to yourself! And to your survival. Flee to a lake, to the forests and groves within your mind, where you can live, prosper, and be at peace with your beloved paintings, your books, and your journeys in search of architectural marvels. Flee, my friend!

And you, "Swan" - both you and your doltish passenger, who believed he could save himself and the world by rescuing some kvetchy ditz - take heed! Her need was only to bewitch and destroy you. Rather than heading off to Brabant, fly! Fly to Combray! Gather Charles up and fly!

By the way, it's more than a little likely, and ought be noted that Charles is almost certainly gay, for, at the end of the day, everyone in Proust's masterpiece is gay. Did they not all reside within one gigantic, hopelessly diseased, homosexual mind? And anyone who rides around smugly preening in a boat dragged about by an also more than likely homosexual "Swan", and who pretends to not be gay himself, is pretty much as believable as the narrator and aforementioned author of In Search of Lost Time, when he doth excessively protest of his heterosexuality and love for women . Take a cottage in the mountains, fellas! Or by a lake! For all your sake! All three of you! Bring some Judy Garland and Maria Callas discs! Head off to the Marais district of Paris, or Nice, some chi-chi gay resort... You'll figure it out, boys.

For all I know, perhaps I am gay as well. I used to frequently wonder if I were asexual, but that was pretty straightforwardly the result of my being terrified of nine-tenths of the girls I knew, with all of whom I was in love. So perhaps I'll leave all that to the three of you - those geometric, Sade-worthy gay orgies in which le pénis de M. Swann is buried up to the hilt in the ass of M. "Swan", who'll likely be busy pecking away at Herr Lohengrin's balls, all of it to a soundtrack of Garland, or Callas, or perhaps Billie Holiday. Keep it upscale though, boys - no Liberace, Barry Manilow, etc. And, do forgive me, I think I'd rather not watch, if it's all the same to you. And if I find that I'm unduly disturbed by the noise, I shall straightway line my room with cork. So, to be clear: I'll be taking a rain check on all the cocksucking and buttfucking, fellas, or, to be more accurate, "un chèque de pluie à perpétuité".

And when you're all done, fellas, and have, hopefully, soaped your bodies and feathers clean in the lake, we'll lay out a spread of crème brûlée, mousse au chocolat, éclairs, macarons - and, needless to say, Madeleines. Following dessert, we shall have "Swan", as in, Avian "Swan", given that he speaks and reads aloud with far more eloquence and taste than any Disney macaw or duck ever could or did, read the President of the Solidarity's "Discourse on Love", from Juliette, by the Marquis de Sade.

Ça vous va ? Eh bien, c'est réglé !

And when that last little theatrical diversion is over, I propose that we piss and shit all over ourselves with the greatest abandon. Afterwards we shall find ourselves lighter - our bowels of shit, our bladders of piss, our balls of cum, and, above all, our hearts and souls emptied of all those deadly poisons we sadly mistook for love.

XXIX.

"The lies - they are so wearisome."

The lies - they are so wearisome. Would that I might claim to have ever worn my real face to the masquerade party. Would that I even had one! When what I do have consists only of a multitude of calculations, bluffs, and chicanery, all intended either to wound or to win affection. The truth lies neither with the one nor the other, nor in between them. I am famished. I am drowning.

And when I see some pair of eyes which seems to bleed with pain, I invariably see myself - the chipmunk in the park who darts about so furiously - in search of what? I do not know, only that it's tragic - this wish to please, this endless dance to win affection, to hold one's tongue, and to never say what's actually on one's mind and in one's heart, for it's only fools that do.

Am I saying what you wish to hear? For that is my intention. I have little interest in listening to the specific content of your answers to the questions which I am asking. I ask them for one reason, and for one reason only: because I am desperately alone. And when I look into your eyes - if and when you finally allow me to do so, that is to say, when you have chosen to return my gaze - but wait! For whatever reason, that happens only when I am speaking. That is the only time when you either allow yourself, or are brave enough, to look up and into my eyes, to hold my gaze. It is never, or almost never, when you are speaking.

And why is that? I know full well! At least for me. For I do very much the same thing, far more obviously and noticeably than you, perhaps for reasons which we share. The truth for me, my dearest friend, is that when I speak, I feel ashamed. When I speak to you, or you to me, it is only then that each of us allows ourselves to glance up into the other's face. And I think I know why that is, at least for me, as I have said.

But there is more, so very much more: because I want you, above all else, to care for me, and though the admission terrifies me, to perhaps even love me.

I don't care what you are saying, as I mentioned earlier - at least not for the most part. I only care that you are saying it, and that our interaction seems to be a thing for which you hunger - that is to say, that you wish to share some part of yourself with me. It's not particularly important to me why exactly you might hunger to do so - that doesn't matter. Only that you do, just that you want it - that's what most matters. Indeed, it is all that matters.

And if I were to tell you what it is I actually want? What it really is my soul is craving? For which it is so famished? I feel certain that you would turn around and flee, just as I would were you to say the very same to me.

I only want what is impossible - and precisely because it is impossible. Were you to look me in the eye and say you loved me, I would crumble into dust. I'd be the boy who wished to die all those years ago, who thrust his hand out from the sea in hopes that she who ought to have loved him didn't hate him, that she was not happy - or, at the very least, did not care - that he was drowning, which seemed far too often to be the case. In the desperate hope for a rescue which was never offered, which never came, and for which he longed, and for which I still long, even now, while knowing full well how obviously absurd and impossible to fulfill such a yearning has always been, and remains.

So you must not - nay, you cannot - say you love me! I won't allow it.

I must massage each conversation with you - or so I constantly tell myself each time we speak. Each word I let drop from my mouth is in service of my effort to keep it all going, with a modicum of feeling and of interest on both our parts - most crucially on yours. I long for some perceptible assurance that you like me, yet, heaven forbid, for it is far too terrifying, don't love me - although it really is only this latter for which I pine, and about which I dream.

It is the thoughts of exactly that which so brutally haunt me when I writhe upon my bed in bursts of a sleep so light it hardly qualifies as sleep at all. There is just this thrashing, this tawdry dance of loneliness - the frantic spasms of a fish ripped from its bowl and made to lie upon a table, where it writhes and gasps in terror, wondering how it might induce the creature looming above it to, dear God, just put it back into the water.

I'm just pretending then, all throughout our talks, as I feel I must. But can't you see that? Every clever thing I craft is just another lie to keep up the connection, for without it I am just this parched and breathless thing, lying on a bed of rusty nails, longing for a body that is warm and onto which I can project my delusions and fantasies - of which I can imagine it the dwelling place of some fanciful and wondrous spirit, of whom at least I can pretend that I am fond.

Dear God - will no one ever hold me? Will this really be the way it ends? With me pouring ashes on the grave of my first wife, at the foot of which I am drowned and suffocated by my own sobs? With the ashes of my dog, who has now also left me wriggling on this, this embalming table? As I suffocate and wrack my brain to try and think of something else to keep this conversation warm and nourishing, in order that I might keep it going, to make of it a thing that gives you pleasure, so that you'll like me? Perhaps even love me? But that cannot and must not be! It is far too dangerous.

Were you to touch me in the ways for which I long, I would burst into a bonfire, at whose crown would stand a child whose freckled face was choked with tears, full of a terror that it cannot be either your or anyone else's job to soothe. That is a role I would, needless to say, sorely like for you to play - and one for which you have most assuredly never auditioned. And yet I have, perversely and selfishly, cast you in it.

And were you to actually acquiesce to play the part I've written for you? Well then! You would necessarily have to be every bit as crippled, tainted, shattered, and scarred as I. But you are not! For no one is. And yet it is you, and only you, whom I wish to play the part, whom I so desperately wish would join me in this mad, fantastical scenario.

Nonetheless, of these things I must never speak! I need to lie, to smile, to placate, to finesse, to ensure the talk goes this way and not that. For if I were to allow what's in my heart to genuinely emerge, be it in words or in a look, you'd see a pair of turquoise pupils staring straight up from the depths of hell, from deep within a sinkhole full of a hunger that no love could ever possibly sate.

The coy and clever iceberg for which you naively took me would then become a raging vent of boiling lava - gushing, scalding, roasting everything in sight, including the both of us - my flesh, your flesh, this tender, fragile thing we had so carefully constructed - our faces hopelessly scarred with mottled hues of pink and red and dusky purple, full of fierce, hazardous crags and coarsely hardened ridges. And I, all the while, trying desperately to resurrect the butterfly I had skewered upon that wall only moments ago, with words I ought never to have uttered, even in a dream. The dream in which I find myself at this very moment, wondering how I will approach you when next we meet - what I'll say and what I won't - so that I might keep all these feathers in the air, which are so very beautiful, and which soothe and nourish me so.

And you? It is you, above all else and others, who are so very beautiful, Bettina. And I do so love you. I would die for you! You must know that. But of course you don't. For if I told you, you'd be frightened - and for good reason - for in so doing there'd be the risk that I'd destroy this fragile thing which seems to thrive only when we both manage to keep the room at temperatures far less than that of all those sweat and lust-filled hothouses in which I dream of lying next to and embracing you, and in which never a word is said by either of us. A place where words are neither required nor wanted.

And when the ache grows too intense to bear, when all the words have faded, when they are no longer needed, the theater of the body will collapse, and the hunger change its shape. It will no longer be only for your voice and for your touch. There shall be this explosive, delicious, milk-white release into a bodiless, empyrean firmament, where you will be the universal consort, the unbroken cosmic loom and womb - that nameless goddess into whom I shall then melt, cast off my very self, and be redeemed - the riverbed of life into whose waters I will dive and by which I shall be absolved and liberated.

And you! The queen who holds the keys to the gates of both silence and infinity, of life, and of death - the placid exhalation of an exhausted soul who finds now that it is free, no longer wandering, and who has arrived, at last, to rest in your embrace.

None of which is true, or ever could be true, much less said - even to myself, much less to you. There is only what has been long established between us - these astonishingly pleasant tennis volleys we share with one another, in which affections are tamped down and fed like crumbs to starving chipmunks racing through graveyards, where they have discovered that the chances of their being clutched and ripped to shreds by birds of prey are somewhat less. And yet, nonetheless! All those hawks and falcons, who hover above them, remain voracious - and in exactly the ways in which I desire you, but cannot and will not ever utter, to you, or even to myself.

Am I smiling now sufficiently? Did that joke land? Was it not charming? Do you like me? Might you even love me? Might you ever come to love me? To perhaps say such a thing in your head, or to yourself, or to utter it one day to me? I know you like me, and that is something! And it will have to be sufficient, for there shall never be anything more in your heart as concerns me. So I sense, and so I believe.

To ask for more would be calamitous - to us, to you, to me, who is not sure that he can keep up this charade, though I am trying as best I can. For if I were to lose my skills at tamping down these passions and words upon this tennis court on which we find ourselves, it would be lethal. And yet how I want to blurt it out this very moment! All that's in my heart! While knowing full well that if a scrap of your affection comes my way, it will be only insofar as I have lied.

And so it is that I lie now, and will go on with my lies, crafting fiction after fiction to soothe myself, to keep the ball aloft. So that when our conversation ceases, and I am alone, I can hold you in my arms in ways to which you would never acquiesce, and from which you would doubtless flee. You will be in me then - a simulacrum of passion, an effigy upon an altar that has little to do with who you are, but rather with what you are in me: an assurance that there is some reason to go on another day.

That is quite the burden, is it not? But fear not - you will not hear of it - not now, and not ever.

For when the pact is within myself, there is no danger. You are safe. There is no risk that at some future volley or charade of ours I will tell you who I am, or what I want, or what I think and feel in my heart and in my guts - this blackness which I know I will never share, and which is literally killing me right now, this very moment, while I am scribbling, while I am dreaming of the lies and tricks and tactics I will employ when next we meet.

For you assume, just as we all do, that what you see and know of me is what I am - that within this home's exterior must be a host of rooms resembling its veneer, that it is not instead a swirling vortex, a canyon, a chain of fire-engulfed mountains, containing countless rooms of my own meticulous invention, brimming with bondage, torture, and death. That what you see is only the artful vinyl siding I have plastered on my spirit for our talks - of these things you must never know.

Surely that is what must lie beneath the veil, my dear Bettina - correct? The very same things which you observe on my surface during our exchanges? Of course! It must be. How could it be otherwise? That is what you think, is it not? Well, of course it is.

You know the one! The one you see? The one you think you know? That witty, charming guy whose jokes are sometimes dark, but who, at heart, is such a lovely fellow? He is the one beneath whom I lurk - fearful, alone, and burning with desire.

But what of all the things that you are concealing, dear girl, both from me and from yourself? Think of all the selves we both are shedding and discarding as we lurch through conversations in which neither of us has a clue what will emerge next from our mouths. That is true of both of us - no less of you than of me.

What we are most likely aware of, what we are able to predict, at least at times, is what we both know full well we almost certainly will never say. For it is dangerous - perhaps even lethal. To what? To this flimsy shelf we have constructed together, stacked as it is with blown-glass filigrees, all likely to shatter if we do not look quite precisely where it is we step and what it is we say. But above all else - attend to what it is we take the utmost care never, ever to say.

Looking out, as we both are, never to offend - keeping all the feathers in the air we are so busy juggling, in the hope that our affections will survive each little chat - hoping that there might be some chance to tweak them even further, to arrange them into ever more fascinating and enticing combinations, to add this or that tasty new confection to the desserts we have been preparing and of which we have been partaking - is it a year now? I am not sure. I only know that it is important, when we part, that I attempt not to obsess about you, dear, and, as a result, impale myself on a razor-sharp harpoon laced with a bitter, eviscerating longing that could very well destroy me.

That I put my thoughts of you inside a dresser drawer, which I then close, in order to seek refuge in all those ancient, lonely lies I have told myself seemingly forever - from when, in the basement all those years ago, as a boy, I longed to die. It never works, this closing of the drawer - never entirely. I am haunted by the thought of you, Bettina, and by the words I will never speak, other than to the gal within me who in so many ways resembles you, and whom I so cherish, and who, though she is not exactly you, came to live within me only because of you, my beloved friend.

All those words of devotion and lunacy that I so long to say to you, Bettina, but never will - words of love, of passion, of the most burning, searing desire, and of madness - of the shedding of our very selves, of our discarding them - wholly, ecstatically, deliriously, while embracing on a cliff overlooking a sea of milk-white nectar, into which we would then dive, with our gazes fastened upon one another, into the most delicious, tantalizing, vast and yawning oblivion.

338

XXX. "Surely this impostor in the mirror..."

Surely this impostor in the mirror has only come so that he might either inform me of what is to come or to inspire my disbelief. Or perhaps to have a laugh at my expense. To ask of me a thing I cannot do, that he knows full well I cannot do. In any event, he is here - to taunt me, express his deep contempt, or - who knows? To perhaps have some sort of chat?

This frightful demon would apparently like to convince me that he is, in fact, me! Which is ridiculous! Am I these creases in this forehead? Or the worry that produced them? These swirls of auburn, silver clouds, that just sit there for evidently no purpose? Are all these allegedly physical phenomena simply dreaming themselves? Are they plotting? Do they clash with one another? Do they exist when I'm not looking?

And these eyes! Am I to understand that I am, somehow, behind them? And those lenses, surgically implanted, am I to think of them as me, as well?

In the space between the mirror and the self that is observing there is laughter, a very great deal of laughter. Can you hear it? Can you explain to me what the joke is?

Perhaps the beard, that must be it! These unkempt tendrils rising like sun-averse, prickly white worms from the deep, damp earth, which seem all to be screaming amidst the laughter which would be deafening if I were listening, but I am not - because I'm watching as the earth, which is my face, begins to bleed amidst my groans and sobs and longings, which it barely hears and largely just ignores. And from this grubby, squalid garden, this long abandoned fissure, rarely looked at or inspected, emerge these writhing, rough, abrasive, milk-white grubs, who are swarming on this face which is not mine, overflowing with their hunger and their boredom and their questions.

All these questions! Who am I? And where am I? Where am I, in fact, located? And whoever it is that asks them - so constantly imagining, expecting me to offer them plausible answers to their questions! But that is far from likely. About as likely as my walking through the park to offer solace to some moss-infested rock that is starving for attention because it's lonely and it's scared, just like these filaments which push up from the pulpy, viscous rot beneath my flesh - praying that they'll find what's on the surface, in the light, might be more kind.

If some are longer than the others, which they are, perhaps they're hungrier. Or could it be because they're bullies? Oh, look! Consider that one! It has just turned up towards the ceiling! And the one which now hangs over my top lip? What does it now want? It has to know the more I look, the more unreal this all becomes - these lips and tongue and teeth, these jagged shards, these moonlit tombstones - sitting there like slaves who have been bound each to the other, in which they sometimes are massaged by that imbecilic muscle, with a mind all of its own.

It's all so stupid! All these imbecilic armies, thrown together in a cavern which is drenched in warm saliva. And only more so when the self that is observing all this nonsense moves its focus towards the drool and slobber pooling there like fetid, toxic waste which ought be spat, nay, begs to be spat, into a toilet or, even better, to be spewed into some well-deserving face. Then the river floods its banks more than before, and the photons in the space between the mirror and the self which - is it me? Is this all me? Are these things me??? This thing that's scribbling, that moves its eyebrows, sticks its tongue out? Surely not, this cannot be! This is a nightmare! How did this happen? How did I get here? How was I plopped into this trap? I can remember, at least I think that I remember, that I was flying not long ago. I had no body, it was boundless, there were spirits all around.

And now I'm tangled up in ropes of flesh and hair and stink and spittle, like a fly whose many legs are bound in slimy straps of filth, who feels the spider fast approaching, hears its hissing in the laughter in the space between the mirror and the self that now has stepped outside its other seeming "self," although I don't recall it chose to - perhaps it had been forced to? I don't know! How could I know?

It's now retreated down some tunnel which recedes behind the eyes which still pretend that they can see a pair of glasses sliding down upon a nose which serves to archive all my past in countless scents and heady perfumes, both of which it files away and hardly ever shares with the thing I feel is me.

It's all so fragile! The way in which I sometimes mouth the words I write, though I would likely not have known that I was doing so, were I not looking at this face which cannot possibly be mine...

If it's some house in which I'm forced to live, it's pretty clear it's been abandoned. And yet I cannot leave, nor can I renovate or buy myself another. If there's a landlord, he's indifferent, and he'll be calling in the lease not all that long from now. Yet when I wish to tell him that the plumbing leaks, that drafts come through the windows, which are filthy, that the walls are slowly crumbling, I can't find him. Though I know when comes the time the rent is due, he will appear, the greedy bastard.

I have been thrown into a squad car by some officers in masks, and I can only watch in horror as it careens down one-way streets, with me encaged in ribs and sinews, behind bars of bones and countless walls of skin. I put a finger in my mouth and bite my nail - perhaps I'll ground myself, this dizziness will stop! My mind is spinning as I'm pulled beneath more waves but yet I still can see that face, that thing which keeps pretending that it's me. Oh, how I hate it!

Since the first time I encountered it I knew it was a trick, some sort of joke. Now that my swagger is a stoop it is no different, it was every bit as bitter then as now. That beardless boy who had no furrows in his brow was just as terrified as I am presently.

I did not then and do not now believe in time, which means there'll be no end to this, this living hell will be eternal! It's all frozen in some stagnant block of stillness which is violence, only violence, since I winked into existence. I'm not winking anymore, nor am I laughing, even smiling, at the countless microbes crawling on my face as if they're marching on some battlefield in which there necessarily can never be a victor, for the violence is the point, the atrophy and devastation, which is infinite, it seems.

That's not the worst though - it's the sorrow and the heartache, leaking out of every pore, which were each and every one tattooed upon this face. I'm just so tired of all this - my jaw is clenching, my teeth are locked, there is this strange taste in my mouth of something vast and cruel and nameless, which is leaking down my gullet to my heart - do I still have one? Yes, I do, at least I seem to, for it's palpitating now - the earth is trembling and there'll be no end to this.

I smell it in the air - my past and future are right now, they're in this room, they're in this very moment...

What are those slanted bits of hair in both my eyebrows? Were they there yesterday, the day before, this morning? I cannot know and do not care to know.

I would prefer my face to not become distorted or misshapen, but why is that? I do not know that either. And why the hell should that still matter, least of all to me, at this late stage?

If there's some mischievous cartographer at work, there's nothing for it - it's a landscape that is crumbling ever faster, and there's nothing I can do. If it's a story, then its pages are now crumpled, and its binding has long been just food for moths, although there seems to be a paragraph or two not there before when it is opened. They've not much interest, all those pages, they lack vigor, they're poorly rendered - filled with vain regrets and thoughts and sorrows barely grasped.

It is a dark, unsparing landscape, and words are hollow things - at least the way that all my words are simply swallowed in a silence which lacks the means to illustrate or bring to life a color seen by only me for which there are no words I know or could possibly invent. And if I weep, that's just an echo too - of throwing anchors overboard, with an effort I cannot maintain, into a sea that's bottomless - this errand of a fool who cannot seem to stop himself from trying, from reaching for some difficult to fathom metaphor, way beyond his skill to capture.

It won't come, it cannot come! For it is nowhere, nowhere I have ever been or have some chance of finding now, because I'm crippled and I'm hiding at this far cry from the surface of my face, by which I'm terrified. I have no wish to travel that long road up to its surface, which would perhaps bring me some solace, but more likely just a bit of clarity I do not want, for the world I look upon only pretends to be familiar - it's been forever altered - which has made of me a ghost behind a door which has been slammed shut and then locked. And I'm just peering through a peephole at the freakish face of someone I don't know, who becomes a thousand others every time he moves that face this way or that...

I understand why people watch horrific films, and place their noses inside books they hope will scare them half to death. It's a distraction from a terror so profound that to contain it in a monster's a relief, for if the monster that's relieved them were to look upon his face with any honesty, he'd rip it off his skull that very moment and run screaming from the room in which he saw it, out the door into the arms of vicious crowds, who'd likely grab up all their pitchforks and then light his faceless skull up with their torches and their laughter, like the laughter that still bubbles through the air between the self that might be me that still is looking at a face that can't be his. I can't accept this! I refuse!

No more now! That's enough! This is a knot I can't untie - it is the world's knot, not just mine. I just happen to be dumb enough to linger in its heart, in its nucleus of fear, locked in a claustrophobic thicket of my past and of my present, all of which are belching long-forgotten nightmares, and as they do so, they're all yawning, drowned in boredom as they are, as they take to farting out once more the most cacophonous of symphonies, composed of all the chaos, shock, and grief that live upon that face which is pretending to be me there, in the mirror, past the space which is still echoing with laughter spewing out from mouths of fiends - the ones who'll hound me to my grave, then stomp upon it, to make sure that I am dead.

When every last nerve's been scraped down to the bone, when what was a face is now a skull in pitch-black darkness, unable to move, to speak, to weep, there's nothing left to either burn or mourn. Just the faintest echoes of my grief, the occasional smoldering ember of rage, and more than a teaspoon full of horror - all of it mixed up with exhaustion, which dilutes them, it is true, but, above all, there's this global, paralyzing numbness, a mournful awe which feels somehow posthumous, a stunned recognition borne of hollowed-out clarity, as if I am a dazed and tired soldier stumbling aimlessly through ruins and seeing only outlines of what mattered once - the ontological nightmare of aging observed by a self, by "my self", whose inner world's now frozen, buried deep beneath this face and limbs and skin which cannot possibly be mine.

Is this some sort of mercy which something within me has now chosen to allow? I cannot forever choke on and be suffocated by my anguish - the soul goes blank! This soul has gone quite blank, at any rate, so much so that it feels as if these words are being thought and written down in their entirety by a dead man, whose corpse is sitting here somehow - don't ask me how! I do not know.

Does that dead man have within himself a part which still can care, or which can love? If he did, what would he see within himself, what would he do? I do not know! I've not a clue! The dead man hides himself in silence - in sleep, and shame, and fear, and lethargy. When nothing hurts any longer, can I not assert, as well, and with an equal assurance, its very opposite?

One who possesses the energy might very well do so. That one is not I.

I, whose haggard face sits atop this collapsed and flattened soul.

XXXI.

"And I, who had been forever fearful of women..."

And I, who had been forever fearful of women, yet burning with tenderness, intense yearning, and the most violent lust for them, while at the very same time sure that I'd never gain a boldness sufficient to even let drop from my mouth a single word in their presence, here I was, somehow - in bed with my very first girlfriend, who was kind and who loved me, or so she at least professed. And, after the weeks, perhaps months, when the thought or the threat of my entering her, of my penetrating her, had repeatedly turned me to jello, we were, at last, happily fucking, this first girlfriend, Alice, and I, banging away in her black-as-pitch dorm room with the most vigorous and joyous late-teenaged glee and abandon, when suddenly she murmured, "Cum!"

A harmless suggestion! Or as such it was intended, and so I ought to have understood it to be. Perhaps she was trying her best to excite me, or was bored, and interested only in getting it all over with. But none of that matters! What happened next remains and feels as vivid today as it did on that night.

What I heard when she uttered that word, that suggestion, was something quite different from anything she could possibly have intended. I heard a command which seemed to rise up from the depths of an infinite black abyss, from whence it had been rudely grunted, with appalling savagery and menace, by a sort of beast - a vicious, terrifying snarl, several octaves lower than could ever have arisen from the throat of my poor, sweet Alice, who now had somehow become this bestial, hirsute, harpy-like creature.

I knew only that I was lying atop, not my sweet and loving girlfriend, but rather upon an inhuman, menacing monster, intent on my demise. Breathless with terror, I jumped up and off her, and bolted towards the light switch, which I frantically switched on, in order to illuminate the very room in which a she-devil, a fiend, had been moments ago about to rip me to shreds, to consume me. I had been quite certain, in those first frightful moments, that I was about to die.

The moment I saw that the woman before me was no demon, but only Alice, my beloved, kind, and caring girlfriend, I fell to the floor, gasping for breath - for hadn't I been fucking a murderous werewolf but a moment ago? A succubus intent on my annihilation?

I had suddenly become the very same boy, now encased in the body of a young man, who had so long ago slept in his grandmother's house, sure that the young, red-headed, seemingly eyeless woman in the oil painting which hung in the hallway was, at any moment, about to leap out from her portrait, run down the hall to my bedroom, and brutally murder me. Later I learned that the sinister-looking young woman who absolutely seemed to me to live within that portrait, who was portrayed in it, was someone I knew quite well, far better than I wished, in fact. It was a painting of my grandmother in her youth, of which some part of me must surely have been aware - that "Mama" who so liked to cruelly insult, threaten, and beat me, and who on so many occasions had taken hold of my hair in order to shove my head down the toilet, at times with her hands, at others with a plunger, or with anything else upon which she might just have cast her glance.

That grandmother had clearly seen in me the victim my mother had made of me, and, as I can see now, the very same victim I still felt myself to be when I jumped up from the bed in Alice's pitch-black dorm room.

I've read and been told that the buzzword du jour for this sort of early childhood experience is "trauma." I do not care for it. It was, rather, an invasion of a soul that had already been crushed, and which made me only more of a cripple, whose every encounter with what I thought or believed to be "feminine" was petrifying, and more than likely lethal. All that had ever been womanish came with this warning, and was, in addition, laced with the promise of, at the very least, my desperate humiliation, and, far more likely, or so it seemed to me, my annihilation. I am not speaking in metaphors here! Blood-crazed succubi do not kid around.

When I jumped up from that bed, I was trying to save my life. There was not a hint of embarrassment, although I'd plenty of uneasiness and self-consciousness in other, not dissimilar, situations. There was no time for it. It was as if I were frantically pushing an alarm to alert I had no idea whom, since there had never before been a soul who had seemed to care, or come to my rescue in the past. I was screaming into what I feared and expected, out of habit, to be a void, broadcasting the likely-to-be-not-responded-to fact that if no one arrived soon, I would momentarily be disemboweled and murdered in that very bed.

I'd always assumed having sex implied closeness, and that when one was close, one was naked, necessarily, and in more ways than one - that exposure meant helplessness, to be at the mercy of the grandmother, the mother, the smile that implied imminent cruelty - the plunger, the toilet, the monsters wearing flesh suits - they who murmured of love while delighting in my torment, and who appeared hellbent on first torturing and ultimately slaughtering me. I was no longer with Alice. I was four years old again, out of my body, regressed to a state in which I was, at least metaphorically, screaming, "Help, I am dying!"All the while knowing full well that there'd be no rescue, solace, or waking from this nightmare. Why? Because there had never been before.

And that was, in fact, the reason I couldn't maintain my erection at first, on those many, long, painful, and deeply embarrassing nights in which I must have been unconsciously assuming that a vagina, Alice's vagina, in this case, must necessarily be a sort of hungry bear trap, salivating in anticipation of its snapping shut, and of the wished-for castration to come. There was a dread which was contained in the apprehension itself, in the space of that opening, in the uncertainty of the moment which, if and when I would manage to surmount it, no longer threatened me. I would no more be hovering, helplessly trapped in some liminal space which was treacherous, which was potentially lethal.

I'd managed it! I had trampled the fences, broken through the barricades. And to make it through the gates of the fortress was to be safe, to be able and to allow myself to relax. To even, what a concept, enjoy both myself and her. Myself with her, beside her, inside of her. At least that's the fable I would tell myself, once I had safely arrived, once I had breached the citadel walls, once I had psychologically slammed shut the door which contained all my primordial terror, at least for that moment.

I was always aroused - that was never the problem. I was always in love, as well. To begin making contact, though, that was always and reliably the moment which most terrified me, the place where the violence was lurking - in the portrait, in the toilet, in the succubus I imagined was lying beneath me in that pitch-black dorm room.

This was all more than understandable. I had been assaulted! Many times! And, I assume because of that, predators seemed able to sniff me out, to know me from afar, in advance, and to say to themselves, "Lucky me! Well then! Here's a little boy that I can FUCK with - that I can hound, oppress, and persecute!"

When one strips off the paint from the canvas of that eyeless young fiend somehow still staring out from that portrait, there are oceans of ancient rot lying beneath it, a gargantuan assortment of vile, poisonous stenches - all of it going back countless generations. I was born a boy who saw women as holy, or who, at least, still told himself it was possible they'd be holy, yet knew full well, from innumerable experiences, that they were far more likely to be lethally dangerous. I wanted them all so much that I'd have offered any one of them my life, at the very same time that I both trusted and expected that they would behave monstrously towards me.

Why? Because every temptation, every murmured "cum," was a threat which was bellowed from landfills of ancestral horror. Every touch of a woman demanded that I give up my body, my dignity, my sanity, my self, my every last breath - on an altar that had been blood-drenched from further back than I could ever possibly recall - on an altar over which harpies cackled, wielded knives, shrieked curses, abominations, and, perhaps worst of all, laughed - there was always the most horrendous laughing! Echoing endlessly in my skull like the sound of ten thousand chainsaws wielded by mobs, nay, vast armies, of murderous viragos and ogresses.

I was simply trying to meekly navigate, in what I believed a desperate attempt to simply survive, through myriads of minefields laid by the most monstrous of maternal lineages, which spanned eons - knowing full well that I was destined to die at any moment - blindfolded, with no map, recourse, or possibility of deliverance.

And yet! Still capable of love, at least of the hope for love. Because I had to believe there was, somewhere, a mother, a lover, a sister - some woman who had managed to remain uncorrupted - some original, primeval "ur-woman" who might save me, who would at least desire to save me, attempt to save me - some gentle priestess with sad, compassionate eyes, who would beckon me into a temple in which I could sleep soundly, without constantly starting up in bed, racked with the dread of some new nocturnal assault. A safe, humane, and compassionate sanctuary, unadorned with portraits of fiends, containing no instruments of torture, no plungers - an entirely imaginary, sacred space, in which women had neither claws nor fangs.

There are demons and monsters in this world who will betray you for sport, simply because it amuses them. It is their nature. But surely there must be others as well? Redeemers? Gentle, benevolent lovers? Saviors? Are there not? Well of course there are not.

When confronted with women, of the real sort, who were perhaps, at least not primarily, monsters, in moments that should have felt more or less safe, which should have been easy, intimate, and perfectly ordinary, I unfailingly expected and waited for the inevitable turn - for it and they had always turned. And there was never any question that it and they would turn again, that they would always turn again. There had never been any other scenario, at least none that I had ever known. I simply knew this. It was a given. And yet I kept looking, looking, looking...

I'm still looking, though the temperature's lower, and my eyes are often now close to wide open. I haven't gone completely or consistently numb in some time. And yet I am still that boy, the one who was so utterly terrified and full of longing, who couldn't approach, who was too petrified to cross the threshold, any threshold.

Oh yes, I can fuck now, as a rule, more or less without a problem, but that's easy! And not at all what I'm talking about. "Fucking" has naught to do with the moment I really long for - that moment of naked vulnerability, in which I am able to let someone in, or feel that I have been offered a place in which I am safe, am loved, am somehow KNOWN. Yet at the moment in which trust is required, I become helpless - I am destroyed. Because for me, the making contact isn't what leads to betrayal, it is the betrayal itself. The lamb is necessarily led to slaughter the instant it reaches out, the second it trusts - that is PRECISELY when the assault comes, in that very moment. Its education, that is to say, that lamb's education, has been long, arduous, complete, and irrevocable.

As a result, every woman appears to me as if she is about to jump out from the canvas behind which she's been hiding, the lot of them - out from the paintings which, underneath their shabby or even lovely façades, their soft colors, their lying and sometimes tender expressions, their serenity, and their promises, I always know precisely what to expect, and what is sure to appear: a plunger, a toilet, the predatory monster they've been all along. At the doorway. Not in some dungeon - no, no, no! At some perfectly innocent-looking doorway which I have been encouraged to open, to only then discover that it was nothing other than a one-way ticket to the scaffold.

I somehow, incomprehensibly and tragically, have managed to remain the boy who believed that some non-existent mother would somehow appear to save him, to come to his rescue. And hence, it has always been required, during fucking, that I have a clear view of my partner's face, and of the expression on that face - a view which absolutely needed to remain unobstructed. There would be precious few fucks from behind in that boy's future, exceedingly vanilla, nothing-to-write-home-about sex life. Of fucks in the ass there were to be next to none. It has been, for the most part, thoroughly generic, and not in the least kinky. For what he and I both wanted, above all else, was simply to hold and to be held.

Yes, for sure! Fucking is fun! At least at times, and with a vanishingly small subset of partners. And it is hardly unpleasant to cum! But all that I really wanted, and all that I continue to want, is simply to lie next to a woman upon whom I can throw a scrim, and, as a result, then imagine a goddess - the most saintly of mothers, or of sisters, any and all of whom I am, for whatever reason, now allowed, even invited, to fuck.

Everyone knows, at least I know, that goddesses are so pure that, although you can touch them, touching is not what you really want from and with these women. You want, rather, to be saved! For a goddess can heal the primordial wound, which is so constantly bleeding, which has drenched every mattress upon which you've ever lain when with a woman - a woman hardly made of flesh and blood, certainly not the sort who are likely to fart in the bed or to wake up annoyed. Rather an unearthly, mythological, quasi-divine princess! An angel! I wanted and continued to want beautiful, vulnerable faces which are completely and constantly visible - uncorrupted by time, by their inevitably moronic personalities, by their endlessly idiotic assertions, and, perhaps most of all, by their most usually monstrously unreasonable requests and needs.

I have felt this on a few precious occasions - this fantastical consummation, this reverent, terrified worship of a woman who, by virtue of her having remained profoundly out of reach, while still somehow managing to appear safe, kind, and compassionate, would then become for me a sort of goddess, an angel who offered me redemption, salvation - into whom I could melt, and because of whom I could cast off all the awfulness of my past, even my very self. These fantasies might last for a night, at best no more than a week, perhaps two, because they consisted simply of my lying beside, needless to say, not the actual, literal woman in question - in her I had very little or even no interest - rather, beside an imaginary, divine, celestial being, an enchantress of my own invention, whom

I fancied I could be more or less sure had no intention of either devouring or murdering me.

And by constantly checking her face, I could be anchored in a "now" that was safe. There was no mask about to slip off - she was not about to momentarily transform into some murderously lethal beast. There would be no shift, no turn! For I had taken the utmost care to pin down that moment with the most elaborate of pragmatic considerations, which had enabled and been fastened securely to the most deeply absurd and ridiculous of fantasies, all of which lit up my soul like a Roman candle, and which made of my heart a thing which, for a moment, I suddenly felt as if I possessed. It was all suddenly, miraculously whole! And I was even allowing it to beat freely, free of the fear of my imminent doom!

There was no longer a potential demon lying beside me, who could annihilate me in the middle of our relations, be those relations carnal, be they faux-emotional, or be they both. I was now to be nourished. That was the main thing. I was to be safe. I had insured it. I had engineered the most meticulous of specifications to insure it, for it was I who had crafted the film! I was now a Hitchcock, who cared but little for his actors, only for the effect he was after. I was a God.

I have since become something of a seer as well, a bit of a prophet. And I have managed to protect something delicate within myself, something sacred, which the world had tried for so long, and on countless occasions, to murder - for which the world never had, and still hasn't, a name. For I have touched goddesses and lived! Yes, I! Me! And I have done and experienced these things with real women! Flesh-and-blood women! Who were not entirely hidden behind scrims and countless applications of imaginary oil paints and fantasies! My successes, in this regard, have admittedly always been less than stunning, and yet they have not been entirely inconsequential.

Nonetheless, to this very day, and until the day I die, the woman I still so desperately want could not possibly ever exist, or, rather, if and when she were to exist at all, it could and would only be in fragments - in a scent, a voice, the words of a long-dead poetess, the ravishing soprano voice of some disembodied singer, in some adorably defenseless girl asleep in my bed, whom I feel relatively sure will not devour me, and who provides me with the raw materials for my endless, rapturous idealizations and hallucinations.

The woman whom I so fiercely desire is, as a result of my history and by necessity, purely mythological. She is my mother, redeemed. She is my savior, who never was and will never become my abuser. Why? Because she has promised, and I believe her! She gives me this promise often! In dreams, in my mind's ear, in the most delicious of visions, mirages, and reveries! She does not, she could not, possibly abide in the real, corporeal world - the world of women with pores, pubic hair, foul vaginal discharges - in this shithouse world in which we find ourselves, the one so full of sweat, spittle, and stink. She lives in me, and only in me. I am the one carrying her. I'm carrying her now, in this moment.

And I am constantly searching for her in beautiful things - in those temples of the mind in which the feminine can be sacred without being monstrous. No one else sees them, or could ever see them, these treasures that I carry so tenderly and guard so vigilantly amidst the ruins of my life, that I partake of so frequently, and even sometimes create. They are nowhere to be found in this world, the carnal, material world - the world of bodies, of lust, of smells, of misery, of the soul-crushing existential angst that inevitably follows coitus.

That world, the tangible, earthly world, is a place containing only surveillance, intrusion, and disgust - a world of toilets, plungers, and mortally dangerous paintings - of violence, humiliation, and annihilation. I, on the other hand, have thankfully become this sorcerer, who roams freely through inner and outer Chernobyls as if they were gardens of Eden, who has become more than a little adept at naming all the incinerated beasts who still lie about within them, within me, including those who still, at times, haunt my dreams. Of not only naming them - of no longer fearing them, of - dare I say it? - of accepting them entirely, even loving them.

I have fashioned the most marvelous of maps, in which all the trapdoors and locked basements are clearly marked, but which also point the way to a multitude of hidden temples and secret wells - to sacred, untouchable sanctuaries, into which only I am permitted. I! Me! Who had for so long lived in a cage deep within the earth, surrounded by barbed wire, thoroughly convinced that criminals worthy of Sade's novels would arrive at any moment - yet who desperately imagined, and who still imagines, that there will come a day when I shall be known, loved, and entirely resurrected from the ashes of my life.

But because to be close invariably meant, nay, guaranteed agony, betrayal, and disfigurement of the self, I have created from these ashes the most delightful and effective of solutions - to idealize and reveal only flashes of myself, knowing full well and expecting that, were I to dare to do more, the onlooker would either flinch, misunderstand, or simply flatten me. Yes, I still collapse into despair, blame myself for wanting too much, want undone what can never be undone - yet at the same time I am, or have, finally, become perfectly aware that no one is coming, that no one will ever be coming. That there will be no goddesses reciting incantations which might reverse what was done all those years ago. That no one ever had, has, or could possibly have the face pure enough, the touch safe enough, or the voice soft enough to erase those nightmares. Other than me! And therein lies the solution. I can do it, and I do.

For I have become quite the alchemist! I can transform rot into truth, psychic filth into beauty. It is a hopelessly and necessarily solitary road, but my road has always been solitary and reclusive. Only a fool would imagine, given my past, that it could ever be anything other than sequestered, cloistered, hopelessly and irrevocably alone.

There will be for me no plateaus of serenity, peace, or contentment, other than aesthetic. Instead there shall be only depictions of beauty, sadness, grief, horror - the truth about the fall, my fall, about the abyss which has been my life.

Oh yes, I am awful! Intolerant and impatient of arrogance, of lack of self-awareness, of cruelties far worse than my own, all those bitter, petty sarcasms and verbal displays of nastiness in which I too frequently indulge - that is to say, of ACTUAL cruelty.

I am sometimes full of, choking on, with, and from, disgust, rage, and contempt. Why? That's not hard. People are walking around garbed, head to toe, in bullshit, and drowning in hypocrisy. Pretending to be emperors, and I needn't trot out or belabor that particular metaphor. But I? I can no longer pretend.

I am simply attempting, and sometimes succeeding, in finding some tiny shred of nobility in my drinking of all these pots of black coffee at high noon, my looking with laser eyes on this empty, arid world, full as it is of braying hyenas, of self-important imbeciles and drones, who've no thoughts or hopes either of serenity, forgiveness, or of wisdom, much less of enlightenment.

The world is a shitshow! Albeit an entertaining one, at least at times - in which people who preach love practice deceit and manipulation, attempt to convince you of their victimhood after decades of their having engaged in passive-aggressive psychological warfare, and who tell themselves lies so filthy and egregious that their souls can no longer breathe.

On this mountaintop, the air is frightfully thin, yes! Dangerously so, at least at times - but the view is vast, and far preferable to the ignorance, depravity, and filth one finds at lower altitudes.

I have seen and been the victim of hosts of demons, she-devils, fishwives and harridans - and yet I have known the occasional angel. And, at this late date? I fucking know who's who. I've even experienced, recently and much to my surprise, the sort of love in which one wants nothing other than the well-being of the beloved, in which there is no need to possess, or to be understood in all the ways I've come to understand are simply not possible.

One spots gold rather easily, after having lived a life drowned beneath counterfeit moneys. When the real thing passes near? A small fire is born, even if it's just a flicker. It is a sacred thing, a thing in which one can warm one's hands, in which I can and do warm my hands - a small yet reliable, smoldering flame, which heats me more than sufficiently in this life which I now lead, the one on these frozen, lonely summits.

Have I been forced to lead it? I suppose I have. No matter - I accept it, all of it.

It is me, it is mine. It is my self, it is my life.

XXXII.

"In the countryside of my soul,
there stand two cathedrals..."

In the countryside of my soul, there stand two cathedrals, very grand and very ancient. They are my home, my place of refuge, my very self. The first is composed of anguish and of rage, and was built laboriously, with great care and the most meticulous attention to every last detail, over many decades, brick by brick. Its scaffolding is utterly familiar to me, for I was its architect. Within me, as well, are its masons, carpenters, sculptors, glaziers, and blacksmiths.

The second is far smaller, and lies deep within a barbed and thistly forest, overgrown with Black Roses, Honey Locusts, and Greenbrier vines. No outsider who is not intent on finding it is likely to stumble upon it. Its stones are black and weatherworn, its spires decayed and rusted. Deep within it, there is a sanctuary in which I often linger, and where any visitor would likely find me, not that he'd wish to do so, or that I'd wish him to. For it is, above all else, solitude which I seek there.

I drink of the waters which gush from its fountains, and in them bathe the pustules with which much of my flesh is covered. In this sanctuary, there is an altar, and upon that altar lies my grief, where it flourishes, glows, and beckons, like the redeemed Grail at the end of Parsifal. It demands of me the most constant obeisance, and I haven't any choice other than to submit, nor any wish not to. My prayers are for the most part devout, although, at times, rather more ambivalent, and, on occasion, even resentful. No matter. It never occurs to me to neglect my devotions.

To recite the daily prayers both nourishes me and leaves me famished, left as I am, when finished, starved of life, of agency, and of hope.

I am a deeply devoted, essentially simple, and profoundly humble monk, whose daily bread consists of little other than attending and conducting services within the walls and in the sanctuaries of these two cathedrals, as well as the procuring and lighting of candles, of washing walls, pews, and various implements of devotion, of sweeping up, of all the lowly and unassuming tasks required of me, services and tasks that cause my heart at times to bleed, and, at others, to shut down entirely. It is a posthumous life I have led these many years, and that I continue to lead.

I am now nothing but a ghost who has walked the earth for many decades, playing at grief as best I can, yet remaining unwilling to offer up more than modest sums at its gaming table, for were I to lose badly there, it would spell death, my literal death, the death of this weak, fragile, and emaciated body in which I find myself still encased. A death which, needless to say, has its appeal at times, but the truth is that this ghost, the ghost who I have become, who is me, is a coward, a limping phantom, a phantom which each day drags itself along the cobblestones and wooden floors of these churches into their sanctuaries and altars, and which retreats every night to once again lie down in its bed, inside the charred and crumbling house in which it pokes and prods the ashes of its life, wondering why and how it has managed to make it through another day, before eventually relaxing sufficiently and allowing itself to disappear for a time in sleep.

This phantom hasn't any need to travel to these churches, for they exist within it, that is to say, within me. And when I die, they shall disappear as well, unnoticed and unremarked upon, as they were in life. Are they beautiful? That I cannot say, nor does it matter. I know of no other churches with which I might compare them, for they are my very self. They are my very eyes, they are my very way of being in the world.

I created and built these edifices, whose congregation consists of me only, and I willingly entered into this sacred, posthumous life, because to have remained alive, in her absence, would have been obscene. Perhaps the sin is somewhat less for me than it would have been for another, given that I am a ghost. Perhaps it's even forgivable. I'd like to think that true. And the fact that I still walk the earth suggests I at least half believe that it is true.

It is without any question true that I have become a thing, a numb, bloodless, seemingly incorporeal being, and yet the embers that I feel occasionally roiling about in my guts suggest I've still got one foot kicking up the grass and moss in some abandoned cemetery, which I have sought, and in which I find myself wildly gazing about in the mad hope that I might one day stumble upon a living woman who is appealing, and of whom I can pretend to myself that I am fond, or, if she is not entirely appealing, at least doesn't appear to hate me, isn't frightened, and does not run away.

I know perfectly well that the wish is foolish, that it is laughable, preposterous. And yet, even now, at this frightfully late date, I have not managed to entirely kill it. It comes unbidden, to soothe and torment me in the altars of these temples which lie within me, and in those deserted graveyards in which I wander.

Were I to scream and unleash all that is contained within me, the sun would turn black and fall immediately from the sky, the land and seas would freeze, the clouds and birds drop like stones. Gargantuan tsunamis would swallow continents, and countless asteroids would be recalled from nearby solar systems to madly rush towards the belly of the earth, and, during all this, all the while, I would but smile contentedly. I would applaud, even laugh. I would, for those moments, feel myself once again alive.

There would no longer be any need of these churches, these ponderous, foul, and hateful synagogues which I created, carry, and bear within me. I would make of Nature my slave. I would destroy her, slice her belly open, rip her womb to shreds, so that she could no longer generate anything of any kind, whether living or inert. This, for me, would be the most delicious and most deserved sort of vengeance, one which would compensate me for the catastrophe which has been my life, and it is precisely the one which so endlessly torments me, because I am unable to bring it about.

I would be reborn in that inferno, had I the power to create it, nay, rather, I would be born for the first time. The locked vault in which I have been so long entombed would be cracked wide open. There would no longer be any need for irony, and for the innumerable, arrogant, eviscerating words which pour so frequently from my mouth. And once my body had shaken for sufficiently long and with sufficient violence, there would descend upon me a sacred silence, a peace of which I've only dreamt and never known, but that I am somehow able to imagine.

I would look upon all the annihilation which I had just caused, and which would now lie before me, with new eyes. And what was left of the world would, as a result, for the very first time, be beautiful. I would no longer have any reasons to feel contempt, or disgust, no longer be forced to listen to the involuntary, farcical protestations of faux love which too frequently dribble from my mouth, drenched, as they are, in artificially sweetened saliva, and the arsenic-laced acids of my stomach and spirit. All those things would simply vanish, for there would no longer be any need of them.

It's hard to envisage who I might then be, who I would perhaps become, who it might be that I'd allow myself to become, or with what tools I might construct this new self. How can a shriveled, hunchbacked golem, who for so long has stumbled about, bleeding hot lava from his pores and spewing it out of his mouth, imagine himself a sort of Olympian God? It's rather more likely that I would simply remain the very same, foul, misshapen creature I am at present, still ranting at the void, suffocated beneath magma, cinders, and ashes, looking about in vain for a person, preferably a woman, who might help, a woman who has never existed, does not now exist, and most certainly will not exist in the devastated landscape about which I so frequently fantasize creating.

No! None of this! Enough! Away with all this fantastical nonsense! I am a devout monk now. Little else. Nothing else. And it must suffice. My duty is to the places of worship I have created, in which I live, and from which I shall never escape.

What I can manage now to do is to grow dumb, like an indrawn breath, to become completely mute, even though my soul still so constantly howls for connection, and my bowels are bloated and distended with longing. No matter. I must cease speaking. I will not flood others, I will not flood, above all, her, with this ache. For her, I will push back this avalanche, push down this spewing jet stream of my hunger and need. Let it all bury me. That process is inevitable and already ongoing. So be it.

I'd much prefer to implode by the side of the road, or starve to death on the top of some frozen mountain, than hurt this woman, whom I so cherish. She is luminous, and because she is luminous, she makes me desperately want to say everything.

And yet that is quite precisely why I shall never speak a word. I want so desperately to say it all - everything! And yet not a word shall ever pass from my lips.

In the presence of others? If and when I happen upon them? I shall likely continue to bellyache, to rage, to hurl my laughable, Lilliputian lightning bolts, because none of them matter. Only she matters.

Longing is not love, although I spent a lifetime confusing the two. Longing carps, complains, and grovels. Love is quiet listening, stillness, prayer. I still feel the need, the hunger, the longing. It eats away at me incessantly. There is this horrid buffalo hump, which houses a ferocious, ravenous beast, at the base of my neck. It has been there for decades, growing ever larger. There are vanishingly few moments in which it neglects to choke me, and the threat of its suffocating me is nearly constant.

There are very few others able to see it. It is my need, my hunger, craving, bitterness, longing. It is the ravenous vulture from whose grip I am never released, and which so ceaselessly feeds on my flesh. Yet, for the most part, it is only I who ever see it, who is aware of its existence, and only me whom it so furiously chokes and attempts to strangle. I have never once observed it to hover over or peck at the flesh of another.

When I speak with her, or am merely in her presence, I am terrified the beast might slip its leash, make of me a sort of lovesick projection machine, a laughable, two-bit bard of desperation, babbling this or that inanity in a ridiculous, thoroughly contemptible effort to feel alive, which I haven't been or felt myself to be for decades, and which, more likely, I've never been, or felt myself to be. And yet, with her, there are these powerful hints and intuitions, wrong-headed as they are, yet so impossible to ignore, that such a thing might be possible.

From what materials do I construct these fantasies? These hopeless ambitions? These almost expectations? Not from anything I ever experienced. Of that I am entirely sure.

Ridiculous. I am ridiculous. This is so altogether ridiculous. I am disgusting. That child within me, who so often whispers, "If someone innocent and kind would only love me, perhaps I'd not be so entirely lost! If someone tender and vulnerable were to simply see me, somehow come to know me, perhaps I might still manage to be touched, cared for, saved!" Dear God! Would it be possible for me, or anyone who has ever had such thoughts, who possessed such an inner voice which spoke to him in so revolting a manner, to be more nauseating and loathsome?

I am starving, yes, but there is no intrinsic shame in being malnourished. That, in and of itself, is forgivable. To break character, however, would be appalling. To let go of that aloof, sardonic, arrogant, cold-as-fuck character, to drop the mask to which I have been so long habituated, and to which I have so long clung, for a duration sufficient to reveal the young boy within? That is impossible.

Everything I have just described is no longer a mask. I am no longer some costumed character, constantly vigilant, constantly on the alert regarding whether or not I need to silence some more authentic self lurking about within me. There is not the slightest chance that I will let rise, or could even let rise to the surface, that vile, needy, naive child, who at times still seems to be slinking around deep within my bowels, much less let him speak, to say his piece. He shall, rather, hold both his tongue and his peace, forever.

I wish him dead, and, indeed, I think he might very well be close to being so. It is, presently, only on rare occasions that I become aware of his lamely stirring within me, deep within my guts, his mucking about there, or imagine that I hear what most usually seem only the faintest echoes of his bitter tears, sighs, and moans.

He awakes in me, when I have the rare misfortune of becoming aware of his presence, not to mention the nagging persistence with which he makes that presence known, when he tugs at my pant leg with his needy, tearful, red, swollen, pinched eyes, the wish to piss on him, to throttle him, to beat him senseless.

To, at the very least, slam the door shut on him in shame, horror, and disgust, taking great care to attempt to ensure that he have no opportunity to show himself again.

That sniveling idiot! That brat! That hideous, snot-filled toddler! The one who still somehow manages to think and believe that there might exist some woman who could tolerate both his beauty and his gore, both the flecks of light and the sewers full of shit within him, which they illumine, someone who stays, in spite of the discomfort which he causes her. He knows, as well as I, that there has never been, is not now, and will never be any such person.

That child, splayed out and weeping on the floor, that bleeding, sobbing, insufferable beggar, who still believes there will be, that there will momentarily appear some good Mommy, a Mommy who will, at any moment, burst through the door, scoop him up, take him in her arms, and make it all stop, make this nightmare end, care for him, love him. My life has been spent standing on the head of a pin buried in the ashes of that foolish, utterly deranged hope, still half wearing the clothes of that contemptible whining boy, who was, and is, shrouded, scourged, and encased within breastplates, and all the other, countless pieces of armor in which he still sometimes walks the earth, and wearing the mask of a man who needs nothing.

Not "wearing"! No, no, no! For they were long ago glued to his face, body, and spirit with the most indestructible of adhesives. Yet there he is still, that vile boy, creaking under the floorboards of every relationship, every betrayal, every loss, every death - weeping, whining, singing his poorly composed and executed elegies. Begging, imploring, astonished at the violence still being inflicted on him, and unable to rise from the floor, pinned to it, as he is, in his disbelief.

Is he not to be once again spat upon? Was that not then, and is it not now, his destiny? What he, in fact, deserved then, and continues to deserve? Of course! Precisely so! That inner child was a victim of fate, of necessity. It was all, almost certainly, although in a way which can never be quite understood, his fault, his doing.

Whether it was karma, some metaphysical bit of folly cribbed from an uncharacteristically foolish, speculative essay of Schopenhauer, or, perhaps, simply a bit of snot that went this way rather than that when the Big Bang crapped this shithole of a universe into existence? The reasons for his lamentable existence and fate do not, ultimately, matter in the least, and they shall never be entirely discovered or enumerated.

What I do know is this: that little piece of shit deserved nothing then, and deserves nothing now. And I, who was once, sadly, he, will take great pains to make quite certain that nothing be exactly what he shall receive from this moment on. Monumental agony, bathed in the contempt of its giver. I hate that little boy. I would do far worse to him than anyone else ever did, had I the chance.

Were he to walk into this room now, in the flesh, or to crawl into it, with his snot-filled nose, with his tear-filled, beseeching eyes, I'd not befriend him. I would eviscerate him, disembowel him, flay him alive, and, like my mother, enjoy every moment of it. It's him I see in everyone, in all those I pretend to loathe in his stead, and in every last aspect of the entire world, which I pretend to loathe as well. But above all else, and above all others, it is him I loathe in my self.

But does not habit turn all this pretense, all this projection, into reality? Is it not them I now truly, that I actually hate? Do I not, having traveled so far, and having become so accustomed, so habituated to such feelings, do I not now honestly wish to incinerate the planet, to gut the sun? I do! Indeed, I do! This is now who and what I am, what I have become. No one, and nothing, other than this.

If this were, at one time, only armor, it has now become flesh, my flesh. That boy is long dead and gone. What remains is only the most impotent of shadows, a phantom.

And yet, I know perfectly well that all it would take would be for some lovely woman, whom I chanced upon, perhaps sitting in an alley - famished, poorly dressed, hopelessly, effortlessly, and deliciously vulnerable - who had given up both on herself and on everyone else, and who was now far too proud and exhausted to beg - for that desperately still longed-for woman to simply say, "I see you are bleeding there, Sir. Is there anything I can do?" And it would all fall away in a heartbeat.

This pose, these church robes, all the ceremonies, altars, sanctuaries, forests. They would disappear, all of them, on the spot. But do not speak to me of such things, of these other, very different shrines, sanctuaries, and places of worship, whose sermons I no longer possess the ears to hear.

I venerate now only the gods of grief and rage. It is to them I have devoted, and to them that I continue to devote, my life. And I could never, and shall never, abandon them. Were that brat to somehow stumble upon one of their premises, I would no longer recognize him. And, whether I did or did not, I would, seeing him for what he is, simply do the Lord's bidding, that is to say, I would slit his throat, flay him alive, and incinerate him upon the altar of my rage without a second thought, in the service of, and within the sanctuary of, what I have become, of who, and what, I now am.

If I could have spared the two of us the pain of being born, of having existed in the first place? That would be another matter. But who is that lucky? Neither he nor I. He knew then what I know now, what it means to be alive. And we both agree. Neither of us should have ever come into this world.

We are mistakes, abominations of Nature, that Nature which I am, at least at times, able to love, appreciate, and take pleasure in, but which I far more often abhor, and wish to annihilate, to extinguish, to massacre.

I find, now and then, that I am tempted to think myself noble. I flatter myself, fancy myself a sort of truth-teller, even something of an admirable fellow. But that despicably grandiose, disgusting notion inevitably disintegrates into dust, moments after I notice myself entertaining it. I recognize it for what it is, and it vanishes on the spot.

And, as a consequence, I am then quite automatically plagued with the most abominable self-loathing, although that, also, on a moment's reflection, reveals itself to be just another variety of vanity, another sort of grandiosity - self-love by another name, self-love simply wearing other clothes. On occasions such as these, it has merely dressed itself up in a sort of fashionable hair-shirt, picked up, perhaps, at some two-bit thrift shop, run by a former social worker, who's lost her license for malpractice, and worn, for a moment, in the hope that self-deprecation might, indeed, be a way to get others to like me. A strategy I have often heard, and which is frequently recommended, although there's not a grain of truth in it.

All of it, all of this, all of them, every last bit - the paralyzed four-year-old on the floor, the nasty sarcastic bastard, the cosmic sadist who would blow up the universe in a heartbeat - all of them would disappear, had I but ninety seconds lying next to the warm body of some woman of whom I could pretend to myself I was fond. But even were that to be the case, I am all too habituated, too accustomed to being all those other selves - the sarcastic one, the spiteful one, the faux brilliant, cynical, burnt-out one, the one who weeps what seem real tears, even in that moment to he that weeps them, but who hates himself for it five minutes later.

This is all so very boring. It is as if I have become a rather shabby and poorly dressed Duchesse de Guermantes, the one of whom Proust so endlessly writes, with an equivalent, though surely less delightful, generalized disdain - hopelessly contemptuous of and bored by all the parties which she resents having to give, but which she nonetheless secretly enjoys, for she knows nothing else, has never known or been taught anything else, and lacks the self-awareness to recognize any of the lies she so long ago learned to tell herself concerning such events and matters.

I am hopelessly, relentlessly contemptuous of and bored by the cruise ship disaster which my life has been, though I still find myself offering up every now and then some stale, cynical witticism which might even manage to get a forced laugh out of this or that passenger, on this or that deck, or in this or that party of this faux Duchesse of my own invention. But of course all this is nothing other than the purest, navel-gazing nonsense. There are no passengers on this ship, attendees at this party, no other worshippers in these churches, monks in these sanctuaries or at these altars. There is no one, other than me. And I am now simply attempting to navigate the ever shorter days of the few years which remain to me with as little suffering as I can manage, all the while lashed to the mast of my self-constructed, two-bit Titanic.

Look at me! I am nothing other than a wannabe Pulcinella, minus the great music. Cynical, cunning, greedy, needy, hypocritical, though still good now and then for the occasional dark, tepid joke. You know the sort, the kind that elicit at best a forced chuckle. But, rather, do not look at me. Please! Look away and not upon me. Not now, nor ever again.

Oh dear! It seems my black heart is beating, unsteadily and feebly, yet nonetheless. Perhaps it wishes to cough up another mediocre tune. I shall, however, take great pains to not allow it the chance. This Pulcinella recognizes full well when something unseemly rises to the level of its being intolerable. For mediocrity is, has always and ever been, intolerable. And, thankfully, having been well taught, this Pulcinella also knows its manners, as well as how to mind them.

XXXIII.

"I speak, you hear nothing..."

I speak, you hear nothing, or, let us say, nothing particularly akin to what I had intended. How could you really? Does one inspect the tennis ball while volleying? I toss it only to the perimeter of you, where it bounces against and then off your flesh, or, if you prefer, it simply disappears within you like a marble falling down a well. It's a negotiation, in which we walk gingerly past one another on a tightrope, while constantly looking down.

I am a well as well, dear. And on the walls of this well, there are pairs of half-blind eyes and half-deaf ears peering and poking out everywhere, which drink in the sensations of your words and of your expressions, which are then handed off to my imagination, where they become very different things. And with you, it is surely very much the same. It's the nature of the game, the steps of the only dances we are permitted to dance with one another. When we converse, the two of us crouch in the basements of our selves as a matter of course, quite unaware that we are doing so. To play a reasonable game of tennis requires the most constant vigilance, does it not? We play out of curiosity, out of loneliness, and out of love. Yet what I know of you is only a sketch, a poorly rendered sketch, of which I am nonetheless so very fond, for it is the sort of sketch which enables me to create a depiction of you in my imagination of which I am many times more fond. What you are, what you really are, in and of yourself, doesn't concern me, not because I am some sort of monster, but rather because it cannot concern me. It is not a thing I can know, to which I can ever have access. I can only be concerned with the canvases I later paint of you in my studio, which belong to me, as you are, doubtless, with yours. If I need something quickly drawn, that is to say, if my imagination is, for the moment, dormant, I might ring you, ask to see you, because I so delight in you, that is to say, I delight in what my idealization of you evokes in me. I have spent innumerable hours after our encounters fleshing you out upon canvases in my studio, in ways that please, stimulate, and arouse me.

We need, however, far stronger liqueurs than are afforded us by mere conversation. And where are we to find them? All I can know of you, when in your presence, is my poorly and rapidly drawn, constantly evolving sketch, which I then carry home when we part, that is to say, firmly grab hold of it, all the while taking great care to preserve its contours, in order that I might eventually set it down within the dwelling place in which my deepest self resides. I carry it to a sort of internal artist's studio, there to slop upon it whatever paints please me, and in whatever context or landscape I wish to place you. What you are, in and of yourself, doesn't concern me, because it cannot concern me, as I have said. And it is not otherwise with you, with your sketches and canvases. It is simply not possible for us to know one another in any real way, my dear, beloved friend. I am ultimately only concerned with and fond of only the canvases in my studio, as you are with those in yours. If I need something quickly drawn, that is to say, if my imagination is hungry, and is, for the time being, dormant, I'll likely ring you, eager for an interaction which might provide me with material, with some up-to-date drafts I can then cultivate and develop at my leisure. And because I like you so very much, rather, because I like what my idealization of you evokes in me, it is likely to be quite the afternoon I'll then be spending in my studio, fleshing you out, as they say, in ways that please me, stir me up, even arouse me. Yes, yes - you are indeed playing a part in a little play for which you've never auditioned! As I am, just as surely, in one of your little potboilers. It's the best any of us can do, it is the nature of the game. Conversation achieves nothing, because it can achieve nothing. For what is called friendship is, ultimately and necessarily, a lie. We are only ourselves when we are alone. We all know that perfectly well. To attend a party is to play pickleball with baboons. And we know that going in.

We gather, in pairs, in groups, just as Schopenhauer said we do, like porcupines - warming ourselves as best we can with one another's heat, while simultaneously bearing the paints, brushes, and canvases upon which we will later soothe, entertain, inspire, and nourish ourselves, and, insofar as we are able, of which we shall then later dream. But all this only insofar as we've been provided with anything sufficiently substantive to evoke these pleasant sensations within us in the first place. As you do indeed provide me, my dear friend, so constantly and reliably.

Now, as for our talk earlier today - why did you say precisely...? Well, you know what it was, surely you do. How many calculations had you made before you uttered it? Did you adjust your words, worry whether or not they would be too honest, or if, having said them, I would continue to be just as fond of you? Or, horror! If it might be something that would, perhaps, be lethal to the friendship? Were you not constantly ushering away the real you, escorting her down the stairs leading to the basement of your very self, where, were she to speak her mind, she'd be far less likely to be heard? And of course I was doing the very same thing, all the while! When we converse, the two of us, my cherished friend, we are treading water, taking care to keep our heads, and most importantly, our mouths free of the pool's ingredients, composed as they are of all those facets of our deepest selves which, by virtue of our having been forced to its surface, are, for the most part, unavailable to us. Each of our pools is bottomless, as is each of our selves, and each of us can only taste of their utmost depths when alone. In the course of any conversation we might have, have had, or will have, we are forced to deny ourselves access to those deepest parts of ourselves. We only delude ourselves when we think otherwise. And yet, here we are. I would not trade our talks for any path which does not lead to you.

You look away when you speak, but quickly raise your eyes to look at me when I speak. And I do very much the same! Why? I am not entirely sure, but it seems to me likely that doing so provides us with the opportunity to dive within ourselves for at least a moment, insofar as the circumstances of the conversation, our mutual comfort, and our individual bravery and persistence allow, in an attempt to be more honest with one another, for you and I have conversations far deeper and more honest than most, which is precisely why they are so infinitely precious to me. Yet, in those moments when we each look away, in the attempt to access deeper parts of ourselves, that is very far from the only thing that we are doing. We are also anxiously asking ourselves how what we are considering saying next might land, if it would, perhaps, be potentially dangerous or poisonous to the friendship, whether we should refashion it or, conceivably, omit it entirely. We are continuously calculating, and it is exhausting. Is it not, my beloved friend? Are you not exhausted by it as well? Of course you are - we both are. Thus, at the very same time we are attempting to be more present and honest, we are busy doing its very opposite.

Let us go then, you and I, my sweet friend, for I am so very fond of you, though do let us also admit to ourselves that, in so doing, in our going "together", we are, at the same time, both of us patients etherized upon a table, that is to say, necessarily prohibited from being and accessing our deepest selves, though through no fault of our own - we are, in fact, doing far better than most. It's simply the nature of such interactions - they necessarily keep us on our surface. Whenever it is I speak to you, listen to you, or craft what it is I might next say to you, the well of my deepest self is not accessible to me, certainly not in anywhere near its entirety. It becomes opaque, and, if and when I do manage to dredge up something from its depths, I never share it with you without first considering its appropriateness, the possibility of its being ill-timed, ill-suited, even perilous, whether uttering it will promote or impede our friendship, if there's some chance it might hurt you, if it were better either reshaped or simply left unsaid.

Were we to come together, my dear, truly come together, not as in the vulgar contraction of pelvic muscles and seminal vesicles, rather, were we to fuse the richness each of us possesses in the very depths of our being, the hoards and riches in the depths of the well that is ourselves, which we are so very careful to squirrel away, and to which we do not have easy or voluntary access, would we not then be undone, would we not go quite mad? Were those parts of ourselves to be understood and embraced, each by the other? Were a few, or perhaps more than a few, bits of what is most profound and intense within ourselves somehow able to merge? That is a foolish and pointless speculation. Nothing other than the purest claptrap. Such things are simply not possible.

So let us go on then, you and I, my beloved friend - let us go on then treading water, as best we can. For what I am able to grasp of you, the sketches, poor as they are, those that I am able to fashion of you, make my soul blossom. They, and you, enable me to experience what is best within myself. If friendship is a lie, if our friendship is a lie, it is a beautiful lie, and one to which I shall cling until the last light fades. If, when we converse, we give and take from one another nothing worth acquiring, why do we so seek it? And why do I seek it so deeply and profoundly with you, above so many others? Because your presence enchants, captivates, and inflames me. When my eyes light upon you, it is like a sudden, brilliant strike of lightning which leaves me breathless and amazed, as if I were some hibernating beast, awakening to spring. I am happy to excuse the faults I see and hear in you - they are nothing to me, for they are outnumbered in countless ways by what is wonderful and divine in you. Yes, I can be sated, even by you, by our meetings, at times even easily or quickly sated, but without you, without them, my beloved friend, I would surely wither and die.

Let us go then. You. And I.

Appendix

To come or to go, that is the question:
A rigorous academic comparison of ejaculatory versus
defecatory pleasure in miscellaneous male subjects

In debates concerning whether the pleasure of the male orgasm is less than, equal to, or surpasses that of taking a massively explosive crap after having been constipated for several days, there are several things the disputants must necessarily consider. To level the playing field of said debate, we shall assume that the fucker in question has not had his orgasm for a good bit of time, perhaps even a period of weeks.

We shall do well to first consider the respective conditions in which the two subjects of our thought experiments find themselves once they have fucked or shat. As Schopenhauer tells us, "Directly after copulation, the devil's laughter is heard," that is to say, the sexual act inexorably chains the one in its grip to a cruel, mindless will, which is concerned only with the propagation of the species, and which cares not a whit for his personal welfare. As a result, after his orgasm, the fucker will more than likely experience an involuntary, transcendental clarity about the meaninglessness both of his previous desire and of the act itself, along with a sense of grief concerning the suffering the act has been engineered to perpetuate, that is to say, the suffering which would necessarily constitute no less than a part, and more likely the majority, of the new sentient being's existence, for which he is responsible. The emptiness he inevitably feels results from his realization that he's been nothing other than a blind, unwitting pawn of this instinctual force, and that he has been once again enslaved by it in order to do its bidding, like a helpless, inert puppet, forced to dance this way and that by a mad puppeteer. He perceives his complicity in an act the sole purpose of which is to create more of the horrid creatures with whom he is forced to interact daily in the course of his life, beings whose existence and suffering are every bit as appalling as his own. And, in addition, there now lies before or beside him the thing with which he has just busied himself, the woman, with and by whom it is expected he is to now speak, and of whom he may be expected, even by himself, to pretend to be fond.

Shitting, on the other hand, is quite another matter. After a bout of constipation, it is a reliably ecstatic experience, one of the very few offered us in this sordid life into which we have all been thrown, the aftermath of which is the purest bliss, a feeling of the most intense euphoria. Think long and hard upon the gargantuan craps in which you have delighted when home alone. Your toilet has behaved as if she were the ultimate lover, the most delicious of paramours, one at your constant beck and call and willing to satisfy your every wish - far purer, more welcoming, and enticing than any conceivable lover of flesh and blood could ever be. She behaves as if she were the most ravishing, generous, and benevolent of sexual partners - a sort of quasi-angelic being, a partner who serenades you with the most exquisitely delicious hymns both to and in bed, where she tenderly rubs your tense shoulders, while uttering a host of promises she fully intends to keep. Her seat is neither warm, nor is it cold. It is cool, like a pillow is cool in the most luxurious of dreams. Just right, just so - perfect. You take a deep breath as your ass parts in spiritual anticipation: it is as if your buttocks are now two beloved elderly neighbors who, having moved themselves to the side of the road, are now smiling broadly and waving you on encouragingly as you urgently and rapidly pass to your destination. You shiver with delight. A gorgeously sculpted log, perhaps two, perhaps three, make their way into the world. Like Olympic divers, they pierce the welcoming waters, making the most lusciously whispered of splashes, and the sounds of those splashes warm your heart every bit as much as they do your bowels. The sensation leaves your entire body tingling. You have suddenly become light, weightless, like an angel, relieved now of all the sufferings of this painful, cruel, and sordid world to which we have all been so brutally condemned. You wipe until you no longer have the need, and see now that the paper has become as white and pure as a forest snow in deepest winter. And although you recognize that pride is a less than admirable emotion, you cannot help yourself. You take several moments to admire and gaze upon your work. You are overcome with immense contentment, enchantment, even elation. After a heartfelt salute, the two of you part ways. The perfect poop. It is a shit-eating grin which now adorns your face, and not one easy to camouflage, although you will take care to not inform others of its origins. You are now quite certain that life will not torture you for many hours to come. You even find yourself tempted to make an anonymous ASMR video recounting the spiritual nature of what you have just experienced, for the generosity of spirit with which you are now overcome, as a result of having shat like this, so copiously and satisfyingly, now produces in you feelings of joy every bit as monumental as were the turds themselves. The Japanese have a word for it: "kaiben." The literal translation is "pleasantly smooth defecation," a perfectly wonderful word, and one which demonstrates how hopelessly impoverished the English language is. We possess no word or phrase to express the sublime pleasure of sitting upon a porcelain throne, and to then be both enveloped within and overwhelmed by the pure ecstasy of pushing out of ourselves this deeply hoped-for, wondrous, and seemingly divine "kaiben." One feels as if one is astral traveling, for one does indeed leave the body on those holy occasions during which the turd winds its way so artfully and sensuously out of the body. Who can possibly describe it, this immaculate anal birth? Who has the words, the music? The feelings of accomplishment, satisfaction, and love which accompany the taking of a massive dump are every bit as profound as those of a new mother gazing in rapture upon her newborn infant, and weeping copious tears of joy.

If you are a simpleton, materialist, or scientific reductionist, you might be tempted to write all this off to the stimulation of the prostate. But if you are one of the aforementioned, you will, when doing so, necessarily bump into the hard problem: that dry, hard, lumpy stool which has perplexed philosophers for millennia. For the stimulation of a prostate in what you would claim is a straightforwardly material world is a thing very different from the transcendent, almost religious ecstasy of "poo-phoria," which is hardly made of matter, including the wondrous matter one has just shat. It is an experience which transcends, and is of a very different nature from, anything in the material world. It is common knowledge that many children of potty-training age go to great lengths to hold their poop in because of the very great pleasure which it affords them. And there are more than a few reports of adults who literally "come" every time they poop, who experience full-blown ejaculations, complete with eyes rolled back in their heads, tremblings, and convulsions, which are accompanied by wild, uncontrollable moaning. Whether he be a child or an elderly adult, when the shitter holds back his poop, and when that poop is begging, screaming, beseeching that it be allowed entry into the world, he will, when finally unleashing it, experience a surge of pleasure so massive that his legs will go weak, he will be left breathless, and his soul will be bathed in the sacred waters of a paradise in which he would endlessly tarry, were he able. These deliriously intoxicated shittings have been known to last up to a half-hour, a third of which often consist of exactly these sorts of jaw-dropping "poo-gasms." Compare now these scenarios of euphoria and bliss with simple post-coital dysphoria, with the feelings of sadness, anxiety, agitation, and emptiness which appear immediately after ejaculation and can linger for hours - for far longer than hours, for lifetimes in fact, in persons given to serious existential reflection.

These experiences are not the norm, and yet the norm never involves anything less than the infinitely sweet feeling of having a now empty bowel, not to mention the potential delight of then standing up from that throne upon which one had just been so pleasurably sitting, and gleefully cutting the poo into countless little artistic slices with the bold stream of one's urine.

Ejaculation provides a quick hit of dopamine, there's no denying it, but it's over rapidly, and is inevitably followed by the dysphoria described above. It is an intense, peak pleasure, but impossibly and infuriatingly transient. The release of semen leaves one drained, depressed, and unmotivated, and for a very straightforward reason: Nature has forced you to do her filthy bidding, and no longer requires anything more of you. Hence she offers you nothing further, other than misery and regret. On the other hand, after a healthy, massive crap, one is reborn, drunk with delight, elated, transported, and left with a supreme and long-lived sense of well-being. It is a cataract of the self, in which the soul discovers, through its relinquishment, its very deliverance, for who has not felt, in that paradoxical moment of possession by dispossession, that emptied fullness in which we are briefly absolved of time's curse, of its fiendish hold upon us, the soul's "excremancipation," in which it experiences not merely relief, that sad and pale cousin of joy, but, rather, a cosmic becoming and transcendence of what was, but a moment ago, a self so endlessly and hopelessly constipated with, and suffocated by, anxieties, hoardings, and bloat. We become the gladsome auditors of the plainchant of the enteric brain, that second cerebrum, whose intestinal choreography has now joyfully delivered us from the mundane landfill of our appetites into the inner sanctum of our very self, that most sacred of spaces, holiest of holies, in which the soul floats free of the body, disentangled from all suffering, viscera, and, best of all, liberated finally of shit. For when the body, which has suffered for so long under the tyrannous and cruel yoke of retention, is able to finally and violently surrender its siege-stones to gravity, there arises, not a madrigal of narcissism, but, rather, a Brucknerian coda of feces - a symphonic, excremental peroration, a feeling that the ledger has, at last, been balanced, that the scales of the cosmic order have been satisfied, that the universe is no longer quite so eagerly battering at the gates of one's abdomen, and that the paltry ego, nay, the world-knot itself, is no longer anywhere near so gnarled and twisted as it was only moments before.

If we now cross gingerly from physiology into psychology, that fetid drawing room where impulses, dressed up as motives, sip aperitifs, we must acknowledge that to shit, the act of shitting, despite its petty everyday crimes of vanity, personal melodrama, and the dull-as-dishwater operettas of third-rate tunes with which it is so often rife, brings with it a recognition through otherness in which the desiring self encounters its own absence, after which there now ensues a duet between the self, as it is imagined, and the ego, which has now, as a result of said shitting, been sufficiently inflated to be ready and able to greet it. In brief, the psyche does not merely evacuate its internal pressure: it composes and gives to this pressure an immense, universal, and colossal significance. The retention which had so infantilized the shitter just moments ago is now undone both by and through the "excremancipation" mentioned above, in which there remain no further breeding grounds for distortion, and no frivolous hoardings which might sour any jealous household gods with which one is burdened. It is as if the soul were now a falcon, loosed from earth's heavy chains, winging its way through the empyrean, untouched by the dust below. Beware that constipation of spirit which continues to stubbornly refuse to let go either of its stools or its stories. That soul shall be left wandering through a museum of fetid heaviness, to which it shall be condemned for all eternity. To be redeemed, it must embrace a brave new ethics of exit, a "letting-go-matics," in which it will learn that every taking must be conjoined with a giving, every savor with a severance. The commode will no longer be simply a throne. It will be the classroom in which humility conducts its most persuasive seminar, the chief concern of which will be the metaphysic of "enoughness," that is to say, that the world, once taken in, must also be let out, that the economy of being is no simple accumulation, but rather one of circulation, and that the truest deliverance consists not in departure from oneself, but, rather, in a humble return to the ordinariness of the commonplace, that prosaic province in which the self finds itself able to encourage its angelic nature to embrace and kiss the animal lying within, to, as it were, shake hands with the janitor of its bowels, nay, to become that very janitor - to revel, embrace, and merge with its custodial nature.

On the other hand, with each ejaculation, there is now the threat of progeny, for with every squirt there comes the threat of a potential mortgage. Whereas each and every bowel movement, noble and brown, necessarily, and by its nature, produces nothing other than the supreme moral victory of emptiness, the blissful transcendence of that nice, "clean-on-the-inside" sensation - a sacred, holy redemption. Tell me all this isn't poetry. Walt Whitman would feel compelled to, at the very least, tweet it. This argument's opponents might now be tempted to claim that masturbation or romance allow for imagination, for a narrative denied the shitter. That with fucking, there is the possibility of delicious yearning - for fantasy, high-end dramaturgy, and that pooping has no foreplay. But that's all the purest rubbish. Prior to an explosive defecation, there has always been the most meticulous, extraordinary foreplay: ceaseless preparation and anticipation, the slow build and promise of feverish intestinal voyages taken on barges, the chambers of which have been loaded full to bursting with lentils, fear, and hope, along with countless intoxicating Arabian Night tales of fiber and fate. The urge rises not like simple, vulgar lust, but, rather, as if making divine prophecies, inevitable and pure. And so the toilet seat awaits, cool as the lover's indifferent thigh. The orchestra tunes, gravity takes its solo, and then... Splish! Splosh! Splat! Nirvana. Can any gooey, sticky, guilt-ridden, post-coital tissue possibly claim the purity of that ivory-pure, alabaster bit of toilet paper, once it has become that divine milk-white and unblemished pearl, so beloved of shitters? Once it has, shall we say, completed its ascent into heaven? The fucker chases pleasures that end in disgust. He comes, then curses both himself and his existence. The shitter finishes lighter, cleaner, and ready to face the day. The fucker busily Googles penance, while the shitter walks merrily through, nay, floats merrily over, the park, the town, the nation, the globe itself. Romance? Those who crow of romance? Their insipid moans are prayers heard only by Mephistopheles. The toilet is the last and most precious confessional booth of our sin-drenched, secular world, in which there is no need of priest, and no small, watery, hypocritical talk to be made. Just silence, porcelain, and the aleatoric hum of the vent fan. Bliss.

Consider what follows. It is taken from the journals of a desperately unrelieved man:

"I haven't taken a shit in nineteen days, nor have I ejaculated. I am, at this point, less a man than a hopelessly pressurized vessel of thwarted natures, a double-locked chamber of unspeakable yearning - my semen boiling upwards, my feces downwards, each seeking its escape, neither permitted its discharge. There is a fullness in me, obscene and philosophical. I am now a veritable Platonic realm of aching blue balls and abdominal agonies. My guts hum like wasp nests. My testicles complain like twin philosophers, suspended upon a meathook in the ninth circle of the inferno. The devil whispers in my sigmoid colon of the tortures to come. Last night, I dreamt of the perfect poop. I saw it descending in slow motion, as if held aloft by the blessed pilgrims of Tannhäuser. It was elegant, sculpted, a turd worthy of Michelangelo. The dream was so vivid that I awoke crying with relief, certain that I had been delivered. But no. It was only air - a false, lying dawn, the betrayal of a deceitful, mendacious sphincter. My stomach, meanwhile, had begun whispering in tongues, each undigested meal a symphony of remorse. I felt only the faint rumblings and sighs of the ghosts who inhabit my bowels.

And then there is my lust, which builds like methane in a sealed mine. Each woman I pass seems to exude not only perfume, but fiber as well - insoluble, mocking fiber. They walk, these lust-drenched beasts, without a care in the world, while ceaselessly, inadvertently, and involuntarily displaying the derision of their perfect digestion - their eyes laxatives, their laughter peristalsis. I cannot look without yearning for both reliefs at once - to come, to go - and, if neither is to be had, to be once and for all, irrevocably, gone.

I have tried everything: walks, prunes, philosophy. My viscera have become a theological paradox. The sperm and the stool have entered into a silent pact of rebellion, as if they were two prisoners refusing parole. Sometimes I imagine that if one escapes, makes it out, the other will too, and that I will simultaneously ejaculate and defecate, an event of such cosmic symmetry it would likely end the universe. Is this why I dare not push? Do I, perhaps, fear transcendence? My mind circles endlessly - which pleasure is greater, which truer? The ejaculation? Violent, specific, with its brief annihilation of self? Or the defecation - serene, expansive, with its so deeply coveted rebirth into cleanliness. The one creates, the other absolves. Creation, absolution - the two crimes of simply being alive. I suspect now that God, if He exists, is a constipated, ferociously horny being, and that even He is eternally denied his relief in both the domains in which he has decreed that his creatures suffer so in order to maintain the tensions implicit in creation. Each star, each thought, each sin, a trapped bubble of divine gas.

I can no longer distinguish between the erotic and the excretory. I cannot dream of fucking a woman without a symphonic soundtrack of voluminous plopping sounds, followed by the most shattering flourishes of orgasmic splashes and flushes. My libido and colon are locked and loaded within a perpetual single prayer. Perhaps this is all that remains of philosophy: the search for the proper outlet. Plato spoke of realms to which we might ascend. I, simpler and more earthly, speak and dream only of evacuation. I am a sort of Job, nay, a Sisyphus, sloshing my way through a seemingly infinite sigmoid colon towards the holy grail of my rectum, a destination at which, it seems, I shall never arrive.

Yet hark! I feel something stirring now! A tremor! My body vibrates like a machine warming to its purpose. Could it be?? Is there to be deliverance???

If I should perish mid-effort, tell them - tell the scholars and the doctors that, although I did indeed love them all, the ejaculators and the defecators both, it is ultimately and quite decisively with the defecators that my heart lies. Nothing could be clearer to me, nothing more true! And thus the tides of my fate now beckon, my providence calls and is seemingly at hand. Thus my calling rises up before me: I am to be the Walt Whitman of shit! Smelling not of my armpits - no, we'll have none of that - but rather of my poops! I shall write endless verse, stanza upon stanza, bathed in the giddiness and beatitudes of my divine excretions, in their stench, and in my boundless love for them. Having expelled and, thank heavens, continuing to now expel, multitudes, I shall spend the remainder of my life creating the most monumental exaltations, panegyrics, and eulogies for the consecrated hailstorms of these golden-brown blessings!

And yet I know full well that every morning I shall once again perform my necessary rituals: those of coffee, fiber, and despair. It shall never be otherwise - but that there shall then come, as a result, again and again, perfect mornings, which shall be countless in their number, in which the air will hum, thick with possibility, full of gentle, gliding descents, and with the near-silent Olympic dives into porcelain pools of those brown, colonic gods whom I so worship, and from whom is never heard a hint of splash, followed eventually by that single, ecstatic, pristine wipe of toilet paper, as stark-white as a readily surrendered flag. I shall then, once again, salute my work, bid it a tearful goodbye, and flush it to the destiny for which it so longs, there to plumb the depths of what will surely and always be its, and my - ongoing, personal, Nirvana.

How pitiful, though, that a man's entire metaphysics can be traced along a few feet of tubing. The philosophers speak of Being and Nothingness. As for me? I LIVE it. Even the most cherished of my dreams are, these days, almost entirely somatic, of incomprehensibly sparkling-clean public restrooms, whose stalls stretch to an infinity populated by angelic hosts, all crying Hosannas for the redemptive peristalsis of my soul. And so it is that I, at the very same time that I celebrate these empyrean mysteries, envy the beasts. The dog squats, the bird voids mid-flight. It is only man that so endlessly sits on porcelain and is forced to philosophize thus.

If I should perish on some future night, ruptured and unspent, let this be my testament: that the chief and foremost pleasure in my life has been, only and ever, the final unfettered overcoming of my hesitation, those great leaps downwards for which I have spent my days in the most constant and resolute of prayers. And that the body, given the chance, can and will turn all of philosophy into nothing more or less than straightforwardly understood plumbing, both inner and outer, and that, short of the final triumph of the grave, the only reliable and constant victory consists in nothing other than that sacred silence which ensues after the sound of the last flush has finally retreated into eternity, when all that has passed through my ass darkly melts into the imperishable weave and fabric of time, is dissolved into the unchanging ether, and becomes irretrievably loosed from the bonds of all that was once mortal."

Abstract

The manuscript above, discovered near the lavatory in Room 7B, is analyzed herein as the first recorded instance of "Simultaneous Ejaculatory-Defecatory Retention Syndrome" ("S.E.D.R.S."). The patient's writings suggest a strong initial conflict between sympathetic and parasympathetic imperatives, which produced in him, in its first early stages, a psychosomatic stalemate at the interface of libido and bowel, a deadlock eventually resolved, with extraordinary relief and pleasure on his part, by and through his massively crapping.

Psychodynamic Interpretation

Following Freud's observation that the child who withholds feces achieves proto-sexual gratification, the subject's abstinence can be read as a regression to what we shall henceforth refer to as his "anal idealism," that is to say, a fixation on what Jung would later call the "Archetype of the Perfect Log," a symbol of both death and deliverance which Jung located in the collective unconscious, which he made up out of whole cloth, and then declared present in all cultures and at all times. The subject's simultaneous dread of and longing for release reflect a

Kierkegaardian anxiety in the face of what the subject perceived as infinite possibility.

Concluding Remarks

Comparative studies reveal widespread tension between creation and elimination. In the case of this subject, the stated dread of potentially creating more horrid creatures with whom he would then be forced to interact, whose existence and suffering he concludes would likely be every bit as appalling as his own, and the various forms of dysphoria he experiences when confronted with the expectation that he speak with the thing lying before or beside him, or even pretend to be fond of it, has historically repeatedly and significantly dampened the pleasure quotient of his orgasms. However, and this is crucial: at the same time, the solitary nature of defecation seems to reliably restore his feelings of existential authenticity. The authors of this study see no downsides to said preference, even to his living only for it and for it alone, nor to his obeisance towards, and constant worship at, its porcelain altar. The defecatory act has become, for him, the equivalent of a symbolic, civic, even religious ritual of individuation - a joyous, festive flush, propelling him towards self-actualization and freedom, as both the overcoming of his individual suffering and the unraveling of what he perceives as the mysterious world-knot which lies at the heart of being, that cosmic labyrinth and tangled skein of being, which so inevitably unnerves him in his times of sustained constipation.

Postscript

The truth is that I've never really had anything significant in the way of talent. The only talents I've ever really possessed or displayed were curiosity, discipline, of the obsessive-compulsive type, and the ability to be moved, none of which has ever been of the slightest use to anyone other than me. These things did, however, enable me to survive in a world in which, had I not had recourse to them, I would surely have died in early childhood. I am, however, perpetually haunted by what seems to me a not-trivial question: was it a good thing that these gifts, such as they were, helped me to survive? A two-part question, naturally. Was it a good thing for me, needless to say, as well as - was it a good thing for those with whom I had human relationships of various kinds? The question of whether my being born in the first place was a good thing, that is to say, whether it was some sort of blessing or boon that I came into this world at all, is a very different one. It is a question to which I have a very straightforward, one-word answer, which you can, perhaps, guess.

It is hardly surprising that I was once again haunted by this enigma, and with a particularly vehement potency, while reading much of what is contained in the volume of poems and prose you now hold in your hands, full as it is of these hopefully well-manicured, and, at times, perhaps quasi-inspired, but, more often than not, extremely intense, relentlessly unpleasant explosions of uncalled-for, egregiously narcissistic, psychic diarrhea, the likes of which would be more than enough to convince any remotely sane person, in whose ranks I would like to believe I belong, at least most usually and for the most part, to never again write such things - nay, to perhaps never again write much of anything at all. Not to mention, in my case, to cease writing music as well. Dear God! All those little, inconsequential ditties I've coughed up over the years. They absolutely do not stand in need of any future offspring or siblings. It seems high time to cease playing them, to perhaps cease even playing the music of other, far greater composers, and to, perhaps sooner rather than later, quite possibly cease playing entirely. At the very least, to most certainly never again have the effrontery to lift a pen in order to write such things with which this volume is so rife, to so much as observe my fingers typing a single word of this sort of stuff. But why stop there? To perhaps never again write a single word of any type, to perhaps never again so much as utter one.

Consider Samuel Beckett, always on about the absurdity of, well, pretty much everything under the sun - waiting, wanting, time, one's intentions, existence, and, not least, and this is crucial, the failure of language. He thought language the behavior of charlatans, that it was necessarily duplicitous, narcissistic, and hypocritical. And yet on he went, coughing up this and that, one "work" after another, to which he unfailingly signed his name, and about which he frequently coached performers and directors, until his very last years. Or John Cage, who loved to so incessantly chatter, at great length and in front of as large and frequent an audience as would have him, about how the role of the composer was no more than to be a "facilitator" of sound and of chance, as opposed to being a creator or shaper of personal expression, seeing not the least irony in giving and writing endless, long-winded, pseudo-Zen-inspired lectures and books concerning how we would all do best to "put aside our egos," and how all previous musics were the purest anathema to him, since they sounded to Cage as if they were rarely anything other than the chatter of hopelessly arrogant people, all babbling away incessantly and in the most unseemly of fashions, and ultimately offering little else other than this or that bit of more-or-less polished self-aggrandizement. And yet he somehow managed never to shut his mouth, stop writing articles and books, choose not to sign his name to his self-described "facilitations," cease performing his "music" in frequently large halls, in front of considerably sized audiences in whose applause he would cheerfully bask, or to think twice about his name having been emblazoned on the entrance to any lecture hall in which he spoke. How are we to describe or understand this sort of behavior? As deeply un-self-aware vanity? Or perhaps as cowardice? Or possibly more straightforwardly and likely - as nothing other than completely conscious, self-serving hypocrisy? As pure, cynical, intentionally malevolent deception? Whichever description one thinks most apt, or whether one finds any of them explanatory, matters very little. The fact remains - they, and other lesser, and far lesser nihilists, absurdists, and pessimists, such as I, have no shame, or at least seem to feel or display no shame, in prattling on relentlessly in whichever manner it is in which each of us favors prattling, all the while displaying a shocking either unwillingness or inability to acknowledge how undignified and ironic our continuing to blab away, scribble away, sing, play, or "facilitate" away might be, that is to say, how utterly revolting, or, at best, of little interest others might find such things - "their" things, "my" things; that is what's most crucial and ironic, that it be "their" things, "my" things. They, I, we, all of us shameless dissemblers and frauds, claim to disparage life, authorship, and meaning with the greatest enthusiasm, all the while expecting others to accept our claims at face value. It seems to occur to not a one of us to SHUT THE FUCK UP, in order that we might retain a modicum of dignity, honesty, and consistency. Of course it "occurs" to us, needless to say, but we're all just enjoying it far too much! We reveal ourselves to be the self-absorbed blowhards we so fundamentally are with every word we write, with every keystroke, in everything we say, sing, declaim, in every last aleatoric car horn, snippet of radio broadcast, and fart we invite into one of our dreadful sonic stews, from which any sane auditor predictably flees.

Most of the pages of this book are worthy of not a great deal more than being perhaps recited in some typically dreadful, embarrassingly overlong TikTok video in which some young lady swoons, begs shamelessly for attention, and cries the most perfectly obvious faux tears, in a desperate and brazen quest for what she imagines will be the kindness and condolences of perfect strangers, one in what is almost always a succession of countless performative pity parties of this sort by such persons, or conceivably shouted from a hastily improvised Hyde Park lectern by some apparently demented, geriatric, scruffy, bearded, unwashed, shaggy-dog of a man, dressed in a hopelessly tattered, dirt-brown overcoat, and sporting a laughably absurd, ill-fitting derby, his arms engaged in the wildest and most laughably histrionic of gestures, his voice a raucous, grating foghorn, fueled by and choking with cough drops, chewing tobacco, more than a little dementia, and a deep and desperately profound resentment.

There is something so wrong, so profoundly undignified, nay, so absolutely disgusting about continuing to speak after declaring speech corrupt, about continuing to write after declaring writing a fraud, about continuing to produce music after declaring the production of music nothing other than the shameless display of its composer's vanity and pride. The logical response would be silence! The honest response would be silence! Of which Cage intermittently professed to be fond, that is until the moment in which he would inevitably cough up his latest, predictably unlistenable horror. And yet here I am, self-publishing this nonsense, for openers, and for at least a few more lines, still talking, typing, dishing out this dreck, this psychic offal, as if the very act of acknowledging its worthlessness somehow absolved me of the indecency of having created it. But that shan't be for much longer, dear reader.

For these are all things that should never have been, and, in my particular case, things which have been composed by a man who should never have been either, but who has, at least and at last, thankfully become a man who has realized that the time for putting an end to all of this hypocritical posturing ought to be now. Ought to have arrived, ought to have already arrived. But how to know if this is to be the case, or if it will ever be the case? How to be sure? Don't ask me! For make no mistake: I can, and often do, disingenuously enjoy coughing up this sort of pretentious, self-pitying, nihilistic vomitus every bit as appallingly and shamelessly much as my betters.

About the Author

Frank Feldman is a neuronal weather pattern, just like you - and a screen upon which a patient, thoughtful, and most likely imaginary reader might find parts of themselves worth paying attention to.

www.ingramcontent.com/pod-product-compliance
Lightning Source LLC
Chambersburg PA
CBHW030619250626
47154CB00006B/1851